NATURAL LAW IN POLITICAL THOUGHT

Paul E. Sigmund

Winthrop Publishers, Inc.
Cambridge, Massachusetts

ii

CONTENTS

INTRODUCTION

One of the prime targets of the current ferment in higher education is the irrelevance of much of contemporary social science to fundamental moral problems. Current student concern is focused on the issues of authority, legitimacy, equality, war, sexuality, and community. These problems are not new to the history of moral and political theory. They have been discussed and analyzed before—and one of the principal methods used to resolve them, at least until the end of the eighteenth century, has been through the appeal to certain basic principles or values inherent in human nature—the theory of natural law.

The methods and assumptions of natural law theory continue to appear in contemporary political and social thought. The hippies' search for community and love, the attack by the New Left and the young on the quality of contemporary life, the demands of the women's liberation movement that the needs and potentialities of women be recognized—all reflect a belief that society should be restructured in a way that is more in keeping with the requirements of human nature. Martin Luther King appeals to the moral law and cites Augustine and Aquinas to demonstrate that discriminatory legislation is invalid. Herbert Marcuse attacks industrial capitalism; because it prevents "the optimal development of the individual." Erich Fromm argues that communitarian socialism will overcome alienation, and promote the "humanization" of society.[1] Their terminology is new but they share with the natural law theorists of the past a teleological value-oriented conception of human nature. Contemporary writers on democratic theory may appeal to human rights rather than to natural rights; to human dignity rather than to the nature of man. Such violent acts as those of the Nazis may be condemned as inhuman rather than as unnatural; as crimes against humanity rather than as crimes against nature. Yet, normative implications are derived from an ideal conception of what it means to be human in a way not unlike that employed by the natural law theorists.

The terminology of natural law is still explicitly employed in certain areas. Catholic moral theology, at least until the last few years, has made it a basic tool of analysis for the resolution of problems in the areas of personal and societal morality which are not explicitly determined by Scripture. In the Catholic cultures of Europe and Latin America, the natural law theories of the papal social encyclicals and of neo-Thomist philosophers such as Jacques Maritain have directly influenced the programs and ideologies of the Christian Democratic parties. Other examples include the political philosopher, Leo Strauss, who has made the idea of "natural right" a central focus of his attention, and Walter Lippmann who argues in *The Public Philosophy* that natural law is a necessary philosophical precondition of genuine constitutional democracy.[2]

Yet the most important formulations and writings on natural law belong to the past—sometimes the very distant past. In some cases, these theories were dependent on views of the world and factual information which have been superseded. But in the critical area of political and moral values it would be "arrogant to

[1] Cf. Herbert Marcuse, *One Dimensional Man* (Boston, 1964), p. 6 and Erich Fromm, *The Sane Society* (New York, 1955), p. 236. For a similar argument which is specifically based on "the essence of man" as understood by "the western tradition" derived from Plato, Aristotle, and "Christian natural law" see C. B. McPherson "The Maximization of Democracy" in Peter Laslett and W. G. Runciman, eds., *Philosophy, Politics, and Society*, 3rd series (Oxford, 1967). pp. 85, 89.

[2] Walter Lippmann, *The Public Philosophy* (New York, 1955), esp. ch. 8 and 11. Lippmann's later views are anticipated in *The Good Society* (Boston, 1937), pp. 344 ff. The classic exposition of the views of Leo Strauss is in *Natural Right and History* (Chicago, 1953). See also Leo Strauss and Joseph Cropsey, eds., *History of Political Philosophy* (Chicago, 1953).

suppose that very little worth knowing is to be found outside the more recent works . . . The best of the profound works of the past, even of the distant past . . . make us aware of what these unsettled questions are. And they present us with the best fruits of creative minds struggling to arrive at answers."[3]

Anyone interested in the development of the systematic study of politics, and in the principal solutions to its recurring problems, as they have been developed in the West, must surely take into account a theory which was a major or dominant theme in political thought from the fifth century b.c. until the end of the eighteenth century. As a philosophy and as an ideology it played a central role in three important historical events—the extension of the influence of Roman civilization and law over Western Europe; the fusion of Christianity and classical culture in the Middle Ages; and the emergence of liberal individualism from the sixteenth to the eighteenth century. The theory of natural law was used in each of these developments to provide a universal, rational standard to determine the nature and limits of political obligation, the evaluation of competing forms of government, and the relation of law and politics to morals. Writers on political thought are still examining and reassessing the great syntheses of Cicero and the Roman lawyers, St. Thomas and the canonists, Locke and the natural rights theorists. Some surprising new relationships have been discovered between the classical natural law theorists and others not usually considered as part of the natural law tradition—e.g., Burke, Rousseau, and Marx. In the twenty years since the publication of Alexander Passerin d'Entreves' *Natural Law* a significant number of new studies and interpretations have appeared which affect and perhaps alter our view of the natural law writers. This work will attempt to evaluate those studies and to use them to reinterpret some aspects of the history of natural law in political thought.

A cursory view of the major theories of natural law reveals that a bewildering variety of doctrines have been associated with the term "natural law." It has been used to justify the universal rule of the Roman emperors; to relate feudal power structures to a hierarchical order in the universe; to express the desires of

[3] Robert Dahl, *Modern Political Analysis* (Englewood Cliffs, N.J., 1963), p. viii.

emerging middle and lower classes for a share of political power; and to justify revolution in America and France. Natural law can be considered then both in terms of its contribution to the developing science of politics and as an ideology—as the symbolic expression of the needs and aspirations of social classes and groups. The symbolism it uses is of a particular variety—an appeal to reason and to an order in the universe and in man. The arguments are rational, even when they appear in a traditional or highly religious context. If modernization, as many writers tell us, is associated with the emergence of rationality, universality, and objectivity in social and political relations, the relationship of natural law theory to modernization in the West may also merit examination from the perspective of natural law.

Yet it is hoped that this work can be something more than a history of ideas and ideologies and that it will be possible to engage in a philosophical evaluation of the worth of natural law as political theory. While it may appear that the variety of forms and content attributed to natural law in the last 2500 years has resulted in considerable confusion about its meaning, there seems to be a central assertion expressed or implied in most theories of natural law. This is the belief that there exists in nature and/or human nature a rational order which can provide intelligible value-statements independently of human will, that are universal in application, unchangeable in their ultimate content, and morally obligatory on mankind. These statements are expressed as laws or as moral imperatives which provide a basis for the evaluation of legal and political structures. While some forms of the theory have associated natural law with scientific "laws of nature" the two are conceptually distinct. Natural law theories contain norms or prescriptions designed to produce or evaluate human conduct, while the "laws of nature" are expressions of observed regularities in human actions or in the physical universe.[4]

The prescriptions of natural law should be distinguished from norms based on custom, tradition, religious authority or revelation, utility (at least in the variety associated with Jeremy Bentham), historical inevitability, racial elitism, emotivism, and

---

[4] Cf. Robert Ardrey, *The Social Contract* (New York, 1970). Ardrey often uses the term, natural law, when referring to the laws of human nature, i.e., psychological constants in human conduct.

the voluntarism of most existentialist writers. Natural law writers have often combined their theories with one or more of the above justifications, but conceptually, natural law forms a distinct approach to the problem of political, moral, and legal obligation.

Besides deriving different substantive principles from natural law, the theorists that we will examine attribute a variety of meanings to nature, which is their source. They have equated the natural with the rational; the divine; the distinctively human; the normally operating; the frequently recurring; the primitive; the elements not subject to human artifice or control; the self-evident; and the nonhistorical. It is therefore necessary in analyzing these theories, to determine in which sense natural law is being used in a given case.

Yet in all its diverse forms, the theory of nature law represents a common affirmation about the possibility of arriving at objective standards, and a common procedure for doing so—looking for a purposive order in nature and man. This affirmation and this procedure have been challenged since the time of the Greeks by classical sceptics, Christian fideists, and modern philosophers and social scientists. Natural law theories have been criticized for their claims to absolutism in the face of the historical and geographical relativity of human mores and political systems; its contents have been viewed as either too vague or too restrictive; its belief in an ordered nature has been attacked for attributing a purposiveness to what is a fluid, aimless and constantly changing reality, both in the universe and in man.

This book will consider these criticisms to determine the extent to which they undermine its claims. The conclusion will attempt to point toward the possible construction of a more dynamic and viable theory based on human needs and potentialities. A reconstruction of the natural law theory (which will suggest that its terminology be abandoned but that its method and goal be retained) will be undertaken because it seems that man can never give up the search for a rational justification of political and moral values. The continuing appeal of theories, like that of natural law, derives from their affirmation that freedom and moral choice are not incompatible with the existence of objective values in man and society; that human existence is meaningful; that human beings possess equal dignity and rights; and that political and legal forms are more than the product of arbitrary will and should be justified in human terms. For these reasons, natural law theories constitute a powerful and attractive alternative to relativist scepticism and to blind faith in traditionalist, religious, or political authoritarianism.

It is paradoxical that the new interest in the questions with which natural law has dealt is often accompanied by a reliance on emotion rather than reason as the way to resolve them. This study is presented in the hope that it may contribute to a renewal of the belief of the natural law theorists in the ability of human *reason* to deal with moral problems. The thanks of the author are due to the participants in his seminars on the subject at Harvard and Princeton, to Samuel Beer, Harvard University, for his helpful comments on the manuscript, and to Alexander Passerin d'Entreves, whose useful study on the subject, published twenty years ago, first stimulated the author's interest in the topic.

BIBLIOGRAPHY

Bird, Otto. *The Idea of Justice.* New York, 1967, ch. 6.

Bryce, James. "The Law of Nature," *Studies in History and Jurisprudence.* New York, 1961, pp. 556–606.

d'Entreves, A. P. *Natural Law.* London: Hutchinson's University Library, 1951.

Jenkin, Thomas P. *The Study of Political Theory.* New York, 1955, ch. 1, 4.

Neumann, Franz. *The Democratic and Authoritarian State.* New York, 1957, ch. 3.

Wolf, Erik. *Das Problem der Naturrechtslehre.* 3rd ed., Karlsruhe, 1964.

1.

NATURAL LAW IN GREEK THOUGHT

The argument from nature begins with the early Greek speculations about the principles which govern the physical universe. From the opening book of Aristotle's *Metaphysics* as well as from fragments of their writings which survive, we know that the pre-Socratic philosophers of the sixth century B.C. spoke of a first principle (*archē*) to which all the elements of nature could be reduced. In the city-state of Miletus on the coast of Asia Minor, Thales (624–526 B.C.) asserted that water was the ultimate constituent of nature, whereas other philosophers ascribed the same role to fire and air. In Sicily, Pythagoras (d. 495 B.C.) explained the universe in terms of mathematical relationships, asserting that a fundamental harmony based on numbers could be found in music, in man, and in the cosmos, and that man should strive to conform his actions to these relationships. Two fifth-century Greek philosophers explained the phenomenon of change in opposing fashions. Heraclitus (d. 478 B.C.) posited change or becoming as the fundamental law of nature. "Everything flows," he said. "Strife is the father of all." Parmenides (b. 515 B.C.) declared that being, rather than becoming, was the basic principle. The last of

1

the pre-Socratics, one who directly influenced Socrates, was Anaxagoras (500–428 B.C.), who lived in Athens for many years and taught the doctrine that mind (*nous*), which he described as material, was the ultimate explanation of the universe.

The Greek interest in the study of the universe to determine its basic principles contrasted with the tendency of other societies of the period to attribute the phenomena of the physical world to supernatural causes. To attribute a secularism to Greek science which it did not possess, however, would be anachronistic. (Thales of Miletus is quoted as saying "All things are full of the gods.") What made Greek religion different was that, perhaps because its gods and goddesses were so anthropomorphic, it seemed to encourage an attitude of curiosity about the external world rather than the attribution of all events and processes to supernatural causes.

The attempt to discover regularities in the universe and explanations for its processes was not divorced from a concern with moral values. As the example from Pythagoras indicates, number provided not only a description of relationships in the universe but also a basis for conduct, a prescription as to how men should act. Balance and limit in action, the avoidance of excess, and harmonious control of the passions by the intellect were the Pythagorean ideals. Regularities in the heavens were described as examples of cosmic justice, and direct applications of these rules to political organization were not unknown. We do not have the texts, but from references in other works it is known that Heraclitus wrote a work on politics, and that Parmenides wrote a set of laws for the Greek city-state of Elea. It also seems from Plato's works that Pythagoras shared his belief in the rule of wisdom in politics and personal ethics. For the pre-Socratics the study of nature thus involved not only analysis, description, and prediction (Thales of Miletus predicted an eclipse of the moon for 585 B.C.), but prescription as well.

Nature was also regarded as a source of norms by the Sophists or professional teachers in Athens. The unparalleled affluence of the Periclean Age (495–429 B.C.), based on the production of silver and the trade and tribute associated with the Athenian Empire, helped to make Athens the intellectual center of Greece. The fact that the Athenian form of government was a democracy during most of the fifth century B.C., and all important decisions were made by an Assembly open to all citizens, put a premium on the development of the arts of persuasion and argument. The Sophists, self-styled teachers of wisdom, responded to this need by offering to teach logic, rhetoric, and philosophy on a professional basis. Their criticism of conventional moral and political beliefs was one of the reasons for the attempts of Socrates and Plato to provide a more permanent basis for knowledge and ethics.

Most of our knowledge of the content of Sophist teaching comes from the writings of Plato, a declared opponent of the Sophists. However, other records seem to confirm the accuracy of his presentation of their views, and on the basis of these sources we can conclude that the relationship of nature to law and justice was a central theme in many of their teachings. The earlier scientific writers had considered politics to be part of a universal pattern in nature. For the Sophists, however, the relationship was one of opposition between nature (*physis*) and the conventional law (*nomos*) of the Greek city-state. The very word for law, related to *nemein* (to assign) suggested that it was the result of human decision, and the origin of Athenian law in the decrees of Solon around 600 B.C., as well as its various subsequent modifications, further emphasized its conventional character.

At least four views seem to have been current among the Sophist teachers concerning the relationship of nature and convention.

1. In the Socratic dialogue, *Protagoras,* we get a representation of the doctrines of the best known of the Sophists, Protagoras of Abdera, whose saying, "Man is the measure of all things," summed up in his rejection of the earlier attempts to find a common element or law in the external world. Part of his discussion with Socrates in the dialogue is devoted to a defense of Athenian democracy against the charge that it allowed policy decisions to be made by the ignorant. Protagoras argues that all men receive a schooling in justice and politics from their families and political communities. They do not acquire these values from nature, but from what today would be called political socialization by the community—although all men have the capacity to acquire these values, and are held responsible if they do not live up to them (*Protagoras,* No. 322–24). In Protagoras' interpretation of the

relationship of nature and conventional law, nature is defined as genetic inheritance and the law is regarded as essentially conventional, acquired in different ways in different societies.

2. In the same dialogue, another Sophist, Hippias, gives nature a moral quality. He argues that equality and universal brotherhood can be deduced from the natural likeness of all men— "I count you all my kinsmen and family and fellow-citizens—by nature not by conventional law. By nature like is kin to like, but law, which tyrannizes mankind, does much violence to nature" (*Protagoras,* No. 337). A similar view is taken by a later Sophist, Antiphon, fragments of whose writings still survive. When he says "By nature all of us in all things are constituted alike, both Greek and barbarian," Antiphon strikes at the fundamental Greek belief in their superiority to the non-Greeks and attacks conventional socioeconomic distinctions. "Those who are born of a great house we revere and venerate: those who are born of a humble house we do not. On this point we are barbarized in our behavior to one another. Our natural endowment is the same for us all on all points, whether we are Greeks or barbarians . . ."[1] Antiphon states the opposition of nature and conventional law more strongly than Hippias. Man-made law is to be obeyed only when one is being observed or can be punished for disobedience, whereas the rules of nature should always be respected, for "the rules of the laws are created by covenant and not produced by nature, while the rules of nature are exactly the reverse." In the view of Hippias and Antiphon, nature provides a moral standard with which to judge conventional law, and the basic similarity of natural endowment of all mankind points to a fundamental equality which is inconsistent with conventional legal distinctions.

3. A different view of the relation of nature and law is presented by Callicles in the Platonic dialogue *Gorgias.* According to Callicles, nature decrees that the strong should rule over the weak, a fact which is demonstrated by the conduct of men, animals, and city-states. The superior rules over the inferior and the stronger state invades the weaker one "according to the law of nature" (*Gorgias,* No. 482). A similar theory is put forward by Thrasy-

---

1 Ernest Barker, trans., *Greek Political Theory, Plato and his Predecessors* (London, 1918, reprinted, New York, 1960), p. 98.

machus in the opening pages of the *Republic,* although it is not as specifically related to nature. That this theory had wide currency in fifth-century Athens is demonstrated by the appeal which the Athenians made to it in their negotiations with the Melians described by Thucydides in his *History of the Peloponnesian War.* When the Melians appeal to justice and the gods against the Athenian threat to violate their neutrality, the Athenians reply, "Among the gods we believe and among men we know that by a law of their nature, wherever they can rule they will" (Bk. V, No. 89). These statements reveal a view of nature as essentially characterized by relationships of domination and submission, and law as a rationalization of those relationships. On its face the appeal to nature seems to be more a psychological observation than a moral justification, but the implication of the argument is that conventional law and morality are either inapplicable or fraudulent, and obedience to them unnecessary for the powerful except in their own interest.

4. After Thrasymachus states his version of this third theory of the relationship between *physis* and *nomos,* the *Republic* presents another view which begins from the same premises but arrives at another set of conclusions. After disassociating himself from the views he presents (Aristotle attributes them to "the Sophist Lycophron" in the *Politics,* No. 1280b), Glaucon, one of the participants in the dialogue, argues (*Republic,* No. 358–362) that law can be viewed as a set of conventional restraints placed on the strong by the weak to prevent the kind of domination described by Thrasymachus. Law is again in opposition to nature in this interpretation, since it enables men to live together in peace by repressing their "natural" tendency to exploitation and oppression.

Yet whether the Sophists viewed it as genetic inheritance, biological characteristic, or psychological drive, nature was the standard which they used to analyze and critically evaluate existing man-made law. Their analysis challenged the prevailing identification of existing laws with justice and nature, and it suggested the frightening possibility of a fundamental disharmony between the physical and psychological characteristics of man and the norms that make it possible for him to live in community. To respond to the challenge of the Sophist criticism, in order to prove that there were objective moral principles for ethics and politics which were not hedonistic, egoistic, or merely conventional, Plato used the same analytical tool that the Sophists had employed—the concept of nature—but he also drew on Parmenides and Pythagoras for theories which could assist him in his enterprise of discovering the permanent bases for the evaluation of moral and political life.

Plato's philosophy is presented in dialogues in which his teacher Socrates takes a principal part. It is difficult to distinguish what is Socrates' doctrine from what is Plato's, since Socrates did not leave any written works. However, analysis of the order of the composition of the Platonic dialogues as well as the picture given to us by other writers such as Xenophon can provide some clues as to the content of Socrates' teaching. Plato's *Apology* and *Crito* reconstruct the last part of Socrates' life, and they indicate that although he maintained that residence in a city obligates one to obey its laws, he also believed that he had a higher obligation which directed him to serve as a gadfly to the conventional opinions of the Athenians, an obligation which finally led to his trial and death. He carried out this role by persistent questioning directed at the refinement and definition of concepts in order to arrive at a better understanding of the objects or actions which they represented. This definition was to be arrived at by analyzing the function or structure of the objects or actions represented by the concept being examined, and it was on this central insight that Plato built his later theories. Socrates did not have a natural law doctrine as such, but (1) he posed the problem of potential conflict between moral and civic obligation; and (2) his belief that the function and structure of a thing determine its essential character and purpose lies at the root of many later natural law theories.

Plato's most important dialogue, the *Republic*, begins from a Socratic base, the dialectical examination of the nature of justice (Book I seems to have been written earlier and may represent an actual Socratic dialogue), but it develops theories which are specifically Platonic. To answer the Sophist theories that justice was either a rationalization of interest or merely a conventional restraint of "natural" impulses, Plato argues that there is a natural harmony both within the individual and between the individual and the community. For the individual this harmony consists of the rule of the reason, assisted by the emotions in restraining and directing man's lower appetites. For society, it consists in the rule of the wiser over the ignorant, the more rational and moral over those less endowed with these qualities. (In accordance with the Socratic theory that knowledge is virtue, reason and moral goodness are equated.) In the *Republic* Plato attempts to prove that the Sophist theory leads only to contradiction, unhappiness, and frustration in the individual because the warring impulses can never be satisfied once they have shaken off the restraints of reason, and in society because tyrannical rulers rise up and oppress the people under the guise of providing them with the direction which they cannot give themselves.

In contrast to the assumption of Athenian democracy that all men should participate in political decisions, Plato argues that knowledge of the true and the good can only be achieved through rigorous training and development of the natural capacities of the most capable citizens so that they can perceive—first the shifting empirical world, later abstract mathematical and geometrical relationships, then logical and ethical truths, and finally the integrating principle of all value, Good itself. The objects of this knowledge are organized hierarchically from the changing uncertainties of appearance through the unchanging realities of mathematical, logical, and ethical Ideas or Forms (which are not mere concepts but have a real existence) to the ultimate unifying source of all value and reality, the Form of the Good.

What has happened to *physis* or nature in the course of this explanation? Plato uses an argument from nature to defend equality for the female members of the ruling ("guardian") class (Bk. V, No. 456), but direct appeals to nature as a source of norms do not appear frequently in the *Republic*. Yet the basic argument of the *Republic* amounts to an assertion that there is an order in nature and human nature which is universal, objective, and harmonious, in which the soul is the most fundamental principle, possessing a threefold internal structure (reason, spirit, and desire) which is the basis of moral obligation. Conformity to this order brings harmony, virtue, and happiness. Violation of it results in disorder, evil, and unhappiness (cf. *The Laws*, No. 889–90). Corresponding to this natural order in man is a parallel hierarchical order in society (the rule of the wise in the *Republic*) and in the universe (described in the *Timaeus*). The rules of ethics and politics, like those of logic, are based on the principle of non-contradiction, but in the case of ethics and politics, noncontradiction means avoidance of opposition between impulse and reason (or the groups in which these characteristics predominate) rather than logical inconsistency. For the realism of some of the Sophists, which was modeled on power relationships in nature, Plato substitutes an ethical and epistemological realism which asserts that an idealized nature is the source of objective and inherent standards of value and can serve as a guide to action—at least for the philosopher who by innate ability, long education, and receptivity to truth is trained in ethics and its social counterpart, politics.

Yet is this appeal to nature an appeal to natural *law?* In one sense it is not, for in Plato's *Republic* and *Statesman* he contrasts the inadequacy of the prospective general statements embodied in law with the flexibility and accuracy of the judgments of free intelligence (*Republic* No. 425; *Statesman* No. 294). Yet in the *Republic* it seems clear that there will be certain basic laws and a constitutional structure of the state (cf. *Republic,* Bk. IV, No. 424) and presumably there would be rules for the guidance of the lowest or producer class. In the *Laws* he argues that laws are necessary because the perfect ruler cannot be found, or if found will not remain perfect once he exercises power (*Laws,* Nos. 691, 713, and 875). In Book X (No. 889) Plato replies to the Sophist argument by affirming the derivation of legislation from nature, not in the same way as in the physical world, but through the application of intelligence to human actions, an act requiring technical competence and art (*techné*), and at the same time adherence to the principles of nature.

Yet in Plato's thought the law still seems imperfect and less than ideal. There is still an element of artifice in it, and although it is based on nature, it can never adequately represent the ideal, even if the legislator urges the citizenry to believe that it does so. To the extent, then, that Plato believed that there were universal principles inherent in nature which imposed a moral obligation on all men, he was enunciating a natural-law theory. Insofar as he viewed any given law as an inadequate representation of the eternal principles of justice, he was asserting a theory of natural (i.e., ideal) justice rather than one of natural law.

The ethical and political writings of Plato's pupil, Aristotle, also raise certain questions about their relationship to the theory of natural law. There is considerable evidence available to those who wish to deny that he did, in fact, subscribe to such a theory. In Book II (No. 1103) of the *Nicomachean Ethics* he describes the acquisition of virtue as the result of good habits rather than the action of nature. Shortly thereafter (Nos. 1107–1109) virtue is portrayed as a mean between extremes which is achieved by avoiding an excess or defect of some quality. In Book VI (No. 1142) politics is called a practical art which does not possess the abstract certainty of theoretical pursuits, and in Book X (No. 1181) some men are said to acquire it through experience even if they lack theoretical wisdom. In all of these sections it appears that decision-making in ethics and politics is not a matter of deriving abstract principles from nature but of utilizing a certain insight and prudence to determine right action. The ethically correct action differs in each case in a way not unlike that described by the modern advocates of situational ethics. In Aristotle's *Politics* as well, much of the discussion is concerned with the proper constitution for a given political, economic, and social environment rather than with the ideal or naturally best constitution.[2]

Yet in the midst of his consideration of virtue as the mean in Book II of the *Nicomachean Ethics,* Aristotle observes that some actions are bad in themselves, regardless of their consequences. He cites adultery, theft, and murder as actions which "it is impossible ever to do rightly." Book V of the *Ethics* also contains an important discussion of "natural justice," which is contrasted with "justice by convention," although the passage is confusing, since it asserts the existence of an unchanging natural justice and at the same time maintains that it is changeable among men, "as are all things human" (*Ethics,* No. 1134b).

In the *Nicomachean Ethics* Aristotle speaks of natural *justice* rather than natural *law* but in his *Rhetoric* he clearly states

---

2 See, for instance, the comparison of the good man and the good citizen in *Politics,* Book III, No. 1276b ff., and the discussion of the best practicable constitution in Book IV, Nos. 1295–97.

a belief in natural law. In two different passages of Book I of that work he refers to "a common law according to nature" (chs. 13 and 15), and in chapter 10 he alludes to a common law which is universal and unwritten. In his argument in chapter 15 he seems to suggest that an appeal to universal law is appropriate if the law of the city-state is contrary to the position which the rhetorician is arguing, but in chapter 13 there is a plain assertion that such a law actually exists and can be known by all men.[3] In both cases Aristotle refers to the lines in Sophocles' *Antigone* in which Antigone cites the "eternal and unwritten law" (although the actual issue—the burial of a brother—involved a religious and ceremonial law rather than an appeal to nature).

From all of these cases it seems clear that Aristotle believed in the existence of some common legal principles which are universal and based on nature. However, aside from the references to the *Antigone,* his work contains no attempt to spell out the details of this universal natural law nor to use it to invalidate existing laws. For later interpreters, however, and perhaps for Aristotle himself, the first book of the *Politics* provides a method for determining what nature intends and it gives several specific examples of norms derived from nature. For Aristotle the essential nature of a thing can be discovered by determining its purpose or end. This in turn can be derived from its structure or normal functioning. *Physis* (nature) is related to *telos* (end); thus, the teleological method can be used to discover nature's purposes and derive values from them. Aristotle uses this teleological analysis to demonstrate that man is naturally social and that government responds to needs which man has by nature (No. 1253). He also attempts to prove that there is a natural hierarchy in nature which decrees that women should be the inferiors of men, children of their parents, and—in contrast to the Sophists' argument about natural equality—that, at least in some cases, slavery is justified by nature because of the natural inferiority in mental and moral capacity of the slave (Nos. 1254–55).

In the next section, Aristotle uses a similar argument to de-

---

[3] The reference in chapter 13 refutes the assertion by David Ritchie in *Natural Rights* (London, 1894), p. 30, that Aristotle's references to natural law in the *Rhetoric* were no more than rhetorical devices designed to win law cases.

velop the first theory of the just war—in this case a war against those "who, though intended by nature to be governed, will not submit. Such a war is naturally just" (No. 1256). Aristotle also condemns usury, arguing that taking interest for lending money, which is merely a medium of exchange and not naturally productive, is an unnatural form of acquisition (No. 1258). In Book II of the *Politics*, the argument from nature is used to defend private property. Aristotle asserts that a system of private property and common use is more consistent with the intentions of nature, which gives man a feeling of pleasure in having certain things as his own, than is the communal ownership proposed for the guardians in Plato's Republic (No. 1263).

After discussing various forms of government as appropriate for different purposes and conditions, Aristotle devotes the last two books of the *Politics* to an analysis of the best state.[4] As he describes it, the ideal state is ruled by aristocrats who have the leisure and education which make it possible for them to achieve the natural purpose of the state—the collective pursuit of the life of virtue. The argument is based on a teleological analysis of the nature of politics. The ideal state is the one most likely to achieve the natural goal of social and political life.

Aristotle, like many other theorists after him, understood nature in two different senses. When he says that virtue is not a product of nature he is speaking of physical determinism; but when he justifies political life, slavery, and the rule of the wise and good, he appeals to nature as containing immanent norms or goals. The application of these norms to given situations requires a special talent, practical wisdom, and one cannot achieve the theoretical certainty of the physical scientist or mathematician in applying these norms; but nature provides guidance for the citizen, the statesman, and the moral man.

The description and evaluation of what is natural and unnatural in social, economic, and political life is not carried out in terms of a systematic law of nature, and Aristotle never specifically links up these discussions with the "natural justice" and

4 This topic had already been alluded to in the discussion of natural justice in Book V, chapter 7 of the *Nicomachean Ethics* where Aristotle states that "There is only one constitution that is according to nature, the best everywhere."

"common law according to nature" of the *Ethics* and *Rhetoric*. When the law of nature later became an important concept in political theory, this connection between natural law and teleology was made, but this only took place long after Aristotle wrote. Yet for him as for all Greek political theorists the concept of nature as a source of norms had a central position, and the interpretation which he gave to it—relating it to ends or purposes—became one of the principal varieties of natural-law theory.

Using concepts first developed by Greek science and responding to the challenge of the Sophist criticism of conventional morality and law, Plato and Aristotle laid the foundations of a theory of natural law. Nature was viewed as harmonious and purposive, and human nature was believed to exhibit an intelligible order from which ethical norms could be derived. For Plato function and structure gave evidence of an ideal order, and the soul in its inherent order was most "natural" of all—a source of ethical values which were ultimately related to the source of all value, the Form of the Good. For Aristotle, nature's structural tendencies or goals could be a guide to politics and ethics, and a conception of a fundamental natural law or natural justice was present in his writings although it was not developed or integrated with the rest of his thought. Neither writer brought these conceptions together in a formal natural-law theory as such. This remained for the Stoics and the political theorists of Rome.

BIBLIOGRAPHY

Barker, Ernest, trans. *Greek Political Theory, Plato and his Predecessors*. London, 1918 (paperback reprint, New York, 1960).

Havelock, Eric. *The Liberal Temper in Greek Politics*. New Haven, 1957, ch. 6–10.

Jaeger, Werner. "In Praise of Law" in P. Sayre, ed. *Interpretations of Legal Philosophies*. New York, 1947, pp. 352–76.

Jaffa, Harry. *Thomism and Aristotelianism.* Chicago, 1952.

Kirk, G. S. and J. E. Raven. *The Presocratic Philosophers.* Cambridge, 1963.

Murrow, Glenn. "Plato and the Law of Nature," in Milton Konvitz, ed. *Essays Presented to George Sabine.* Ithaca, New York, 1949, pp. 17–44.

Taylor, A. E. *Socrates.* New York, 1933.

Wild, John. *Plato's Modern Enemies and the Theory of Natural Law.* Chicago, 1953.

Wormuth, Francis. "Aristotle on Law" in Milton Konvitz, ed. *Essays Presented to George Sabine.* Ithaca, New York, 1949, pp. 45–61.

ARISTOTLE ON NATURAL LAW

Nicomachean Ethics*

Natural and legal justice

Of political justice part is natural, part legal,—natural,
that which everywhere has the same force and does not exist
by people's thinking this or that; legal, that which is originally
indifferent, but when it has been laid down is not indifferent,
e.g., that a prisoner's ransom shall be a *mina,* or that a
goat and not two sheep shall be sacrificed, and again all the
laws that are passed for particular cases, e.g., that sacrifice
shall be made in honor of Brasidas,[1] and the provisions of decrees.
Now some think that all justice is of this sort, because that
which is by nature is unchangeable and has everywhere the
same force (as fire burns both here and in Persia), while they
see change in the things recognized as just. This, however,
is not true in this unqualified way, but is true in a sense;
or rather, with the gods it is perhaps not true at all, while with
us there is something that is just even by nature, some not
by nature. It is evident which sort of thing, among things
capable of being otherwise, is by nature; and which is not
but is legal and conventional, assuming that both are equally
changeable. And in all other things the same distinction will
apply; by nature the right hand is stronger, yet it is possible
that all men should come to be ambidextrous. The things
which are just by virtue of convention and expediency are

---

*From *The Nicomachean Ethics of Aristotle,* translated by Sir David Ross,
Book V, chapter 7, Nos. 1134b–35a, by permission. Copyright © 1925 by Clarendon
Press, Oxford, England.

1 Thucydides, *The Peloponnesian War,* Book V, p. 11.

like measures; for wine and corn measures are not everywhere
equal, but larger in wholesale and smaller in retail markets.
Similarly, the things which are just not by nature but by
human enactment are not everywhere the same, since constitutions
also are not the same, though there is but one which is
everywhere by nature the best. . . .

The Politics*

ARISTOTLE

Book I:

. . . He who thus considers things in their first growth
and origin, whether a state or anything else, will obtain
the clearest view of them. In the first place (1) there must be
a union of those who cannot exist without each other; for
example, of male and female, that the race may continue; and
this is a union which is formed, not of deliberate purpose,
but because, in common with other animals and with plants,
mankind have a natural desire to leave behind them an image
of themselves. And (2) there must be a union of natural
ruler and subject, that both may be preserved. For he who can
foresee with his mind is by nature intended to be lord and
master, and he who can work with his body is a subject, and
by nature a slave; hence master and slave have the same
interest. Nature, however, has distinguished between the female
and the slave. For she is not niggardly, like the smith who
fashions the Delphian knife for many uses; she makes each
thing for a single use, and every instrument is best made
when intended for one and not for many uses. But among
barbarians no distinction is made between women and slaves,
because there is no natural ruler among them: they are a
community of slaves, male and female. Wherefore the poets
say, "It is meet that Hellenes should rule over barbarians"; as if
they thought that the barbarian and the slave were by
nature one.

Out of these two relationships between man and woman,
master and slave, the family first arises, . . . The family is
the association established by nature for the supply of men's

* From Aristotle, *Politics,* translated by Benjamin Jowett, Book I, 2, Nos. 1252–53.
Copyright © 1885 by Clarendon Press, Oxford, England.

everyday wants, . . . But when several families are united, and the association aims at something more than the supply of daily needs, then comes into existence the village. . . .

When several villages are united in a single community, perfect and large enough to be nearly or quite self-sufficing, the state comes into existence, originating in the bare needs of life, and continuing in existence for the sake of a good life. And therefore, if the earlier forms of society are natural, so is the state, for it is the end of them, and the [completed] nature is the end. For what each thing is when fully developed, we call its nature, whether we are speaking of a man, a horse, or a family. Besides, the final cause and end of a thing is the best, and to be self-sufficing is the end and the best.

Hence it is evident that the state is a creation of nature, and that man is by nature a political animal. . . .

The Rhetoric*

ARISTOTLE

Book I:

10. . . . Let injustice, then, be defined as voluntarily causing injury contrary to the law. Now, the law is particular or general [*lit.:* common]. By particular, I mean the written law in accordance with which a state is administered; by general, the unwritten regulations which appear to be universally recognized. . . .

13. Let us now classify just and unjust actions generally, starting from what follows. Justice and injustice have been defined in reference to laws and persons in two ways. Now there are two kinds of laws, particular and general. By particular laws I mean those established by each people in reference to themselves, which again are divided into written and unwritten; by general laws I mean those based upon nature. In fact, there is a general idea of just and unjust in accordance with nature, as all men in a manner divine, even if there is neither communication nor agreement between them. This is what Antigone in Sophocles evidently means, when she declares that it is just, though forbidden, to bury Polynices, as being naturally just: "For neither to-day nor yesterday, but from all eternity, these statutes live and no man knoweth whence they came." . . .

15. . . . For it is evident that, if the written law is counter to our case, we must have recourse to the general law and equity, as more in accordance with justice; and we must argue that, when the dicast takes an oath to decide to the best of his judgment, he means that he will not abide

* From Aristotle, *The "Art" of Rhetoric,* translated by John Henry Freese, Book I, Nos. 1368b, 1373b, 1375a–b, by permission. Copyright © 1926 by Harvard University Press.

rigorously by the written laws; that equity is ever constant
and never changes, even as the general law, which is based
on nature, whereas the written laws often vary (this is why
Antigone in Sophocles justifies herself for having buried Polynices
contrary to the law of Creon, but not contrary to the unwritten
law: "For this law is not of now nor yesterday, but is
eternal . . . this I was not likely [to infringe through fear
of the pride] of any man"); and further, that justice is real
and expedient, but not that which only appears just; nor the
written law either, because it does not do the work of the law;
that the judge is like an assayer of silver, whose duty is to
distinguish spurious from genuine justice; that it is the part
of a better man to make use of and abide by the unwritten
rather than the written law.

SOURCES

Plato, *Protagoras,* Nos. 320–25, 337.
——, *Gorgias,* Nos. 466–88.
——, *Apology,* No. 26.
——, *Republic,* Bks. I, II; V, No. 456; Bk. VI, Nos. 507–09;
   Bk. IX, Nos. 588–91; Bk. X, No. 597.
——, *Laws,* Bk. III, Nos. 690–91; Bk. IV, No. 712; Bk. VI,
   No. 757; Bk. IX, No. 875; Bk. X, Nos. 889–92.
Aristotle, *Nicomachean Ethics,* Bk. II, No. 1103, 1107–09;
   Bk. V, No. 1134b; Bk. VI, No. 1142; Bk. X, No. 1181.
——, *Politics,* Bk. I, No. 1254–56; Bk. II, No. 1263; Bk. III,
   Nos. 1276, 1287a, 1293b–94b; Bk. VII, Nos. 1323–25.
——, *Rhetoric,* Bk. I, 10, No. 1368b; Bk. I, 13, No. 1373b;
   Bk. I, 15, No. 1375.

2.

NATURAL LAW IN ROMAN THOUGHT

The earliest statement of a comprehensive theory of natural law appears in the writings of Cicero (106–43 B.C.), the Roman statesman and politician. His statements on the subject are heavily influenced by earlier writings along similar lines by the philosophers of the Stoic school in Athens, of which only fragments survive. Stoicism originated in Greece around 300 B.C. in the teaching of Zeno of Citium. (The *stoa*, or porch, where Zeno taught has been reconstructed in the Athenian *agora* or marketplace.) Zeno's own teacher, Crates, was a member of the Cynic school which rejected the contemporary Greek values of the city-state, political participation, property, family, learning, and reputation, considering the life of virtue as the only important value and the community of the wise and virtuous in the city of the world (*cosmopolis*) as the only valid form of social life. Zeno softened the radicalism of the Cynics' criticism, but retained the view that political life was only a relative good, whereas in the ideal state all men would live together as "one herd in accordance with nature." Both Zeno and a later head of the Stoic school in Athens, Chrysippus (232–206 B.C.) are known to have written works on the state, but only secondary accounts of their contents remain. The "nature" of which they spoke seems to have been both a material and a moral order. Both man and the universe were believed to be governed by "right reason which pervades all things and is identical with Zeus, lord and ruler of all that is."[1] This reason was expressed in law which, in Chrysippus' words, is "the ruler over all the acts both of gods and men. . . . For all beings that are social by nature, it directs what must be done and forbids what must not be done."[2]

In the second century B.C., Stoicism was subjected to criticisms which were not unlike those put forward earlier by some of the Sophists in fifth-century Athens. Carneades (213–129 B.C.) denied the existence of natural justice and described all law and politics as based on individual or national self-interest. His views are represented in Cicero's *On the Commonwealth*, where Cicero also reproduces the arguments of Panaetius (185–110 B.C.), the leader of the Stoic school, who replied to him. Cicero states that the first two books of his work *De Officiis* (*Moral Duties*) are based upon a work by Panaetius, and modern scholars have argued that Book I of the *Laws* and the first three books of the *Commonwealth* are also dependent upon him.[3] In Panaetius' reconstruction of Stoicism, the opposition between reason and the lower nature which had been emphasized in early Stoicism was modified, and the earlier insistence on the limitation of reason to a few wise men was abandoned. For Panaetius, all men possess the common capacity to participate in divine reason, and the whole human race shares a fundamental equality and universal brotherhood.

This was the version of Stoicism which was imported into Rome in the middle of the second century B.C. After the conquest of Greece in 146 B.C., Greek philosophical ideas were taken over with enthusiasm by the Roman upper classes, and the members of the personal circle of the Roman General, Scipio Africanus the Younger, were especially attracted to Stoicism as modified by

1 "Diogenes Laertius," VII, quoted in Donald Kagen, *Sources in Greek Political Thought* (New York, 1965), p. 261.

2 The opening words of Chrysippus' book *On Law*, quoted in the introduction to George H. Sabine and Stanley B. Smith, eds., *Marcus Tullius Cicero, On the Commonwealth* (Columbus, Ohio, 1929), p. 22.

3 See the references in note 56, page 29 of the Sabine and Smith introduction to *On the Commonwealth*.

Panaetius. The members of the Scipionic circle appear as characters in Cicero's dialogues, the *Laws* and the *Commonwealth*, and develop ideas with which Cicero undoubtedly sympathized.

Cicero himself lived several generations later. He was born in 106 B.C. of a family of the equestrian rank, possessing some wealth, but not a part of the hereditary aristocracy. In his youth he studied law and philosophy and spent some time at the Platonic Academy in Athens. Most of his life was devoted to an active career in law and politics, but he also found time to do considerable writing. *The Commonwealth* (*De Re Publica*) was written during the period of the First Triumvirate, between 54 and 51 B.C. *De Officiis* or *Moral Duties* was written in 44 B.C. *The Laws* (*De Legibus*) is the last of Cicero's works, on which he was still working at the time of his death in 43 B.C. While not highly original in content, these works summarized the political and philosophical thinking of Stoicism and transmitted it to the medieval and modern worlds.

The doctrine of natural law received its classic expression in Book III, chapter 22 of Cicero's *The Commonwealth*. "There is a true law, right reason in accord with nature; it is of universal application, unchanging and everlasting. . . . It is wrong to abrogate this law and it cannot be annulled. . . . There is one law, eternal and unchangeable, binding at all times upon all peoples; and there will be, as it were, one common master and ruler of men, God, who is the author of this law, its interpreter and its sponsor." The same linkage of law and reason occurs in *The Laws*, where Cicero says, "Law is the highest reason implanted in nature, which commands what ought to be done and forbids the opposite" (*Laws*, Bk. I, 6). It is "right reason applied to command and prohibition" (*Laws*, Bk. I, 12) and "the primal and ultimate mind of God whose reason directs all things either by compulsion or restraint" (*Laws*, Bk. II, 4).

The "reason" of which Cicero speaks is not only the ability to conceptualize and engage in logical and mathematical manipulations. It is *right* reason, a moral faculty which enables man to distinguish between good and evil, and to perceive what is in accordance with man's nature. The content of the true natural law is not spelled out, although it is asserted to be eternal and unchangeable. From the discussions in the works of Cicero it seems to include, as a minimum, a duty to contribute to society, a concern for justice, and a respect for the life and property of others.

In contrast to the views of Aristotle and Plato, Cicero's natural law also seems to imply moral (although not social and political) equality. Cicero asserts that "no single being is so like another . . . as all of us are to one another" and bases this equality on the fact that "reason which alone raises us above the level of beasts . . . is certainly common to us all and, though varying in what it learns, at least in the capacity to learn, it is invariable" (*Laws*, Bk. I, 10). Yet, on the other hand, Cicero defends the institution of slavery with an argument similar to that of Book I of Aristotle's *Politics* (*The Commonwealth*, Bk. III, 25), and he condemns democracy as the worst form of government (*Commonwealth*, Bk. III, 33 and 35). It seems that the equality of men consists only in their innate capacity for moral action before "bad habits and false beliefs" (*Laws*, Bk. I, 10) have corrupted them.

Cicero was a conservative in Roman politics, and he appealed to natural law as the moral justification of existing laws rather than as the basis for radical change. While he asserted that "to invalidate this (natural) law by human legislation is never right" (*The Commonwealth*, Bk. III, 22), he did not hint at any possibility of annulling positive law in cases of conflict. His discussion was more concerned with demonstrating that existing Roman laws were in accord with nature than with showing where they violated its provisions. An illustration of this tendency occurs at the end of Book II of *The Laws* where, following an account of Roman burial customs, including the provision that graves be sixty feet apart, the speaker expresses his gratification that the claim for satisfaction.

Cicero's defense of the just war in *The Commonwealth* (Bk. III, 23) is the *locus classicus* of the attempt to distinguish between moral and immoral warfare. In reply to the assertion that all existing states are based on conquest, he justifies the wars carried out by the Romans on the grounds that they were fought either to redress an injury or to repel an invader. He adds that a just war should be formally declared and only initiated after a formal claim for satisfaction.

Once again in this instance, Cicero is attempting to justify existing Roman conduct by an appeal to the higher law. Yet as the subsequent history of the just-war doctrine indicates, once such a standard is defined it becomes a potential source of criticism of the existing order. While many wars can be justified by an appeal to a previous injury or to self-defense, some cannot, or at least there can be argument on the subject. Moral standards become more precise when they take legal form, and even if there is a danger of casuistry or pharisaism, at least an attempt has been made to get beyond an appeal to tradition, community consensus, or a vaguely conceived virtue of the Platonic or Aristotelian variety.

In his later work, *Moral Duties (De Officiis)* Cicero argues that men are naturally social and that we have a duty to be kind to others and to share the goods of nature with them. As in *The Commonwealth,* he attempts to refute the sceptical moral theory that self-interest is to be followed rather than the principles of morality. "To take away wrongfully from another and for one man to advance his own interest by the disadvantage of another man is more contrary to nature than death, than poverty, than pain, than any other evil . . . " (*Moral Duties,* Bk. III, 5).

Passages in the treatise also reflect the modification of Stoic ideas by Roman influences. Thus the ideal of public service is praised, while earlier Stoics would have regarded political participation as irrelevant to the life according to nature. The murder of tyrants is especially praised, since the Romans had always regarded the assassination of Tarquin as an act of service to the republic of the highest moral worth.

The term, *jus gentium,* or "law of nations" appears for the first time in Cicero's writings at the beginning of *The Commonwealth* (Bk. I, 2) in Book III, chapters 5 and 17 of *Moral Duties,* and in two minor works[4] it is described as a common law of mankind, which is closely related to natural law.

In the nineteenth century, Sir Henry Maine in chapter 3 of his classic work, *Ancient Law,* asserted that the term, *jus gentium,* was used to refer to the decrees of the Roman *praetor peregrinus* deciding cases between Romans and members of non-Roman tribes, and was considered by the Romans as a part of "the lost code of nature." This theory (which is repeated in most histories

---

[4] Cicero, *Partitiones Oratoriae,* ch. 37, No. 130: "Common legal principles are by nature. Particular laws are either written or those unwritten principles contained in the law of nations (*jus gentium*) or the customs of our ancestors." See also *Tusculan Disputations,* Book I, ch. 13, No. 37: "The consensus of all nations (*gentium*) is to be considered the law of nature."

of political thought) has now been discredited by legal historians. According to more recent research, the praetor's decrees were a part of the *jus honorarium,* while *jus gentium* was not a legal term but a philosophical one which was used to translate the Greek *koinos nomos* or common law.[5] It did not refer to a lost code in the past, but to the common elements in all legal systems. It was related to natural law to the extent that these universal common practices appeared to support a belief in a universal law of nature underlying the variety of legal formulations.

The close relationship which Cicero had asserted between natural law as a rational standard for all legal systems and *jus gentium* as an indication of its universal acceptance, began to break down in the writings of the Roman lawyers. Justinian's legal collection, known as the *Corpus of Civil Law* (533 A.D.) is divided into three parts—the *Digest* of earlier writings of prominent legal experts, the *Institutes,* a handbook for law students, and the *Code* of laws then in force in the Empire. In the opening passages of the *Digest* we can identify the sources of some of the contradictory statements which appear in the *Institutes,* the more influential of the two works. It is clear from the *Digest* and from surviving versions of his own legal writings that Gaius, one of the earlier (second century A.D.) Roman legal writers represented in the collection, still identified natural law and *jus gentium* with one another as Cicero had done earlier. Ulpian, however, writing in the third century, distinguished them declaring that the *jus gentium* "falls short of natural law" and that in its provisions regulating slavery it was contrary to the law of nature, "for by the law of nature all men were born free" (*Digest,* Bk. I, i,4). In addition to asserting the original freedom of all men, the *Digest* also stated that "as far as the natural law is concerned," all men are equal (L, xvii, 32)—a condition that slavery clearly violated. Natural law represented in this case an ideal order of things, while *jus gentium* contained the provisions in common practice among men. Ulpian devoted considerable attention to the legal regulations concerning slavery, thus demonstrating that he was no more ready than Cicero to use the natural law to invalidate existing societal arrangements.

[5] On this point see discussion in Fritz Schultz, *A History of Roman Legal Science* (Oxford, 1946), pp. 73, 137; Barry Nicholas, *An Introduction to Roman Law* (Oxford, 1962), p. 56.

Though without immediate legal application, the ideal of original freedom and equality was derived from the law of nature in the writings of the Roman lawyers. When the study of Roman law was revived in medieval Europe, this ideal was transmitted to the Middle Ages in the *Digest* and *Institutes,* and it was appealed to by various radical reform movements in defense of human freedom and equality.[6]

Ulpian also differed from Gaius in his definition of natural law. Whereas the Stoics and Gaius had defined it as the set of rules prescribed by reason, for Ulpian it was "that which all animals have been taught by nature. . . . From it comes the union of man and woman called by us matrimony, and therewith the procreation and rearing of children; we find in fact that animals in general, the very wild beasts, are marked by acquaintance with this law" (*Digest,* Bk. I. i, 1). Because of its prominent position in both the *Digest* and the *Institutes,* this definition was also influential in later ages, although, since it departed from the Stoic identification of natural law and reason, it was not as universally accepted as the assertion of the original natural freedom and equality of men.

Although the civil law was not seen as wholly subordinated to the natural law it was a useful concept for the interpretation and development of the law. Thus natural relationships such as that of parent and child could be interpreted as implying certain legal obligations under natural law, and the doctrine that property was originally held in common under natural law was used as the basis for determining the limits of private ownership (cf. Bk I, Title viii of the *Digest*). Slaves were held to possess certain natural obligations with legal consequences while a freed slave acquired legal rights by virtue of his reinstatement to natural freedom. A further use of natural law was as a synonym for normal conduct so that, for example it was held that self-defense when attacked was justified as innate in every human being. Natural law was thus used to develop and apply the law, but not to invalidate it.[7]

[6] See examples cited in Paul E. Sigmund, "Hierarchy, Equality, and Consent in Medieval Christian Thought," J. Roland Pennock and John W. Chapman, eds., *Equality* (New York, 1967), ch. 8.

[7] Cf. Ernest Levy, "Natural Law in the Roman Period," *Natural Law Institute,* vol. II (Notre Dame, Ind., 1949), pp. 50 ff. See also Title VIII of *The Digest, infra.*

Christianity was another vehicle for the transmission of Stoic natural law ideas. Although Christianity was suspicious of pagan thought as tainted with sin (Tertullian asked "What is Athens to Jerusalem? What is Cicero to the Psalms?"), elements of Stoic thinking bore resemblances to Christian conceptions, and in some cases were incorporated directly into Christian sacred writings. St. Paul's speech on the unknown God made on the hill of the Areopagus in Athens as reported in the Acts of the Apostles (Acts, 17) quotes from a Stoic poet and describes all men as "of one blood." In his epistle to the Galatians, he asserts that "There is neither Jew nor Greek, there is neither bond nor free, there is neither male nor female; for you are all one in Christ Jesus" (Gal., 3). Most important of all was his incorporation of a type of natural law doctrine into Christian teaching in his epistle to the Romans: "For when the gentiles which have not the Law [of Moses], do by nature the things contained in the Law, these, having not the Law, are a law unto themselves in that they show the work of the Law written in their hearts, their conscience bearing witness thereof" (Romans 2:14–15).[8] In this passage Paul states that men can know the moral law from the promptings of their consciences; but unlike Stoic writings on the subject, there is no mention of a special role for reason. Rather, a process of direct moral intuition seems to be involved, and the potential elitism of Stoic rationalism gives way to a more universalistic Christian emphasis on the role of conscience.

It was easy for the early Christian writers to take over the Stoic doctrine of natural law, particularly when, as in the writings of Seneca (1–65 A.D), the concept of nature also included an ideal of a lost Golden Age of equality and liberty which resembled the Christian belief in a Garden of Eden and the Fall of Man (Seneca, *Epistle XC,* No. 5).

The theory of natural law had only a secondary importance in the writings of the Fathers of the Church such as Ambrose,

---

8 Paul also attacks Roman sexual practices as "against nature" (Romans 1:26) and (a contemporary note) declares that "nature itself teaches that for a man to wear his hair long is degrading" (I Cor. 11:14). For a somewhat labored argument that Paul did not hold the natural law doctrine, see Felix Flückiger, *Geschichte des Naturrechts,* Vol. I, (Zurich, 1954), pp. 295–97.

Augustine, and Gregory. Nature, although corrupted by sin, was the product of God's creative action and therefore could not be viewed as totally depraved. Nature, if defined as man's state before he was corrupted by the Fall, could serve as an ideal standard which, although difficult for fallen men to observe, would be the model to which they could aspire. Christian writers understood Stoic theories of man's original freedom and equality in these terms. Man, as God created him, was not intended to be subject to the coercive domination of government or of slavery (Augustine, *The City of God,* Bk. XIX, 15). Property would not have been necessary if all cooperated and supported one another freely. Thus, Isidore of Seville, the last of the Fathers of the Church, specifically mentioned "possession in common of all things and one liberty for all men" as a part of the natural law (*Etymologies,* Bk. V, 2). Only as a result of man's sin was property established, and the coercive mechanism of government needed to repress evildoers and punish the wicked. As for slavery, "when men's nature was as God created it, no man was a slave either to man or to sin. However, slavery is now penal in character and planned by that law which commands the preservation of the natural order and forbids its disturbance" (Augustine, *The City of God,* Bk. XIX, 15). In striking contrast to Aristotle's view, this theory asserted that property, government, and slavery were all against the nature of man before the Fall. Yet Augustine viewed all of these institutions as necessary for man and thus in a sense natural in his fallen state.[9]

The patristic ambivalence towards nature is most evident in the writings of St. Augustine, whose spiritual autobiography, the *Confessions,* reveals that fallen nature was a reality for him in the strong passions which he tried in vain to control before his conversion. When Augustine retells the story of Alexander and the pirate in the *City of God* (Bk. IV, 4), and the pirate asserts that the only difference between himself and Alexander is one of scale, the moral of the story is different from its significance in Cicero,

---

[9] Ernst Troeltsch, *The Social Teaching of the Christian Church* (New York, 1936), Vol. I, 154, attempts to resolve the ambiguity by distinguishing between an "absolute" and a "relative" natural law in patristic thought; but this distinction is not found in the writings of the Fathers.

where it was related as a view to be refuted (*The Commonwealth,* Bk. III, 14). For Augustine, it illustrates a central truth, unless rulers are guided by Christian justice and truth, "what are kingdoms but large-scale robber-bands?" The only way to achieve true justice is through revelation—not through reason; not through nature, but through faith. The city of the world which loves only itself inevitably is disordered and dominated by evil passions. Only the community of those who love God can ever find the peace which is "the tranquillity of order" (*City of God,* Bk. XIX, 13).

Yet there is another nature which is not characterized by corruption and wickedness. By nature, man, as God created him, was free; and even now, when sin has made slavery necessary, man can retain his internal freedom, provided that he does not become a slave to sin. A peace consisting in an "ordered concord of obedience and rule" (*City of God,* Bk. XIX, 13) is possible on earth. This order is defined as the "distribution which allots things equal and unequal, each to its own place." Nature is still a moral standard and sinful actions are defined as contrary to nature.[10]

Cicero's definition of a just war is criticized by Augustine, who nevertheless defends the right of a ruler to wage a just war and relates this right to the natural law. "The natural order which seeks the peace of mankind, ordains that a monarch should have the power to undertake war if he thinks it advisable, and that the soldiers should perform their military duties in behalf of the peace and safety of the community." Like many Christian thinkers after him Augustine combines this with a Scriptural argument interpreting Christ's words about rendering to Caesar the things that are Caesar's (including tax money to be used for military purposes) and his praise for the centurion as indications that he was not opposed to war as such. Augustine's hierarchical view of the structure of the natural order is also demonstrated when he indicates that in cases where the righteousness of a war is in doubt,

---

10 "If it is a vice and can be rightly blamed, it must be against nature. All vice from the very fact that it is vice, is against nature" (*De Libero Arbitrio,* Bk. III, 13, 38, translated as *The Problem of Free Choice* by Dom Mark Pontifex, Westminster, Md., 1955, p. 180). See also the *Confessions,* Book III, ch. viii, and *The City of God,* Book XIX, ch. xiv, for similar statements.

the soldier is obliged to follow orders "because his position makes obedience a duty."[11]

For Augustine, a natural moral order built into the universe by God is still a standard, even if, because of sin, men have departed from it or refuse to recognize it. Augustine was a theologian and an active churchman rather than a lawyer or closet philosopher, but a belief in a natural order and natural law played a role, even though a subordinate one, in his thought. Through him and the other Fathers of the Church, the Stoic natural law theory was transmitted largely unchanged to the Middle Ages.

From inchoate beginnings in Greek thought, the Stoic philosophers developed a natural law theory which was the basis for most subsequent thinking on the subject. They viewed nature as permeated with reason, which was understood to be a moral force from which ethical norms could be derived. All men by the use of their reason were capable of perceiving universal moral laws—among them their duties to society and their fellow men, their original equality and freedom, and the necessity for moral limits on warfare.

A religious dimension was added to this rational conception of nature as the source of ethical norms, since a rational God was the source of the reason that permeated the universe. Christian thought combined this with a belief that God had written this law in men's hearts through the promptings of conscience. In the works of the Roman lawyers, natural law was both related to and distinguished from *jus gentium,* the common legal provisions in the various legal systems of mankind. For one writer (Ulpian) natural law linked man to the animal world, since nature was defined as the instinctual element which men share with animals. Most commonly, however, natural law was understood to be a rational ethical ideal which underlay existing legal arrangements and provided a standard by which to judge and interpret them. In this form it became part of the common heritage of the Christian West in the writings of Cicero, the Roman lawyers, and the Fathers of the Church.

---

11 St. Augustine, *Contra Faustum,* Bk. XXII, ch. 75, translated in Henry Paolucci, ed., *The Political Writings of St. Augustine* (Chicago, 1962), p. 165.

BIBLIOGRAPHY

Barker, Ernest. *From Alexander to Constantine.* Oxford, 1956.

Carlyle, A. J. *A History of Medieval Political Theory in the West.* Vol. I, Edinburgh, 1903, pt. 2, ch. 3–4.

Herbert, Deane. *The Political and Social Ideas of St. Augustine.* New York, 1963.

d'Entreves, A. P. *Natural Law.* London, 1951, ch. 1.

Dodd, C. H. *New Testament Studies.* Manchester, 1953, ch. 6.

Flückiger, Felix. *Geschichte des Naturrechts.* I, Zurich, 1954, ch. VIII.

Levy, Ernest. "Natural Law in Roman Thought," Natural Law Institute, *Proceedings.* Vol. II, Notre Dame, Ind., 1948, pp. 43–72.

Maine, Henry. *Ancient Law.* London, 1870, ch. 3.

McIlwain, Charles H. *The Growth of Political Thought in the West.* New York, 1932, ch. 4.

Reesor, Margaret. *The Political Theory of the Old and Middle Stoa.* New York, 1951.

Sabine, George H. and Stanley B. Smith, eds. *Cicero, On the Commonwealth.* Columbus, Ohio, 1929, Introduction.

Schultz, Fritz. *A History of Roman Legal Science.* Oxford, 1946.

Watson, Gerard. "The Early History of Natural Law," *Irish Theological Quarterly.* Vol. XXXIII (1966), pp. 77 ff.

Wormuth, Francis D. "Astraea and Diké: Ius Naturale in Roman Law," in Morris D. Forkosch, ed. *Essays in Legal History in Honor of Felix Frankfurter.* Indianapolis, 1966, pp. 585–99.

The Digest of Justinian*

Title i: On Justice and Law

1. Ulpianus (*Institutes* 1). When a man means to give his
attention to law (*jus*), he ought first to know whence the term
jus is derived. Now *jus* is so called from *justitia;* in fact,
according to the nice definition of Celsus, *jus* is the art of
what is good and fair. (1) Of this art we may deservedly
be called the priests; we cherish justice and profess the knowledge
of what is good and fair, we separate what is fair from what is
unfair, we discriminate between what is allowed and what
is forbidden, we desire to make men good, not only by putting
them in fear of penalties, but also by appealing to them
through rewards, proceeding, if I am not mistaken, on a real
and not a pretended philosophy. (2) Of this subject there
are two departments, public law and private law. Public law
is that which regards the constitution of the Roman
state, private law looks at the interest of individuals; as a matter
of fact, some things are beneficial from the point of view
of the state, and some with reference to private persons. Public
law is concerned with sacred rites, with priests, and with
public officers. Private law has a threefold division, it is
deduced partly from the rules of natural law, partly from those
of the *jus gentium,* partly from those of the civil law. (3)
Natural law is that which all animals have been taught by
nature; this law is not peculiar to the human species, it is
common to all animals which are produced on land or sea, and
to fowls of the air as well. From it comes the union of man
and woman called by us matrimony, and therewith the procreation
and rearing of children; we find in fact that animals in general,
the very wild beasts, are marked by acquaintance with this
law. (4) *Jus gentium* is the law used by the various tribes of

* From *The Digest of Justinian,* translated by Charles Henry Monro, Volume I
by permission. Copyright © 1904 by Cambridge University Press.

mankind, and there is no difficulty in seeing that it falls
short of natural law, as the latter is common to all animated
beings, whereas the former is only common to human beings
in respect of their mutual relations; . . .

Manumissions also are comprised in the *jus gentium*.
Manumission is the same as dismissal from *manus* (hand), in
short the giving of liberty; as long as a man is in a state
of slavery he is subject to *manus* and *potestas* (control), by
manumission he is freed from control. All this had its origin
in the *jus gentium*, seeing that by natural law all were born
free, and manumission was not know, because slavery itself
was unknown; but when slavery came in through the *jus
gentium*, there followed the relief given by manumission; and
whereas people were once simply called by the one natural
name of "man," by the *jus gentium* there came to be three
divisions, first freemen, then, as contradistinguished from them,
slaves, and then, in the third place, freedmen, that is persons
who had ceased to be slaves.

Hermogenianus (*Epitomes of Law 1*). It was by this
same *jus gentium* that war was introduced, nations were
distinguished, kingdoms were established, rights of ownership
were ascertained, boundaries were set to domains, buildings
were erected, mutual traffic, purchase and sale, letting and
hiring and obligations in general were set on foot, with the
exception of a few of these last which were introduced
by the civil law.

Ulpianus (*Institutes 1*). The civil law is something which
on the one hand is not altogether independent of natural
law or *jus gentium*, and on the other is not in every respect
subordinate to it; so that when we make addition to or deduction
from universal law (*jus commune*), we establish a law of
our own, that is, civil law. (1) Now this law of ours is either
ascertained by writing or without writing; as the Greeks say,
"of laws some are in writing and some are not in writing."

Gaius (*Institutes 1*). All nations which are governed by
statutes and customs make use partly of law which is peculiar
to the respective nations, and partly of such as is common
to all mankind. Whatever law any nation has established
for itself is peculiar to the particular state (*civitas*), and is called

civil law, as being the peculiar law of that state, but law
which natural reason has laid down for mankind in general
is maintained equally by all men, and is called *jus gentium,* as
being the law which all nations use.

Ulpianus (*Rules* I). Justice is a constant, unfailing disposition
to give every one his legal due. (1) The principles of
law are these: Live uprightly, injure no man, give every man
his due. (2) To be learned in the law (*jurisprudentia*) is to be
acquainted with divine and human things, to know what
is just and what is unjust.

Paulus (*On Sabinus* 14). The word *jus* is used in a
number of different senses: in the first place, in that in which
the name is applied to that which is under all circumstances
fair and right, as in the case of natural law (*jus naturale*);
secondly, where the word signifies that which is available
for the benefit of all or most persons in any particular state, as
in the case of the expression civil law (*jus civile*). . . .

Title viii: On the Division of Things and Their Respective Natures

Marcianus (*Institutes* 3) . . . Some things are by natural
law common to all, some belong to a community (*universitas*),
some to nobody, most things belong to individuals; and
they are acquired by various titles in the respective cases. (1) To
begin with, by natural law, the following are common to all:
air, flowing water, the sea, and consequently the seashore.

Florentinus (*Institutes* 6). Moreover pebbles, gems and
generally things which persons find on the seashore at
once become theirs by natural law.

Marcianus (*Institutes* 3). Accordingly no one is debarred
from entering on the seashore for the purpose of fishing, so long
as there is no meddling with houses, buildings, or monuments;
these not being, like the sea itself, subjects of the *jus
gentium.* . . .

SOURCES

Cicero, *The Commonwealth* (*De Re Publica*), Bk. I, ch. 25; Bk. III, ch. 11, 14–15, 22–23, 25; Bk. VI, ch. 16–18.

——, *Moral Duties* (*De Officiis*), Bk. I, ch. 16; Bk. III, ch. 3–7, 17.

——, *The Laws* (*De Legibus*), Bk. I, ch. 6–7, 10, 12; Bk. II, ch. 24.

Justinian, *The Digest*, Bk I. Titles i, viii.

St. Augustine, *The City of God*, Bk. IV, ch. 4; Bk. XIX, ch. 12–15.

——, *Contra Faustum*, Bk. XXII, ch. 74–79.

The New Testament, *Acts of the Apostles*, ch. 17.

——, St. Paul, *Epistle to the Romans*, ch. 1–2.

——, St. Paul, *Epistle to the Galatians*, ch. 3.

3.
MEDIEVAL THEORIES
OF NATURAL LAW

In many histories of political theory, the medieval period is discussed almost exclusively in terms of the political thought of St. Thomas Aquinas. Yet medieval scholarship in recent years has given increasing attention to another important source besides that of the philosophers and theologians—the writings of the canon lawyers. In the history of natural law theory, as in many other areas, the canon lawyers made interesting and original contributions and transmitted important elements of the classical theories.

The systematic study of canon law may be said to have begun with the publication of the *Concordantia Discordantium Canonum* (c. 1139), better known as the *Decretum*, by the Bolognese monk, Gratian. Other collections of church law had been published earlier, but the *Decretum* became the basis of instruction in the faculties of canon law which were developing in the medieval universities in the twelfth and thirteenth centuries. With the addition of the official collections of papal legislation in the thirteenth and early fourteenth centuries, it formed the basic law of the Roman Catholic Church until 1918, when the present Code of Canon Law was promulgated.

The opening section of Gratian's work was influenced indirectly by Roman law and directly by the writings of the Fathers of the Church, especially Ambrose, Augustine, and Isidore of Seville. Drawn as it was from different sources, it contained apparently contradictory statements which Gratian sometimes, but not always, tried to reconcile. At the outset, Gratian seems to equate natural law with Scripture (both of which are said to command the observance of the Golden Rule), and a few lines later divine law is described as coming from nature. This description is followed by a definition of natural law drawn from Isidore of Seville (560–636) in which he asserted that natural law "holds everywhere by an instinct of nature." Isidore held that "the union of man and woman, the generation and rearing of children" were a part of that law, thus reflecting the influence of the Roman lawyer Ulpian, who associated natural law with animal instinct. Later commentators on the *Decretum,* however, rejected this view and restricted natural law to the specifically rational and human.[1]

Isidore's statement that among the provisions of the natural law were "the possession in common of all things and one freedom for all men" was quoted by Gratian in *Distinction I.* Along with a similar statement by Augustine in *Distinction* 8, it reasserted for the Middle Ages the patristic conception of an original "natural" state of communal ownership and liberty. Like the Church Fathers, however, the medieval canon lawyers argued that as a result of sin, practices such as slavery and property had been introduced which departed from these ideals (*Decretum,* C. 12, qu. 1, c. 2); and they discussed church laws regulating these institutions without ever considering the possible legal application of Gratian's statement that "anything . . . which is against natural law is . . . null and void" (*Decretum,* D. 8).

However, the canon law retained a belief that universal human freedom and communal ownership represented a more ideal "natural" state of human existence exemplified by life before the Fall. In Rufinus' commentary on the *Decretum* this belief was formally incorporated into canonist theory through the concept of admonitions (*demonstrationes*) of the natural law. "These things

---

[1] See the excerpts from Rufinus (c. 1170) translated in Ewart Lewis, *Medieval Political Ideas,* vol. I (New York, 1954), pp. 37–38, and the references to Huguccio in Walter Ullmann, *Medieval Papalism* (London, 1949), p. 39, no. 2.

which nature neither forbids nor commands, but shows to be good, especially . . . one freedom for all men and common possession of all things."[2] (Rufinus goes on to explain that slavery and property are now established by civil law because of human passions and sin.)

While it was not applied to property or slavery, Gratian's assertion that natural law could be used to nullify existing legal provisions was actually implemented by the canon lawyers in other cases. "Natural and divine law" were cited in church courts in medieval Europe to annul arbitrary customs and local laws. With the existence of the ecclesiastical courts to give it application, the conception of natural law as a higher set of norms invalidating irrational legislation began for the first time to have an operative significance.

The formula, "natural and divine law," was characteristic of the canon lawyers' close association, and even at times confusion of the two types of law. Whereas Aquinas differentiated divine law, defined as God's direct revelation in Scripture, from natural law, God's commands as revealed in his creation; for the canon lawyers the distinction was not so clear. Natural law was divine law since it came from God, and Scripture contained further evidence of the natural law, although Gratian himself recognized that not everything contained in Scripture could be considered as still binding. (He distinguished in D. 6 of the *Decretum* between the "mystical," i.e., ceremonial, and the "moral" precepts of the Scriptures. See *infra.*)

With such a loose definition of natural law, it was evident that some provision had to be made for possible changes and interpretations. For the canonists the solution to this problem was easy; the pope could dispense from the law (although not from articles of faith and decrees of the early councils). Under certain specified conditions, he could take away liberty, dissolve the marriage bond, and even annul the obligations of oaths.[3]

The canon law was an important influence in transmitting patristic conceptions of natural law to medieval Europe, in particular the belief in freedom and communal ownership as the

[2] Cf. discussion by Rufinus translated in Ewart Lewis, *Medieval Political Ideas,* Vol. I, pp. 38–39.

[3] Cf. Ullmann, *Medieval Papalism,* ch. 3.

original and natural state of man. What it added was the assertion that a conflict between natural law and an existing legal provision was grounds for annulment of the positive law. And as in the writings of the Fathers of the Church, the natural law was related directly to God and divine revelation, thus giving it a theological reinforcement which made it an important part of medieval thought. The canon lawyers did little, however, to develop the concepts taken over from the Roman writers. The creative thinking was done by the theologians, and especially by the greatest of the medieval writers on theology, St. Thomas Aquinas.

St. Thomas Aquinas (1225–74) was a Dominican monk who taught at the University of Paris and in Italy a century after Gratian. His theological works were written in order to respond to the challenge to the Catholic faith posed by the reintroduction of Aristotle's writings into Western Europe at the beginning of the thirteenth century. Aquinas wrote no separate treatise on law, but a section of his *Summa Theologica* (Pt. I–II, qu. 90–97) is devoted to a discussion of the subject. In contrast to the canonists, Aquinas distinguished natural and divine law very clearly from each other. According to Aquinas the *natural law* is that part of the *eternal law*, God's plan for the universe, in which man shares by his reason; the *divine law* is God's direct revelation to man through Christ and the Scriptures. Since "grace does not contradict nature, but perfects it," the divine law confirms the natural law, but it also adds precepts which could not be known by reason alone. To complete the Thomistic fourfold division of law, *human law* is the application to specific circumstances of the precepts of reason contained in the natural law. Like all law, it is a "rational ordering of things for the common good, promulgated by the one in charge of the community." If it departs from reason, "it has the quality not of a law but of an act of violence."

When Aquinas elaborates on the specific content of natural law, it is clear that he is attempting an ingenious synthesis of elements which had often been opposed in the writings of earlier writers. He begins with the principle that "good is to be done and evil avoided," which he describes as a self-evident premise comparable to the principle of contradiction in logic. Like all basic principles of morality, this principle is perceived by a process of direct moral intuition through a special capacity (Latin: *habitus*) called *synderesis,* which is sometimes equated with and sometimes distinguished from conscience.[4] Arguing that the good of man is related to God's purposes as manifested in the way in which he designed man, Aquinas focuses his attention upon what he calls the "natural inclinations," placed in man by a rational and purposive God as guides to his fulfillment or end. These inclinations (we might call them drives) are organized in a hierarchical scheme based on the Neoplatonic and Augustinian view of the cosmos as composed of various grades of being which differ qualitatively. They correspond to and indicate man's natural purposes, intended for fulfillment by their author, God. The natural law contains the precepts related to man's drive to preserve himself, which he shares with all living things; those related to his animal drives such as sex and the rearing of children (cf. Ulpian's view of natural law as based on animal instincts); and those which mark him as specifically human—his need for society, his desire for knowledge and for God.

This passage (*Summa Theologica,* Pt. I–II, qu. 94, conclusion) is the only detailed account of the content of the natural law in Aquinas' writing. However incomplete, it is more specific than earlier references in the writings of the Stoics, the Roman lawyers, and the Fathers. However, a careful review of Aquinas' references in the *Summa* reveals that there are other principles which he includes in the natural law. Among the practices which Aquinas condemns as opposed to nature in the *Summa* are theft (with some reservations concerning the prior right of a starving man to food), adultery, homosexuality, usury (following Aristotle on the nonproductive nature of money), drunkenness, gluttony, suicide, murder, and the violation of promises. Among the commands of natural law he includes the care of children by their parents, reverence for God, charity to the poor, and obedience to the law.[5]

---

[4] *Summa Theologica,* Pt. I, qu. 79, a. 12; Pt. I–II, qu. 94, a. 1. On the translation of *habitus* and the meaning of *synderesis,* see Volume 28 of the Blackfriars editon of the *Summa Theologica* (London, 1964), p. 45, notes b and 3. A major part of the *Summa Theologica* is contained in Anton C. Pegis, ed., *The Basic Writings of St. Thomas Aquinas,* 2 vols. (New York, 1945). A useful collection of excerpts (taken out of scholastic form but with original Latin text on facing pages) is A. P. d'Entreves, ed., Aquinas, *Selected Political Writings* (Oxford, 1954).

[5] *Summa Theologica,* Pt. I–II, qu. 94, a. 3 ad 2 and 3; Pt. II–II, qu. 57, a. 2 ad 2; qu. 64, a. 5; qu. 66, a. 7; qu. 78, a. 1 ad 3; qu. 81, a. 2 ad 3; qu. 88, a. 3 ad 1 and a. 10 ad 2.

The application of these principles to concrete situations is difficult. We may know the fundamental principles of morality directly, but when we attempt to apply them to complex situations (Aquinas calls this arriving at particular determinations by the use of the practical reason) there is less certainty.[6] The example that Thomas cites of a conflict between the obligation to return property and loyalty to one's country seems to indicate that even with knowledge of the natural law it is difficult to arrive at "particular determinations" because they involve a conflict between applicable moral principles.

The fusion of Stoic and Roman Law ideas of natural law with Aristotelian notions of teleology and the incorporation of these concepts in a Christian framework was the contribution of Thomas Aquinas to the development of natural law theory. His theory is at the same time more precise and more subject to varying applications than those which preceded him. Rather than simply referring vaguely to reason as the source and content of natural law, Thomas points to natural (and divinely intended) purposes in man as indications of the precepts of that law. Nevertheless, he is also aware that the complexities of human life make it impossible to set down a hard and fast rule for every situation.

Aquinas' theory is more satisfactory than those which preceded him, but it is still open to criticism. How do we know, for instance, which of our inclinations or purposes are natural and which are not? Perhaps Aquinas would reply that the answer is self-evident from the notion of human nature—but we must ask, What is contained in the notion of human nature? For Aquinas human nature seems to be a set of ideal goals and purposes that all men can perceive by *synderesis*, those who do not being either ignorant or depraved.[7] Yet controversies over moral values indicate that not all share the same "self-evident" conception of human nature or would even agree that looking for a relatively stable set of goals in man is the best way of approaching morals and politics.

Disagreements on moral values are also often based on different priorities of values or conflicts between several competing

---

[6] *Ibid.*, Pt. I–II, qu. 63, a. 1; qu. 91, a. 3; qu. 94, a. 4, 5.

[7] Cf. *Summa Theologica*, Pt. I–II, qu. 94, a. 4: "In some the reason is perverted by passion, or evil habit, or an evil disposition of nature."

values. A deductive natural law system which derives all morality from one basic value does not usually face this problem, but the pluralism of Aquinas' approach inevitably suggests that moral dilemmas may be posed by conflicts between man's duties to society and to God (church and state), to preserve himself and preserve social institutions (war and compulsory military service), to provide for himself and his children and to contribute to society (the social function of property), and so on.[8]

Aquinas' treatment of the *jus gentium* or law of nations also attempted to synthesize conflicting earlier views. The Roman lawyers had recognized that at least some institutions (e.g., war and slavery) which were common to all nations were not part of the law of nature. At the same time they saw in the universal existence of certain kinds of laws a proof of the existence of the law of nature; and one Roman law writer, Gaius, identified the law of nations and natural law. Aquinas took a different but related view. He classified *jus gentium* as a part of positive law but described it as closely connected to the natural law. "To the law of nations belong those things which are derived from the law of nature as conclusions from premises, e.g., just buyings and sellings and the like, without which man cannot live together—which is part of the law of nature since man is by nature a social animal, as is proved in Aristotle's *Politics*. But those things that are derived from the law of nature by way of particular determinations belong to the civil law. . . ."[9]

Aquinas was also obliged to attempt to reconcile the divergent views of Aristotle and the Church Fathers on the conventional or natural character of slavery and property. Aristotle had held that

---

[8] Some interpreters have seen in Aquinas a deductive theory of natural law because of his comparison of moral reasoning to scientific deduction (*Summa Theologica*, Pt. I–II, qu. 91, a. 3) and his assertion that all precepts of the law are based on the first principle of the practical reason that "good is to be done and evil is to be avoided" (*Summa Theologica*, Pt. I–II, qu. 94, a. 2). See, for example, Morton White, *Religion, Politics, and the Higher Learning* (Cambridge, Mass., 1959), pp. 124 ff. However, the context of Aquinas' discussion seems to indicate a more pluralistic approach. For an argument that Aquinas is a "pragmatist" rather than a "classical rationalist," see Michael Novak, "The Traditional Pragmatism," *A Time to Build* (New York, 1967), ch. 17.

[9] *Summa Theologica* Pt. I–II, qu. 95, a. 4; but cf. also Pt. II–II, qu. 57, a. 3, where Aquinas seems to accept and to attempt to reconcile the Roman law definitions.

both were justified by nature (cf. Aristotle, *Politics,* Bk I, No. 1254, and II, No. 1263–64) whereas patristic opinion considered the two institutions to be opposed to man's original nature—and in the case of slavery, the Roman law writers agreed.

In his discussion of natural law Aquinas attempts to reconcile the two views through the concept of "additions" to the natural law made necessary by new conditions (*Summa Theologica,* Pt. I–II, qu. 94, a. 5). While nature did not originally provide men with these institutions (and therefore Isidore of Seville's "common possession" and "one freedom" can be said to be more natural), "they are adoptions of human reason which are useful for human life and in these cases the natural law is not altered but added to."

Discussions of slavery and property elsewhere in the *Summa,* however, indicate that Aquinas has differing views on the character of the two institutions. Private property is defended as "not contrary to the natural law but an addition thereto devised by human reason, which is necessary to human life." (*Summa Theologica,* Pt. II–II, qu. 66, a. 2.) His arguments are similar to those of Aristotle (to whom he attributes the doctrine that "possession of material things is natural to man"). Men take better care of what is their own and there is likely to be less confusion and disagreement when property is divided, although there is an obligation "to help one's neighbor in need" (*Summa Theologica,* Pt. II–II, qu. 66, a. 7), and if a property holder refuses to recognize this obligation, his property may be taken from him ("private property, common use" in Aristotle's formulation in Book II of the *Politics*).

In the case of slavery, although Aquinas mentions Aristotle's argument that it is useful for the slave to benefit from the guidance of a wiser man (*Summa Theologica,* Pt. II–II, qu. 57, a. 3 ad 2), he states elsewhere that slavery is the result of sin and could not have existed "in the state of innocence" since by natural law all men are equal. Furthermore, since "all men are equal by nature" a slave still has rights of self-preservation and marriage and family life which are not subject to his master's will (*Summa Theologica,* Pt. II–II, qu. 104, a. 5).

Thus it appears that Aquinas views slavery as a convenient institution but does not accept Aristotle's contention that slavery is naturally justified. Natural law, in fact, places sharp limits on the institution. The slave is not Aristotle's "living tool."[10] Property, on the other hand, seems to be more than a useful institution. While specific rules of property are devised "by human agreement," the institution itself is now "necessary" because of man's egoism and disputatiousness since the Fall. On balance, therefore, it seems that Aquinas leans more to Aristotle than the Fathers on the question of property, while the reverse is true of slavery.[11]

Aquinas does not compromise on another issue on which Aristotle and the Fathers disagreed—the natural justification of government. Although the Fathers considered government to be an essentially coercive institution which was only necessary because of the sinfulness of men, Aquinas follows Aristotle in viewing it as a means to the fulfillment of the social and political nature of man. Answering a statement of Augustine that man was not under the domination of man before the Fall, Aquinas says that government would always have existed, since men may differ on ways to attain the common good and there must be an authoritative determination of common action. Moreover, government enables society to benefit from the insights of the morally and intellectually superior as to the best way to achieve the common good. Even rule by infidels can be justified on the basis of reason and the *jus gentium* (*Summa Theologica*, Pt. I, qu. 96, a. 4; Pt. II–II, qu. 10; qu. 12, a. 2).

From his acceptance of slavery and his emphasis on the legislative role of the "one who has the care of the community" it is apparent that Aquinas does not consider social and political equality as part of the natural law. Despite man's original natural equality, the moral and intellectually superior have a special claim to rule, and there is no reference in Aquinas to consent of the ruled as a requirement for political legitimacy. Aquinas mentions cases in which a free community has a right to legislate for itself

---

[10] A possible way to reconcile the Aristotelian and patristic views would be to hold that a consequence of the Fall has been to produce the "natural slave" of Aristotle who needs the moral direction of a master, but even in his argument as to the usefulness of guidance by a wiser man Aquinas says, "Considered absolutely the fact that this particular man should be a slave rather than another man is based, not on natural reason, but on some resultant utility."

[11] Cf. also *Summa Theologica*, Pt. I, qu. 92, a. 1, ad 2; qu. 96, a. 4; and *Supplement*, qu. 52, a. 1.

(*Summa Theologica*, Pt. I–II, qu. 97, a. 3 ad 3), and favors a limited popular role in government (*Summa Theologica*, Pt. I–II, qu. 95, a. 4; qu. 105, a. 1), but he describes monarchical rule as most in accord with nature (*De Regimine Principum*, ch. 2). This hierarchical outlook on society is further reflected in a passage in the *Summa Theologica* in which St. Thomas asserts that just as there are three orders on each of the levels of the angelic hierarchy, so in every city there is a threefold order: "Some are supreme as the nobles, others are lowest as the common people, while others hold a place between these" (Pt. I, qu. 108, a. 4).

Both in governmental forms and in legislation Aquinas allows for a considerable element of relativity in the application of general principles to particular situations. The common good which he cites as the end of legislation is not some single fixed good such as that Plato envisioned, but a complex of the particular and the general which varies from country to country and changes as man devises new applications of natural law principles (*Summa Theologica*, Pt. I–II, qu. 94, a. 5).

Nevertheless some standards which may not be violated remain. For the waging of war, for instance, Aquinas lays down strict conditions. In order for war to be just, it must be declared by a legitimate authority (private wars, common in Aquinas' time, are forbidden), the cause must be just, and the war must be waged for a good purpose—to restore peace and restrain evil, not for aggrandizement (*Summa Theologica*, Pt. II–II, qu. 46, a. 1).

No less than the canon lawyers, Aquinas insists that a law which violates natural law is not law but a "corruption of law" and "an act of violence" (cf. *Summa Theologica*, Pt. I–II, qu. 93, a. 3 ad 2; qu. 95, a. 2; qu. 96, a. 4). It is not clear, however, who is to determine when such a conflict exists. Aquinas would presumably regard the natural law as self-evident, at least to the wise. Since he considers the pope to be the authoritative interpreter of the divine law, which in turn confirms parts of the natural law, the question of excessive subjectivity in interpreting the natural law does not pose a serious problem for him.

The role of the divine law as a guide for natural law in the Middle Ages is a reminder that Aquinas' theory of natural law should not be taken out of the theological context in which it appears. As he indicates (*Summa Theologica*, Pt. I–II, qu. 5, a. 5), nature alone cannot bring man perfect happiness. Man's highest end is the contemplation of God in the Beatific Vision in heaven. Natural law is only an imperfect way of knowing God's purposes while man is still on earth, and it cannot bring him to his true fulfillment. Divine revelation provides a much more complete guide, and the life of grace enables man to attain heights of spirituality which he could not attain by nature. Even if it were possible, a life of natural virtue in Aristotelian terms would not completely satisfy man nor fully perfect him. (The belief that man could attain salvation by his own unaided natural powers had been condemned by the Church as the Pelagian heresy many centuries before.)

It appears, therefore, that Aquinas' system of natural law is and must be incomplete. He could not admit the Aristotelian possibility that nature could provide fully for man's fulfillment. The theological doctrine of Original Sin and the Fall of Man compelled him to combine in his thinking two notions of nature—the first being man's uncorrupted nature in the state of innocence, and the second man's present sinful state in which coercive government and property are necessary and slavery is useful. Similarly, his belief in the necessity of divine grace led Aquinas to assert that human nature could not arrive at its true goal—the direct vision of God—without divine assistance, and to combine a recognition of the necessity of the supernatural life of grace with the Aristotelian naturalism which pervades much of the rest of his theory.

Nevertheless, the incorporation of Aristotelianism into Christian thought gave a renewed emphasis to the attempt to ground morals and politics on values inherent in man's nature—and the scholastic synthesis of the diverse strains in earlier thought has endured and even outlasted the universal acceptance of Christianity which it assumed. Today this synthesis forms the basis of contemporary neo-Thomism and the grounds for Christian Democratic natural rights, theories which are applied to a modern secular political context different from the world of St. Thomas.

BIBLIOGRAPHY

Carlyle, R. W. and A. J. *A History of Medieval Political Theory in the West.* Vol. II and V, Edinburgh and London, 1927–38.

d'Entreves, A. P. *The Medieval Contribution to Political Thought.* London, 1939, ch. 2.

Jaffa, Harry. *Thomism and Aristotelianism.* Chicago, 1952.

Lewis, Ewart. *Medieval Political Ideas.* Vol. I, New York, 1954, pp. 6–69.

Lottin, O. *Le droit naturel chez St. Thomas et ses predecesseurs.* Bruges, 1926.

O'Connor, D. J. *Aquinas and Natural Law.* London, 1967.

Ullmann, Walter. *Medieval Papalism.* London, 1949, ch. 2, 3.

———. *A History of Political Thought in the Middle Ages.* Baltimore, 1965, ch. 6–8.

Weigand, Rudolf. *Die Naturrechtslehre der Legisten und Dekretisten von Irnerius bis Accursius und von Gratian bis Johannes Teutonicus.* Munich, 1967.

The Concordance of Discordant Canons or Decretum (1139)*

GRATIAN

Part I: Divine and Human Law

Distinction I: The human race is ruled in two ways: by natural law and by custom. Natural law is what is contained in the Old and New Testaments, which commands every man to do unto another what he would have done unto himself and forbids him to do unto another what he would not have done unto himself. Therefore Christ says in the Gospel, "Whatever you wish men to do unto you, do the same unto them. For this is the Law and the Prophets" (Matthew 7:12).

Canon 1 (Book V, ch. 2, Isidore of Seville, *Etymologies*): *Divine laws come from nature; human laws from custom.* "All laws are either divine or human. Divine laws come from nature; human laws from custom, and therefore the two differ, for different laws please different peoples.". . .

Canon 6: *What are the kinds of law?* (*Ibid.*, ch. 4). "Law is either natural law, or civil law, or the law of nations (*jus gentium*)."

Canon 7: *What is natural law?* (*Ibid.*) "Natural law is the law which is common to all nations because it holds everywhere by an instinct of nature and not by any legislative enactment. Such things are included in it as the union of man and woman, the procreation and education of children, possession in common of all things, one freedom for all men, the acquisition of what is taken from the heavens, the earth, and the sea—also, the return of a thing which has been left in trust or of money which has been lent, and resistance

* Translated by Paul E. Sigmund from *Corpus Juris Canonici*. Copyright © 1879 B. Tauchnitz, Leipzig.

to violence by force. For this and anything like this is never considered unjust, but natural and equitable."

Canon 8 (*Ibid.,* ch. 5): *What is civil law?* "Civil law is whatever a people or a state has adopted as its own for a divine or human reason."

Canon 9 (*Ibid.,* ch. 6): *What is the law of nations?* "The law of nations includes the occupation and establishment of fortified places, wars, captivity, slavery, rights of return, treaties of peace, armistices, the obligation not to injure ambassadors, (and) the prohibition of marriage with foreigners. This is called the law of nations because nearly all nations observe this law.". . .

Distinction 5: Natural law is first among all laws in time and in dignity. For it began with the emergence of rational creation and it does not change with time, but remains immutable. But since natural law is described above as contained in the Old and New Testaments, and certain practices contrary to what is commanded in the Old Testament are now allowed, the natural law does not seem to have remained immutable. For the Old Testament commands that a woman shall cease to enter the Temple for forty days if she bears a male child and for eighty days if she bears a female child, while now there is no prohibition against entering the church immediately after giving birth. . . .

Distinction 6, Canon 3: . . . The natural law is contained in the Old and New Testaments, but not everything that is found in the Old and New Testaments proves to be part of the natural law. There are moral precepts in the Old Testament such as "Thou shalt not kill," and there are mystical precepts such as those concerning the sacrifice of a lamb and other similar precepts. The moral commands are part of the natural law, and therefore no one can show that they have been changed. But the mystical commands appear to be foreign to the natural law, although they are found to be connected with it in their moral significance. Therefore they seem to have been changed as to their superficial appearance, but their moral significance proves to be unchanged. . . .

Distinction 8: Natural law differs from custom and from

legislation. By the natural law all things are common to all
men. Not only do we believe that this was the case for those
of whom we read, "The multitude of believers were of one
heart and one spirit" (Acts 4:32), but we also find that it
was taught by philosophers at an earlier time. Thus Plato
teaches that that city is most just in which no citizen has
any desire for things of his own. But by custom and legislation
one thing is mine and another someone else's. Therefore
Augustine says:

Canon 1: *By divine law all things are common to all men,
but by statute law, one thing is mine and another someone
else's (Tract VI on the Gospel of St. John,* ch. 1). "By what
law do you defend the property of the church—by the
divine law or by human law? We have the divine law in the
Scriptures, and the human law in the legislation of kings. How
does anyone possess what he possesses? Is it not by human
law? By divine law 'The earth is the Lord's and the fullness
thereof' (Psalm 23)." . . . The natural law prevails over
custom and legislation in dignity. Anything that is accepted by
custom or included in legislation which is against natural law
is to be considered null and void. Therefore Augustine says:

Canon 2: *No one may do anything against natural law
(Confessions,* Bk. III, ch. 8). . . .

Canon 4: *Custom is to yield to truth and reason*
(Augustine, *On Baptism, against the Donatists,* Bk. III, ch. 6).
"Once the truth is evident, I answer clearly, let custom yield
to truth. Who would doubt that custom ought to yield to
manifest truth." Likewise, "Let no one set custom over
reason and truth, for reason and truth always overcome
custom." . . .

Therefore it is clearly evident that custom yields to
natural law.

Distinction 9: That statute law yields to natural law is
proved by many authorities. For Augustine says:

Canon 1: *The laws of princes ought not to prevail over
natural law (Epistle L).* "When the emperors adopt bad
laws contrary to the truth, the good believers are tried,
and those who persevere receive the crown (of martyrdom).
When they adopt good laws against falsehood, criminals

are deterred and the learned corrected. Those who will not obey the laws of the emperors which are adopted in keeping with God's truth will receive a great punishment, but those who do not obey the laws of emperors that are adopted in violation of God's truth will receive a great reward.". . .

Therefore, since nothing is commanded by the law of nature but what God wishes, and nothing forbidden but what God forbids, and since there is nothing in the canonical scriptures other than what is found in divine law and divine law is consistent with nature, it is clear that whatever is demonstrably contrary to the divine will or canonical scripture is also opposed to natural law. Hence, when a subject is considered as part of the divine will, or the canonical scriptures, or divine law, it is also under natural law. Therefore, any ecclesiastical or secular legislation which is shown to be contrary to natural law must definitely be rejected. . . .

ST. THOMAS AQUINAS ON
NATURAL LAW

The Summa Theologica

*Whether There Is in Us a Natural Law**

. . . the Gloss on Rom. 2:14: "When the Gentiles, who have not the law, do by nature those things that are of the law," comments as follows: "Although they have no written law, yet they have the natural law, whereby each one knows, and is conscious of, what is good and what is evil."

I answer that, Law, being a rule and measure, can be in a person in two ways: in one way, as in him that rules and measures; in another way, as in that which is ruled and measured, since a thing is ruled and measured in so far as it partakes of the rule or measure. Therefore, since all things subject to divine providence are ruled and measured by the eternal law, it is evident that all things partake in some way in the eternal law, in so far as from its being imprinted on them, they derive their respective inclinations to their proper acts and ends. Now among all others, the rational creature is subject to divine providence in a most excellent way, in so far as it partakes of a share of providence, by being provident both for itself and for others. Therefore it has a share of the eternal reason, whereby it has a natural inclination to its proper act and end; and this participation of the eternal law in the rational creature is called the natural law. . . .

* From *The "Summa Theologica" of St. Thomas Aquinas,* Part II, Section I, Question 91, Article 2 (I–II, qu. 91, a. 2), translated by the English Dominicans, Vol. III, by R. and T. Washbourne, Ltd. London, 1915. American edition, copyright © 1947 by Benziger, Inc. Used by permission.

Whether the Natural Law Contains Several Precepts, or Only One*

. . . The precepts of the natural law are to the practical reason, what the first principles of demonstrations are to the speculative reason; because both are self-evident principles. . . .

. . . Now a certain order is to be found in those things that are apprehended universally. For that which, before aught else, falls under apprehension, is *being,* the notion of which is included in all things whatsoever a man apprehends. Therefore the first indemonstrable principle is that *the same thing cannot be affirmed and denied at the same time,* which is based on the notion of *being* and *not-being:* and on this principle all others are based, as is stated in [Aristotle's] *Metaphysics.* Now as *being* is the first thing that falls under the apprehension absolutely, so *good* is the first thing that falls under the apprehension of the practical reason, which is directed to action: since every agent acts for an end, under the aspect of good. Consequently, the first principle in the practical reason is one founded on the nature of good, viz., that *good is that which all things seek after.* Hence this is the first precept of law, that *good is to be done and pursued, and evil is to be avoided.* All other precepts of the natural law are based upon this: so that whatever the practical reason naturally apprehends as man's good or evil belongs to the precepts of the natural law as something to be done or avoided.

Since, however, good has the nature of an end, and evil, the nature of the contrary, hence it is that all those things to which man has a natural inclination are naturally apprehended by reason as being good, and consequently as objects of pursuit, and their contraries as evil, and objects of avoidance. Therefore, the order of the precepts of the natural law follows the order of natural inclinations, because in man there is first of all an inclination to good in accordance with the nature which he has in common with all substances:

* *Ibid.,* Pt. I–II, qu. 94, a. 2.

inasmuch as every substance seeks the preservation of its own being, according to its nature: and by reason of this inclination, whatever is a means of preserving human life, and of warding off its obstacles, belongs to the natural law. Secondly, there is in man an inclination to things that pertain to him more specially, according to that nature which he has in common with other animals: and in virtue of this inclination, those things are said to belong to the natural law *which nature has taught to all animals*,[1] such as sexual intercourse, the education of offspring and so forth. Thirdly, there is in man an inclination to good according to the nature of his reason, which nature is proper to him: thus man has a natural inclination to know the truth about God, and to live in society: and in this respect, whatever pertains to this inclination belongs to the natural law; for instance, to shun ignorance, to avoid offending those among whom one has to live, and other such things regarding the above inclination. . . .

[1] *Digest,* I, i, 1.

SOURCES

Gratian, *Concordantia Discordantium Canonum,* Dist. I, V, VIII, and IX.

St. Thomas Aquinas, *Summa Contra Gentiles,* Bk. III, ch. 1–3, 37, 48.

———, *Summa Theologica,* Pt. I, qu. 79; 92, a. 1; 96, a. 4. Pt. II, Section I (I–II), qu. 51, a. 5; 63, a. 3; 90–97. Pt. II, Section II (II–II), qu. 10; 12, a. 2; 57, a. 2–3; 64, a. 5; 66, a. 2 and 7; 78, a. 1; 81, a. 2; 88, a. 3 and 10; 104, a. 5; Supplement, qu. 52, a. 1.

4.

FROM MEDIEVAL
TO MODERN
NATURAL LAW

I: Ockham, Suarez, and Grotius

Alexander Passerin d'Entreves distinguishes the modern forms of the theory of natural law from earlier versions in terms of three principal characteristics. Modern natural law theory is rationalist, individualist, and radical.[1] Natural law in the modern period, frees itself from its close association with theology and the medieval church; it breaks with the hierarchical and group-oriented aspects of medieval theory; and it becomes a revolutionary ideology or justification for the transformation of political, economic, and social relationships. To study how these characteristics emerge, it is necessary to examine the thought of three writers frequently associated with important changes in the mean-

[1] A. P. d'Entreves, *Natural Law* (London, 1951, paperback reprint, New York, 1965), ch. 3.

ing and application of natural law—William of Ockham, Francisco Suarez, and Hugo Grotius.

The extent to which the writings of William of Ockham (1290–1349) on the subject of natural law mark a departure from the normal pattern of medieval thought is still a subject of controversy. His metaphysical nominalism appears to represent a radical epistemological individualism since Ockham breaks with the moderate realism of Aquinas by asserting that universals are only names (*nomina*) for similarities among existing individual things rather than, as for Aquinas, a recognition of their real essences. On this basis it would seem difficult for Ockham to hold that there is a universal law based on essential relationships inherent in nature, as earlier writers had asserted. Nevertheless, he does in fact write about natural law, and indeed develops a rather sophisticated version of it which incorporates major elements of the traditional theories of the Roman lawyers, the Church Fathers, and Aquinas.

For Ockham, the term "natural law" can be used in three different senses. First, it means the unchangeable dictates of natural reason, such as the Commandment "Thou shalt not commit adultery." Such dictates are always binding. Second, it refers also to precepts such as universal freedom and communal ownership which are based on "natural equity" in effect before the Fall of Man. These precepts are no longer binding because sin has made necessary the establishment of the institutions of private property and slavery which are contrary to those precepts. Third, it can also apply to principles derived "by evident reason from the law of nations or from some human deed . . . and this can be called conditional natural law (*jus naturale ex suppositione*)."[2]

Ockham cites as one provision of natural law in the third sense the requirement that rulers should be elected by consent— probably the first time in the history of political thought that governmental legitimacy was defined as derived from consent based on natural law. In support of this assertion, he quotes from canon law the statement of Gratian that no one should be set

---

[2] *The Dialogue,* Part III, Treatise II, Book III, ch. 6, translated by Francis Oakley in Ralph Lerner and Muhsin Mahdi, eds., *Medieval Political Philosophy: A Source Book* (New York, 1963), pp. 500–501.

over unwilling subjects (D. 61, c. 13), and argues that the consent of the community is required because "What touches all should be approved by all,"—a maxim that Ockham probably drew from the "Rules of Law" at the beginning of the Canon law collection known as the *Liber Sextus,* published in 1298.[3] Ockham adds that subjects can relinquish or transfer to others their right of election (he cites the case of the Holy Roman Empire) but if they have not done so, these rights belong to the people by natural law in the third sense, "given the fact that someone is to be placed over others as prelate, prince, or ruler." [4] "Evident reason" and the nature of law and government are sufficient to demonstrate the necessity of consent for legitimate rule.

The importance of consent in Ockham's political thought is also evident in his description of the law of nations (*jus gentium*). Like Aquinas, he holds that as part of human law but instead of linking it directly to natural law as Aquinas does, he states that it "derives its force as law from the agreement of all men proscribing the contrary." [5] A shift has been initiated in the meaning of *jus gentium* which is finally completed in the theory of Grotius, three centuries later.

In his discussion of natural law in the first sense Ockham affirms the existence of certain immutable principles, such as "Thou shalt not commit adultery," but he does not indicate how these principles can be perceived by human beings who can only see similarities between individual things, and give these similarities general names. Perhaps Ockham was merely inconsistent, as George Sabine asserts. More likely, as Ewart Lewis surmises, he believed that man could have a direct intuitive knowledge of cer-

---

[3] The maxim has a long history, going back to discussions in Roman law of water rights and the participation of guardians in the disposition of the estate of a minor. (See Gaines Post, "A Romano-canonical Precept, 'Quod Omnes Tanget,' in Bracton," in *Studies in Medieval Legal Thought* [Princeton, 1964], pp. 163–228.) Ockham's citation of the text is significant, since later conciliarist writers such as Henry of Langenstein (1330–97) followed him in making use of it to support the natural right of the community to choose its rulers. Nicholas of Cusa (1401–64) added an argument from original natural equality which in his theory was transformed from a description of an earlier state of innocence into the basis for a prerequisite of express or tacit consent for the legitimacy of government in church and state. (See except.)

[4] *Ibid.,* p. 503.

[5] *Ibid.,* p. 498.

tain moral principles inherent in his own nature, although in the external world he could only have a real knowledge of individual things.[6] Ockham himself did not deal with this problem which was implicit in his nominalism, although a later nominalist, Thomas Hobbes, was able to develop an empiricist natural law which did not depend on the ability of man to perceive ultimate essences or natures.

Another aspect of Ockham's metaphysics which had direct implications for his natural law theory was his emphasis upon God's will rather than his reason as the ultimate source of law. Drawing on a religious tradition which could be traced to the Old Testament, Ockham refused to accept any limitation upon God's omnipotence and freedom in relation to his creation, and he therefore rejected the rationalistic conception of divine legislation which had been developed by the medieval scholastics. For Ockham, the natural law could not be considered a limit upon God's free creative activity. It was binding now because God had commanded it and had so ordered nature that we could perceive moral imperatives within it. In ordinary circumstances God did not alter the content of natural law, but there was nothing intrinsically impossible about his doing so by means of his absolute power. He could make adultery right, or command someone to hate him if he willed it, and the mere categories of human reason could not restrain him. However, in the present order of things he had willed that the precepts discoverable by human reason should also coincide with those which were commanded by the Divine Will.[7]

Although Ockham was in difficulty with the medieval Church because of his support of the Spiritual Franciscans in their controversy with the papacy over evangelical poverty, his views on metaphysics and theology received wide currency because of the

[6] George Sabine, *A History of Political Theory,* 3rd edition (New York, 1961), p. 306; Ewart Lewis, *Medieval Political Ideas,* Vol. I (New York, 1954), p. 333, note 28.

[7] Cf. Francis Oakley, "William of Ockham and the Voluntarist Tradition," *Natural Law Forum,* Vol. VI (1961), especially pp. 64–72 and evidence cited there. Note that the problem discussed is the compatibility of Ockham's natural law theory with his voluntarist ethics, not his nominalist epistemology. It is common to link and even to confuse Ockham's voluntarism and his nominalism (e.g., A. P. d'Entreves, *Natural Law* [London, 1951], p. 69) but they are conceptually distinct.

adoption of his theological method as the *via moderna* (as opposed to the *via antiqua* of Aquinas) in some of the faculties of theology of the medieval universities. The controversy over the comparative importance to be given to God's will and his reason as the predominant element in the natural law continued in succeeding centuries. The case of Gabriel Biel (1425–95) demonstrates that there was no necessary connection between Ockham's nominalism in epistemology and his voluntarism in theology and law. Biel adhered to Ockham's nominalism in his denial of the real existence of universals, and yet asserted a thoroughgoing rationalism in his attitude to natural law. In a statement which was echoed by many other writers in the next two centuries, including Grotius, he asserted that "Even if, which is impossible, God did not exist . . . if anyone acted against right reason . . . he would still sin."[8]

The controversy over the relationship of will and reason in God continued in the writings of the Spanish theologians in the sixteenth and seventeenth centuries. The best known of the Spaniards, Francisco Suarez (1548–1617) summarized the argument and attempted to adopt an intermediate position. In Book II, ch. 6 of *On Laws and God the Lawgiver,*[9] he agrees with the adherents of the rationalist school, among whom he mentions his fellow-countryman Gabriel Vasquez (1549–1604), that the fundamental order on which the natural law is based is a reflection of God's immutable and rational nature. He shares with the voluntarists, however, the view that the binding force of the natural law is God's will. All law, he says, is based on a superior's command, and since God has no superior he cannot be said to be subject to the natural law. Since he is our superior, it is his will which makes the natural law binding on us, even if we are able to perceive its intrinsically rational character before we are aware of his intention that we obey it.

In some ways Suarez' discussion anticipates elements of the later attack on natural law for fallaciously deriving value statements from statements of fact. Merely to observe a rational relationship, says Suarez, is not to perceive any moral obligation of

[8] Translated from the Latin quotation in Gierke, *Political Theories of the Middle Age* (London, 1900), p. 174.

[9] Translated by Gwladys L. Williams, et al., in *Selections from Three Works of Francisco Suarez S.J.* (Oxford, 1944).

performance; a superior will is necessary to impose that obligation upon us. (Suarez does not answer the further question, Why is one obliged to obey a "superior?".)

For his interpretation of the relationship of reason and will in law Suarez claimed the authority of Thomas Aquinas. It is true that Aquinas had defined law as "a rational ordering by the one who has the care of the community" (*Summa Theologica*, Pt. I, II, qu. 90), thus including in his definition both the rational content of law and the exercise of will by a superior. However, the problem had not been posed in such clear terms in the thirteenth century. The specific question to which Suarez addressed himself— Can God command us to hate him, and if not, is this inability not a denial of his omnipotence?—was only suggested as a result of the speculations of Ockham and the later medieval scholastics.

Two episodes in the Old Testament which had been mentioned by Aquinas—God's command to Abraham to kill his son, and his instruction to Osee to have intercourse with a prostitute— also suggested that the natural law might be annulled by direct divine action, a theory which Suarez denied, describing the two cases as situations in which divine intervention altered the circumstances of the actions so that the natural law, properly defined, did not apply. Killing one's offspring and having intercourse with someone other than one's wife were not forbidden if they were done at the command of God, who is the absolute lord of men's lives and bodies.

Some of the theories of consent which had emerged at the end of the Middle Ages reappear in Suarez' writings. Like Nicholas of Cusa, he grounds the requirement of consent for political legitimacy on the concept of man's natural freedom. "In the nature of things all men are born free, so that, consequently, no person has political jurisdiction over another person" (Bk III, ch. 2). Like Ockham, he bases the law of nations or *jus gentium* on universal consent, but he goes one step further than Ockham by specifically denying Aquinas' assertion that its provisions are derived as conclusions from natural law. "The precepts of the *jus gentium* were introduced by the free will and consent of mankind. . . . We should not confuse the *jus gentium* with the natural law, neither is it necessary solely on account of inferences, although they may be many, to give that name to what is simply natural law. For the [fact that a precept calls for] reasoning, does not exclude the true and natural necessity of that precept."[10]

The role of consent as the basis of *jus gentium* takes on a particular importance when Suarez distinguishes between two senses in which *jus gentium* can be used. For Suarez the term can be defined either as the common provisions in existing legal systems or (more properly, he declares) the law governing "the relations of various peoples and nations to each other."[11] The two definitions demonstrate that Suarez' theory marks a transition between the classical understanding of the law of nations as the common legal principles shared by all nations and its modern meaning as international law, which is based on the consent of sovereign nations and consists of the mutual obligations and agreements among nations in such areas as international commercial relations, diplomacy, and war.

Hugo Grotius (1583–1645), the Dutch Protestant writer often regarded as the founder of international law, was influenced in certain important respects by the writings of the Spanish scholastic theologians. This influence is obvious in the very examples which he uses in his work *The Law of War and Peace* (1625) to demonstrate the immutability of the natural law. Like Gabriel Biel, he asserts that the natural law would be binding even if, "which cannot be conceded without the utmost wickedness" (*Prolegomena,* par. 11), God did not exist. Grotius also resembles some of the scholastics in equating the precepts of the natural law with mathematical formulae. "Just as even God cannot cause that two times two should not make four, so He cannot cause that that which is intrinsically evil be not evil" (Book I, ch. 1, sec. x, par. 5). Both of these examples had been used by the theological rationalists in their arguments against the Ockhamite voluntarists so that it is difficult to argue, as a number of commentators have done, that Grotius' statement marks the beginning of the separation of natural law from theology.[12] Moreover, Grotius himself added the disclaimer quoted above reaffirming his own belief in God, and when he defined natural law as "that which is in conformity with

10 Francisco Suarez, *On Laws and God the Lawgiver,* Book II, ch. 17, No. 8.
11 *Ibid.,* Book II, ch. 19, No. 8–10.
12 See, for example, George Sabine, *A History of Political Theory,* p. 422, and Carl J. Friedrich, *Inevitable Peace* (Cambridge, Mass., 1948), p. 122.

the rational nature," he was careful to add, "and therefore is commanded and forbidden by God, the author of nature."[13]

Grotius separated natural law from the *theologians* in the sense that he used it for a secular purpose, the creation of an international legal system, rather than as an adjunct of theological speculation, but he did not develop his theory independently of theological assumptions; and in fact he was considerably influenced by the "natural theology" of the scholastics. Nevertheless, although the notion of independent validation of natural law by reason was a very old one, it had a different significance at a time when Catholics and Protestants were seeking a basis other than religion to regulate the relations of states. Grotius' solution was to make use of natural law, long familiar in the West, but given a new importance because of the religious division in Europe.

The founders of Protestantism—Luther and Calvin—had not made much use of natural law, but they were compelled by their very adherence to Scripture to accept St. Paul's statement that the Gentiles "show the work of the law written on their hearts, their conscience also bearing witness" (Romans 2:15). Although Luther was suspicious of all legal systems, and he was especially critical of the canon law of the Roman Catholic Church, he occasionally referred to a higher law of nature which could be used to criticize the inadequacies of human law in secular affairs, and to regulate the relations of non-Christians who did not recognize the Christian law of love.[14] This natural law could not be codified, but it could be known through the conscience, although, because they were sinful, most men were not likely to observe it. Similarly, John Calvin had defined natural law as "that apprehension of the conscience which distinguishes sufficiently between the just and

[13] Hugo Grotius, *The Law of War and Peace,* Book I, ch. 1, sec. 10, par. 1 (pp. 38–39 in the Francis Kelsey translation, Oxford, 1925).

[14] "[In disputes about restitution] if neither is a Christian, or if either is unwilling to be judged by the law of love, you may . . . announce to them that they are acting against God and the law of nature even though they may obtain absolute justice through human law. . . . When you ignore love and natural law, you will never succeed in pleasing God, though you have devoured all the law-books and jurists." *On Secular Authority* (1523), Part II, sec. 3, in John Dillenberger, ed., *Martin Luther, Selections from His Writings* (New York, 1961), pp. 400–01. See also passages cited in John T. McNeill, "Natural Law in the Thought of Luther," *Church History,* X (1941), pp. 211–27, and "Natural Law in the Teaching of the Reformers," *Journal of Religion,* XXVI (1946), pp. 168–82.

unjust and which deprives men of the excuse of ignorance while it proves them guilty by their own testimony."[15] Yet for both writers a more important guide to right living was the gospel, in particular the Christian law of love, and only divine grace enabled sinful man to perform good actions. Natural law understood as the promptings of conscience rather than as a rational system of law had a place, though a distinctly subordinate place, in Lutheran and Calvinist thought of the sixteenth century. Not until the seventeenth century, when Grotius, a Calvinist of the Arminian or free-will variety, constructed his system of international law upon a natural law basis, did Lutheran and Calvinist Europe begin to see the potentialities of a doctrine that it had assumed but largely ignored. The enthusiastic reception which *The Law of War and Peace* received created new interest in the subject of natural law and transformed it from an occasional reference in Cicero and Roman law or a theological construct of the scholastic philosophers into the conceptual underpinning of the emerging system of international law.

Grotius' comparison of natural law principles to a mathematical equation suggests that he intended to develop a system based on deduction from a few self-evident truths, but in fact his system was as much inductive as it was deductive. The fundamentals from which he began were the social nature of the man and the principles which must be observed in order for him to live in society. Thus, because experience shows that the keeping of promises is necessary for social life, the doctrine *pacta sunt servanda* (treaties should be observed) became a principle of natural and international law. Property, too, became necessary as society developed. Once the need for it had been established, the obligation to respect it became a part of natural law rather than an addition to, or departure from it as in earlier theories.

Grotius considered just wars "in accord with the first prin-

---

15 John Calvin, *Institutes of the Christian Religion* (John T. McNeill, ed.), Book II, ch. 2, par. 22, Philadelphia, 1960, p. 282. See also Book II, ch. 8, par. 1, pp. 367–68, and Book IV, ch. 20, par. 16, p. 1504. For commentaries, see Arthur Cochrane, "Natural Law in Calvin," in Elwyn Smith, ed., *Church, State Relations in Ecumenical Perspective* (Pittsburgh, 1966), pp. 176–217; and David Little, "Calvin and the Prospects for a Christian Theory of Natural Law," in Gene Outka and Paul Ramsey, eds., *Norm and Context in Christian Ethics* (New York, 1968), ch. 6.

ciples of nature" and he derived the right to wage war from the fundamental natural right of self-defense. Political absolutism was justified by Grotius on the basis of the right of a people to hand itself over to a ruler, and, in a statement which was later attacked by Rousseau, Grotius defended the natural-law basis of slavery either as the result of a voluntary surrender of a person or persons to one recognized as superior or the consequence of crime or defeat in a just war.[16]

Grotius' conception of *jus gentium* clearly departs from that of those who preceded him (with the exception of Suarez). *Jus gentium* in Grotius' interpretation is no longer the law of nations in the sense of the common elements in all legal systems; it is a law *between* nations, the complex of legal obligations established by express or tacit consent between nations, i.e., international law. The relationship of this law to natural law may be very close, as when the nations decide to give force to natural law provisions, or it may be quite remote as when a previously indifferent matter is outlawed in international law, or specific penalties are applied. It is significant, then, that Grotius classifies *jus gentium* as a type of "voluntary law," noting that its provisions are the result of agreement among various nations. Although ultimately based on the natural-law right of nations to regulate their contacts with each other, the law of nations itself is positive or conventional law, established by consent among nations, and many of its specific provisions derive their binding force solely from the agreement of the nations involved.

Referring once again to d'Entreves' three characteristics—rationalism, individualism, and radicalism—we can only perceive the beginnings of a shift in the meaning of natural law in the writings of Ockham, Suarez, and Grotius. Ockham and Suarez were both Roman Catholic churchmen and while their theories were rational in form, their contents were closely related to their theological views. Grotius, the most modern of the three, was not a rationalist in the sense of one who considers theology irrelevant to his thinking. His theory was deeply influenced by the writings of later medieval theologians, and resembled them in many ways. It is true that in a religiously-divided Europe an appeal to im-

---

[16] Grotius, *The Law of War and Peace*, Book II, ch. 5, sec. 31–32; Book III, ch. 7, sec. 1 (see excerpts.)

mutable principles of reason and nature had a different significance from a similar appeal by a medieval Catholic theologian, but this appeal never denied the relationship between those principles and God, the author of reason and nature. It was to a kind of natural theology that Grotius appealed rather than to the modern rationalist's denial of the relevance of God to political theory.

As to the radicalism and individualism of the early modern theories with the exception of the increasing references to consent (which was closer to a consensus of the community than to modern individual consent) in the formulation of national and international law, there was no marked change in the method or conclusions of the writers of this period which would indicate that their theories were markedly different from the earlier writings. The emphasis was still upon law rather than upon rights, upon society and man in general rather than upon the individual. Ockham's nominalism has been cited as a possible source of greater individualism in the interpretation of moral obligation, and a similar connection could be drawn between Suarez' emphasis on the principle of individuation in metaphysics and the importance of consent in his political thought. Yet neither figure developed a genuine individualism in his political thought. Nor were any of the theories discussed in this section particularly radical. Ockham discussed the people's right to elect the pope but accepted the existing arrangements in the Empire. Radical implications could be drawn from the consent theories of Nicholas of Cusa and Suarez but neither churchman drew them. Grotius justified slavery and political absolutism as in accord with natural justice. Not until the writings of Thomas Hobbes did a genuinely radical and thoroughly individualist natural law theory appear. To this theory we turn in the next chapter.

BIBLIOGRAPHY

Chroust, Anton Hermann. "Hugo Grotius and Scholastic Natural Law," *New Scholasticism*. Vol. XVII (1943), pp. 101–133.

Cochrane, Arthur. "Natural Law in Calvin," in Elwyn Smith,

ed. *Church, State, Relations in Ecumenical Perspective.* Pittsburgh, 1966, pp. 176–217.

d'Entreves, A. P. *Natural Law.* London, 1951, ch. 3.

Gierke, Otto. *Political Theories of the Middle Age.* London, 1900, pp. 172–74.

Hamilton, Bernice. *Spanish Political Thought in the Sixteenth Century.* Oxford, 1963, ch. 1.

Lewis, Ewart. *Medieval Political Ideas.* Vol. I, New York, 1954, pp. 13–15, 333–34.

Little, David. "Calvin and the Prospects for a Christian Theory of Natural Law," in Gene Outka and Paul Ramsey, eds. *Norm and Context in Christian Ethics.* New York, 1968, ch. 6.

McNeill, J. T. "Natural Law in the Thought of Luther," *Church History.* Vol. X (1941), pp. 211–27.

———. "Natural Law in the Teaching of the Reformers," *Journal of Religion.* Vol. XXVI (1946), pp. 168–82.

Oakley, Francis. "William of Ockham and the Voluntarist Tradition," *Natural Law Forum.* Vol. VI (1961), pp. 65–83.

Post, Gaines. *Studies in Medieval Legal Thought.* Princeton, 1964, pp. 163–228.

Shephard, Max. "Occam and the Higher Law," *American Political Science Review.* Vol. XXVI (1932), pp. 1005–23; Vol. XXVII (1933), pp. 24–38.

Sigmund, Paul E. *Nicholas of Cusa and Medieval Political Thought.* Cambridge, Mass., 1963, ch. 6.

De Concordantia Catholica*

NICHOLAS OF CUSA

Consent and Natural Law: Book II, chapter 14

. . . All legislation is based on natural law, and if it
contradicts natural law, that legislation cannot be valid (*Decretum,*
D. 9, *Cum ergo,* and c. *Constitutiones.*) Now since natural law
is naturally based on reason, all law is connatural to man
in its root source. The wiser and more outstanding men are
chosen as rulers by the others, to draw up just laws by their
naturally clear reason, wisdom, and prudence, to rule the
others by these laws, and to decide cases for the preservation
of peace, as is contained in *The Decretum,* D. 2, *Responsa
prudentum.* From which we conclude that those better endowed
with reason are the natural lords and masters of the others,
but not by any coercive law or judgment imposed on someone
against his will. For, since all are by nature free, every
rulership, whether it consists in a written law or is living law
vested in a prince, which forces subjects to abstain from
evil deeds and directs their freedom towards the good by fear
of punishment, is based only on the agreement and consent
of the subject. For if men are by nature equally powerful
and equally free, the true properly ordered authority of one
ordinary man who is equal in power cannot be naturally
established except by the election and consent of the others.
Also, law is established by consent (*Decretum,* D. 2, *Lex;*
D. 8, *Quae contra,* where it says, "An agreement of every race
and city among themselves" etc. "There is a general agreement
of human society to obey their kings" etc.). Note that
because it is generally agreed that it is convenient for human

* Translated by Paul E. Sigmund from *De Concordantia Catholica, Libri Tres,*
Vol. II and III, edited by Gerhard Kallen (Hamburg, 1959–65).

society to wish to obey kings, and because in a properly ordered government an election of the ruler ought to take place by which he is set up as judge of those who elect him, rightly ordered lords and rulers are constituted by election, and established in the same way as general judges over those who elect them. . . .

Book III, Preface

. . . Legislation, however, should be adopted by all those who are to be bound by it, or by a majority chosen by the others,[1] because it should benefit the whole, and what touches all should be approved by all, and a common decision is only produced by the consent of all or a majority. And there can be no excuse for not obeying the laws when everyone has imposed the law on himself. "For it is not proper for laws to be well framed but not obeyed," as Aristotle says in Book IV, chapter 7, of the *Politics*.[2] And so also those who adopt them should interpret them. For it is necessary that a kingdom be governed by law, for love and hate are present in all men, and it is better for a commonwealth to be governed by law than by the best man as king, as Aristotle concludes in Book III, chapter 9, of the *Politics*. . . .[3]

[1] A garbled version of Marsilius' argument in *Defensor Pacis,* D. 1, c. 12, par. 3 (English translation by Alan Gewirth, New York, 1956; paperback reprint, 1967).

[2] Aristotle, *Politics,* No. 1294a (Book IV, ch. 8 in modern editions).

[3] Aristotle, *Politics,* No. 1286a (Book III, ch. 15 in modern editions). Nicholas borrowed these references from Marsilius and probably had not read Aristotle at this time. See Paul E. Sigmund, "Marsilius and 15th Century Conciliarism," *Journal of the History of Ideas,* Vol. XXIII, no. 3 (July, 1962), pp. 392–402.

On the Law of War and Peace*

HUGO GROTIUS

Prolegomena

6. . . . Among the traits characteristic of man is an
impelling desire for society, that is, for the social life—not of
any and every sort but peaceful, and organized according to
the measure of his intelligence with those who are of his own
kind. . . .

8. This maintenance of the social order, which we have
roughly sketched, and which is consonant with human
intelligence, is the source of law properly so called. To this
sphere of law belong the abstaining from that which is another's,
the restoration to another of anything of his which we may
have, together with any gain which we may have received from
it; the obligation to fulfil promises, the making good of a loss
incurred through our fault, and the inflicting of penalties
upon men according to their deserts.

9. From this signification of the word, law, there has flowed
another and more extended meaning. Since over other animals
man has the advantage of possessing not only a strong bent
towards social life, of which we have spoken, but also a power
of discrimination which enables him to decide what things are
agreeable or harmful (as to both things present and things
to come), and what can lead to either alternative: in such
things it is meet for the nature of man, within the limitations
of human intelligence, to follow the direction of a well-tempered
judgment, being neither led astray by fear or the allurement
of immediate pleasure, nor carried away by rash impulse.
Whatever is clearly at variance with such judgment is understood
to be contrary also to the law of nature, that is, to the nature
of man. . . .

* Translated by Francis W. Kelsey, by permission of The Carnegie Endowment
for International Peace, Classics of International Law, Oxford, 1925.

11. What we have been saying would have a degree of validity even if we should concede that which cannot be conceded without the utmost wickedness, that there is no God, or that the affairs of men are of no concern to Him. The very opposite of this view has been implanted in us partly by reason, partly by unbroken tradition, and confirmed by many proofs as well as by miracles attested by all ages. Hence it follows that we must without exception render obedience to God as our Creator, to Whom we owe all that we are and have; especially since, in manifold ways, He has shown Himself supremely good and supremely powerful, so that to those who obey Him He is able to give supremely great rewards, even rewards that are eternal, since He Himself is eternal. We ought, moreover, to believe that He has willed to give rewards, and all the more should we cherish such a belief if He has so promised in plain words; that He has done this, we Christians believe, convinced by the indubitable assurance of testimonies.

12. Herein, then, is another source of law besides the source in nature, that is, the free will of God, to which beyond all cavil our reason tells us we must render obedience. But the law of nature of which we have spoken, comprising alike that which relates to the social life of man and that which is so called in a larger sense, proceeding as it does from the essential traits implanted in man, can nevertheless rightly be attributed to God, because of His having willed that such traits exist in us. . . .

17. But just as the laws of each state have in view the advantage of that state, so by mutual consent it has become possible that certain laws should originate as between all states, or a great many states; and it is apparent that the laws thus originating had in view the advantage, not of particular states, but of the great society of states. And this is what is called the law of nations, whenever we distinguish that term from the law of nature. . . .

Book I, Chapter I

X: Definition of the law of nature, division, and distinction from things which are not properly so called

1. The law of nature is a dictate of right reason, which points out that an act, according as it is or is not in conformity with rational nature, has in it a quality of moral baseness or moral necessity; and that, in consequence, such an act is either forbidden or enjoined by the author of nature, God. . . .

4. It is necessary to understand, further, that the law of nature deals not only with things which are outside the domain of the human will, but with many things also which result from an act of the human will. Thus ownership, such as now obtains, was introduced by the will of man; but, once introduced, the law of nature points out that it is wrong for me, against your will, to take away that which is subject to your ownership. . . .

5. The law of nature, again, is unchangeable—even in the sense that it cannot be changed by God. Measureless as is the power of God, nevertheless it can be said that there are certain things over which that power does not extend; for things of which this is said are spoken only, having no sense corresponding with reality and being mutually contradictory. Just as even God, then, cannot cause that two times two should not make four, so He cannot cause that that which is intrinsically evil be not evil. . . .

Book I, Chapter II: Whether it is Ever Lawful to Wage War

I: That war is not in conflict with the law of nature is proved by several considerations

. . . 4. In the first principles of nature there is nothing which is opposed to war; rather, all points are in its favor. The end and aim of war being the preservation of life and limb, and the keeping or acquiring of things useful to life, war is in perfect accord with those first principles of nature. If in order to achieve these ends it is necessary to use force, no inconsistency with the first principles of nature is involved, since nature has given to each animal strength sufficient for self-defense and self-assistance. . . .

5. Right reason, moreover, and the nature of society, which must be studied in the second place and are of even greater

importance, do not prohibit all use of force, but only that use
of force which is in conflict with society, that is, which
attempts to take away the rights of another. For society has
in view this object, that through community of resource and
effort each individual be safeguarded in the possession of what
belongs to him. . . .

Book III, Chapter VII: On the Right Over Prisoners of War

**I: According to the law of nations all persons captured in a
war that is public become slaves**

1. By nature at any rate, that is, apart from a human
act, or in the primitive condition of nature, no human beings
are slaves, as we have said elsewhere. In this sense it is
correct to accept what was said by the jurists, that slavery is
contrary to nature. Nevertheless, as we have shown also in
another connection, it is not in conflict with natural justice
that slavery should have its origin in a human act, that is,
should arise from a convention or a crime.

2. But in the law of nations, which we are now discussing,
slavery has a somewhat larger place, both as regards persons
and as regards effects. For if we consider persons, not only those
who surrender themselves, or promise to become slaves, are
regarded as slaves, but all without exception who have been
captured in a formal public war become slaves from the
time when they are brought within the lines, as Pomponius
says. And no crime is requisite, but the fate of all is the
same, even of those who by their ill-fortune, as we have said,
are caught in the enemy's territory when war has suddenly
broken out. . . .

SOURCES

Calvin, John, *Institutes of the Christian Religion,* Bk. II, ch. 4 and 8; Bk. IV, ch. 20.

Grotius, Hugo, *The Law of War and Peace,* Prologue; Bk. I, ch. 1; Bk. II, ch. 5; Bk. III, ch. 7.

Luther, Martin, *On Secular Authority,* Pt. II, sec. 3.

Nicholas of Cusa, *De Concordantia Catholica,* Gerhard Kallen, ed., Hamburg, 1959–65, Bk. II, ch. 14; Bk. III, Preface.

Suarez, Francisco, *On Laws and God the Lawgiver,* translated in Gwladys L. Williams *et al., Selections from Three Works of Francisco Suarez S.J.,* Oxford, 1944, Bk. II, ch. 6, 17–19.

William of Ockham, *The Dialogue,* Pt. III, Treatise II, Bk. II, ch. 26–28; Pt. III, Treatise II, Bk. III, ch. 6, translated in Ralph Lerner and Muhsin Mahdi, eds., *Medieval Political Philosophy: A Source Book,* New York, 1963, pp. 494–505.

5.

FROM MEDIEVAL TO MODERN NATURAL LAW

II: Hooker, Hobbes, and Locke

If we continue to use d'Entreves' definition, it would be difficult to classify Richard Hooker (1553–1600) as a modern natural law theorist. In his *Laws of Ecclesiastical Polity* (1593) he acknowledges his dependence upon the thinking of the scholastics, especially Thomas Aquinas, and his theory closely resembles that of the Angelic Doctor. For Hooker, too, there is a hierarchy of laws ranging down from God to particular human societies. He retains the eternal, divine, and human law of the Thomistic system, but he broadens the meaning of natural law to include all "natural agents" while what Aquinas would call the natural law Hooker terms the "law of reason" (*Laws of Ecclesiastical Polity*, I, iii, i). He does not make any reference to the special moral faculty of *synderesis* which Aquinas mentions, but his description of how the reason comes to know self-evident moral principles

(*Laws of Ecclesiastical Polity,* I, v, 5) does not differ substantially from that of Aquinas.

There are important differences from Aquinas' theory in Hooker's approach, however, which are significant for the future development of natural law in the writings of John Locke. No less than Aquinas, and in some ways more clearly, Hooker stresses the love of God as the first commandment of natural law, but immediately thereafter he continues with a demonstration that the second great commandment of the natural law is love of neighbor, and argues that this law follows from the "relation of equality between ourselves and them that are as ourselves . . . we all being of one and the same nature" (*Laws of Ecclesiastical Polity,* Bk. I, ch. viii, sec. 7). Natural equality had been a truism in natural law thinking since the beginning of the Christian era, and it had occasionally been used to argue for a general theory of community consent. Hooker alludes to it only to support duties of mutual charity, forbearance, and justice. Later, however, John Locke cited these references when he made natural equality the basis for his doctrine of consent to government.

Hooker himself seems to have seen a relationship between equality and consent, although not as explicitly as Locke. As Hooker outlines it, government arises partly out of the natural inclinations of man (the Aristotelian argument) and partly out of the recognition that the growth of "envy, strife, contention, and violence among men" occasioned by man's partiality "towards himself and them whom he greatly affecteth" made it necessary to agree upon a government with authority to rule and govern. "So that in a word all public regiment of what kind soever seemeth evidently to have risen from deliberate advice, consultation, and composition between men, judging it convenient and behoveful, there being no impossibility in nature considered by itself but that men might have lived without any public regiment" (*Laws,* Bk. I, x, 3–4). It is clear from this statement that despite his Aristotelian belief in the natural sociability of man, Hooker had a view of a prepolitical situation not unlike what later theorists called the state of nature, although he himself did not use the term. To explain the transition from life in "those times wherein there were no civil societies" (*Laws,* Bk. I, x, 3), he refers to the need for consent, "without which consent there were no reason that one man should take upon him to be lord or judge over another"—apparently a reference to natural equality. He combines this argument from equality with Aristotle's opposing argument for the natural right of the noble, wise, and virtuous to rule, but finally decides in favor of consent in order to preserve peace and because the only really natural title to superiority is that of the father in the family.

The consent which Hooker describes, however, is original consent at the time of the formation of the government rather than the periodic renewal of consent of the type implied in modern democratic government. It is true that he believes in some kind of continuing tacit consent to legislation ("laws there are not which public approbation has not made so," *Laws,* Bk. I, x, 8), but lacking any action by the community as a whole to withdraw its consent to law and government, all members continue to be bound to obedience. Consent is therefore corporate rather than individual, revolution is possible but highly unlikely, and the movement from a pregovernmental patriarchal society is more a gradual process than a conscious rational decision. Hooker's natural law theory is conservative in intent and in effect.

Using the standards of individualism, rationalism, and radicalism, one finds it difficult to classify Hooker as a modern natural law theorist. His theory of consent and equality is couched in terms of the community rather than the individual. It does not call for a radical change in existing institutions. It is related directly to God, and much of what Hooker takes to be natural law is derived from Scripture. The first two principles of his natural law are variations of the two great commandments mentioned by Christ in the New Testament, and his division of the law of nations into primary and secondary precepts, based on man's nature before and after Adam's Fall (*Laws,* Bk. I, x, 13), is itself dependent on Christian revelation. The underlying assumption which Hooker shared with Aquinas, that faith does not contradict reason but perfects it, leads him even more than it does Aquinas to use Scripture as a guide to natural law and to assume that a natural ethics and a natural theology will lead to many of the conclusions contained in the Old and New Testaments.

Yet Hooker's natural law is the Law of Reason, and his theories of consent, equality, and the pregovernmental state are more fully developed than those of earlier writers. In the hands of

John Locke, these theories provided many of the ingredients of the most influential and important of all the modern theories of natural law—that contained in the *Second Treatise of Civil Government.*

If there is a radically individualistic break made with the classical and medieval tradition of natural law anywhere it is in the *Leviathan* (1651) of Thomas Hobbes (1588–1679). So different is Hobbes' theory that there are some who deny that it can be called a natural law theory at all.

The first important difference is the sharp disjunction which Hobbes makes between natural right and natural law, a distinction which recalls the old *jus-lex* dichotomy of Roman law. But where the Roman distinction is made between a general system of law and right (*jus*) and a particular legal principle (*lex*) contained within it, Hobbes contrasts a right of nature—man's right to do anything that will preserve his life—with the laws of nature —the instrumental and hypothetical rules of reason regarding the best means to self-preservation. In accordance with his natural right, man has unlimited liberty to do as he sees fit to preserve himself in a state of nature before society and government are created. Natural laws however, prescribe how to end "the war of all against all" of the state of nature limiting man's natural liberty for the sake of greater security and protection.

Hobbes begins his analysis with two assumptions: 1) the existence of a state of nature or the absence of organized society and government; and 2) the dominance of a single drive in man, that of self-preservation, which may and often does place a man in competition with other men who have a similar drive and are physically equal in their capacity to inflict death upon one another. The only solution to this situation for Hobbes is absolute submission to a sovereign through a social contract by which all agree to surrender their natural liberty to him in the interest of maintaining peace. The only limit on this submission is that the sovereign may not threaten the life of the citizens, since this is the reason for which the original agreement or contract was made. The freedom which man had before submission to government is what Hobbes calls natural right—his liberty to defend himself in any way he sees fit. The obligations which he recognizes as instrumentally related to appropriate means to produce a stable social and political order where life is no longer "solitary, poor, nasty, brutish, and short" are what Hobbes calls the laws of nature. Yet, as he recognizes (*Leviathan,* ch. 15), his so-called laws of nature are not laws at all, but only "theorems" or practical rules of survival which are effective only if a number of conditions are fulfilled, notably the condition that all others must observe the same rules. The reason they are not laws is that no law can be conceived as binding unless it is backed by irresistible force—"covenants without the sword are but words"—and only in civil society is there mutual recognition of the obligation of obedience and the certainty of enforcement by the sovereign.

Yet Hobbes goes on to say that "the same theorems, as delivered in the word of God that by right commandeth all things are properly called laws." A number of recent works on Hobbes' political thought have argued from this passage that his natural laws are more than prudential maxims; they are natural laws in the traditional sense.[1] Using Hobbes' own definition of law, they assert that Hobbes considers that God provides the necessary sanctions in the next life and will enforce the provisions of the natural laws; if man recognizes this fact, he should, by Hobbes' own definition, feel moral obligation, not mere calculating self-interest, as the basis for submission to the sovereign. Only in this way, they claim, can we explain Hobbes' assertion that the laws of nature are always binding in intention, *in foro interno,* even if the necessary conditions to make it possible to observe them *in foro externo* do not exist (*Leviathan,* ch. 15).

Other writers have criticized this interpretation, noting that although Hobbes believes that all men can arrive at a knowledge of God as First Cause by reason, only certain men, "as many of mankind as acknowledge his providence," believe that God "governeth the world and hath given precepts and propounded rewards, and punishments to mankind" (*Leviathan,* ch. 31). As a legal system, therefore, this theory leaves a logical gap between the requirement that God be recognized as enforcing the laws of nature in order for them to be truly obligatory laws, and the

---

[1] A. E. Taylor, "The Ethical Doctrine of Hobbes," in K. C. Brown, ed., *Hobbes' Studies* (Oxford, 1965), pp. 35–36; Howard Warrender, *The Political Philosophy of Hobbes* (Oxford, 1957); F. C. Hood, *The Divine Politics of Thomas Hobbes* (Oxford, 1964).

admission that this recognition is not immediately evident to all men, as is the fear of death.[2]

If this criticism is correct, the laws of nature have a different meaning in Hobbes' thought from that which they had in earlier writers. Yet they seem to involve something more than a calculation of short-term self-interest. Given the proper circumstances, they demand a restraint on one's impulses and conformity to general law which in many ways resemble action on moral principle. The principle which Hobbes derives from nature begins as "Preserve yourself," but he extends its meaning to include "Preserve yourself by respecting, where it exists, the peaceful social order which permits all to preserve themselves." Some actions which might appear to be related in the short run to self-preservation are ruled out after a peaceful social order has been established. Once the commonwealth has been created, there is a moral obligation to obey the sovereign who maintains order. Hobbes says that this obligation is derived from consent, but in reality it seems to involve the choice of the interest of the community, which coincides with the long-term interest of the individual, over action on the basis of impulse or immediate self-interest. This choice may appear to be nothing more than a prudential calculation but it has the elements of universality and conscious choice of the general over the particular that characterize moral action.[3] Those who choose short-run self-interest, or who commit such "irrational" acts as suicide or dying for principle are considered insane or unreasonable, for they are violating a rational, "natural," and moral law derived from the universal and immutable desire of all men (if they are aware of their true interests) to avoid a violent death.

Self-preservation through rational conduct is the single "natural law" in Hobbes' system, despite the fact that he never de-

[2] Cf. Michael Oakeshott, *Rationalism in Politics* (London, 1962), pp. 266–273; John Plamenatz, "Mr. Warrender's Hobbes," in Brown, *Hobbes' Studies* (Oxford, 1965), pp. 73–88; M. M. Goldsmith, *Hobbes' Science of Politics* (New York, 1966), ch. 4; J. W. N. Watkins, *Hobbes' System of Ideas* (London, 1965), ch. 5; David Gauthier, *The Logic of Leviathan* (Oxford, 1969), ch. 5.

[3] The interpretation of Hobbes on this point depends on one's definition of morality. For an argument that Hobbes was not writing about morality at all, but constructing "a naturalistic system of hypothetical imperatives," see J. W. N. Watkins, *Hobbes' System of Ideas* (London, 1965), ch. 5.

scribes it in this way. It is not a law in the sense in which Hobbes defines a law, an injunction backed by irresistible force, but it is—and should be—the goal of all men's efforts, both a psychological constant in man's nature and the source of political obligation. If one redefines his basic terms, Hobbes can be considered a natural law theorist, not because of the role of God in his system, but because he derives universal moral principles from attributes of human nature.

Yet this is a very different type of natural law. Whereas the earlier natural law theory was pluralistic, Hobbes' theory is unitary; whereas the earlier theory had asserted a natural order in the universe and in society, he asserts the inevitability of conflict in the desires and actions of men and argues the necessity of imposing order by human contrivance; where earlier writers had posited a hierarchy of values, Hobbes asserts a single goal, self-preservation, which man shares with all living beings; whereas the earlier tradition had defended the natural superiority of the wise and/or a moral claim to equal treatment, Hobbes defends an equality in the common fear of death and the capacity to inflict it on one another; in contrast to earlier theory, which had viewed society and politics in terms of corporate groups, Hobbes begins with the individual and views society as a collection of individuals.

Hobbes' views provoked a reaction in England and on the continent,[4] and subsequent writers on natural law were required to take account of them. When a chair of the Law of Nature and of Nations was established in Heidelberg in 1661, Samuel Pufendorf (1632–94), a German who had been lecturing on related subjects in Sweden, was invited to lecture and write on these topics. In 1672 he published *De Jure Naturae et Gentium* (*On the Law of Nature and Nations*),[5] which combined some of the ideas of Grotius with a critical review and partial incorporation of Hobbes' ideas.

Pufendorf rejected the right of nature of Hobbes and concluded that men are rational and moral in the state of nature. "The natural state of man even when considered apart from commonwealths is not one of war but of peace," so that "it is quite wrong for a person . . . to designate as natural a state which is

---

[4] Cf. John Bowle, *Hobbes and his Critics* (London, 1951), and Samuel L. Mintz, *The Hunting of Leviathan* (Cambridge, 1969).

[5] English translation by C. H. and W. A. Oldfather (Oxford, 1934).

in the main produced by the neglect and misuse of a natural principle" (*On the Law of Nature*, Bk. II, ch. 2, sec. 9). Like Aristotle and Grotius, Pufendorf recognized man's natural sociability and his need for the assistance of society in order to develop himself fully. Yet he also based his analysis of government upon a hypothetical contract (in fact two contracts, one of association and the other establishing a government) entered into by the free agreement of equal individuals in a state of nature (*On the Law of Nature*, Bk. VII, ch. 2, 6–8) and he spoke of self-love as the most fundamental principle of natural law, describing man as "at all times malicious, petulant, and easily irritated, as well as quick and powerful to do injury" (*On the Law of Nature*, Bk. II, ch. 3, 15). Pufendorf resolved the contradiction between his Hobbesian and Grotian views of man by positing the existence of two "natural inclinations . . . implanted by nature"—one to self-love and the other to sociability. Self-love is the stronger of the two, but man recognizes that "the more he loves himself the more he will endeavor to love others, for no one can hope with any reason that men will want of their own accord, to make any effort to increase the happiness of those whom they know to be malevolent, perfidious, ungrateful, and inhuman . . ." (*On the Law of Nature*, Bk. II, ch. 3, 17). Pufendorf's writings thus combined the individualism and pessimism about human nature of Hobbes with the belief in man's potential rationality and sociability of the older tradition. During the century after its publication, his theory was one of the best-known systematic presentations of natural law. It was translated into English and French, used by Locke, criticized by Rousseau, and quoted by the American revolutionists.[6] Yet after the middle of the eighteenth century Pufendorf's influence declined sharply while that of one of his readers, John Locke, continues to excite interest and controversy to the present day.

In the most influential work on natural law ever written, *The Second Treatise of Civil Government*, John Locke (1632–1704) acknowledged the influence of Hooker and gave clear evidence of extensive borrowing from Pufendorf.[7] Yet he never acknowledged

---

[6] See Leonard Krieger, *The Politics of Discretion: Pufendorf and the Acceptance of Natural Law* (Chicago, 1965), Epilogue.

[7] Locke quotes Hooker in sections 5, 15, 60, 61, 74, 90, 91, 94, 111, 134, 135, and 136. Pufendorf's influence is clearest in sections 58, 65, 74, 105 and Locke praised

a debt to Hobbes. The extent of Hobbes' influence on Locke has been the subject of considerable debate, some aspects of which we are compelled to examine here. On several occasions, Locke insisted that he did not know Hobbes' work, but the fact that there is some evidence to the contrary has led several writers on Locke to suspect that there is much more of Hobbes in Locke's theory than at first appears. In the two most important books which contain this theme, *Natural Right and History* by Leo Strauss (Chicago, 1953) and *Locke on War and Peace* by Richard Cox (Oxford, 1960), Locke is accused of adopting the Hobbesian view of natural law and cleverly disguising his beliefs by frequent allusions to Hooker.

In the first place, the evidence of Locke's direct knowledge of Hobbes' works is not conclusive. He had a copy of the *Leviathan,* but lent it out in 1674 and did not get it back until 1691. The *Second Treatise* was written between 1679 and 1681 and published with minor changes in 1689.[8] In the second place, after the publication of Strauss' book, but before Cox's book appeared, an early (1664) work by Locke on natural law, contained in the Lovelace collection at Oxford, was published as Locke's *Essays on the Law of Nature* (W. von Leyden, ed., Oxford, 1954). In the *Essays,* which were written before 1664, Locke takes a traditionalist view of the natural law which is far removed from that of Hobbes. Man is naturally sociable, and it is possible for him to arrive at a knowledge of the principles of the natural law by using his reason on the evidence of sense-experience. God's will is the formal cause of the obligation to obey the precepts of natural law, but their material content is derived from rational relationships in nature (*Essays* I and IV) and "the external order of things" (*Essays* VII). Obedience to the natural law brings good results, but utility cannot be the basis for morals, because if morality were equated with self-interest, anarchy would result (*Essays* VIII).

After the publication of the *Essays,* Professor Strauss attempted to defend his point of view, basing it on Locke's assertion that the

him in his correspondence. See introduction by Peter Laslett to *John Locke, Two Treatises of Government,* 2nd edition (Cambridge, 1967), pp. 22 and 74–75.

8 Laslett, *John Locke ,Two Treatises of Government,* p. 71. Cox mentions (p. 5, n. 1) the return of the book in 1691 as evidence that Locke knew the *Leviathan,* but omits the more important date when it was lent out, since this would undercut his whole case.

consensus of mankind was not an indication of the content of the natural law. For Strauss, this demonstrated that Locke had broken from the classical and medieval tradition, which had cited universal consent as a proof of natural law.[9] Yet the classical and medieval natural law theorists had always recognized that at least one institution, slavery, was universally accepted and yet was opposed to nature; and Richard Hooker noted the divergence of contemporary practice from the ideal standards of natural law and attributed this to original sin (*Laws of Ecclesiastical Polity,* Bk. I, vii, 11). Characteristically, Locke did not utilize this religious explanation of departures from natural law, but he was acutely conscious of the variety of moral standards through history and in different parts of the world—a greater variety now since the practices of the American Indians and of the Asians had become known to Europe. Yet for him the lack of the consensus of mankind did not affect his basic argument that natural law could be known by the reason on the basis of rational analysis of experience.

The *Second Treatise of Civil Government* departs from the traditional natural law theory, in the central position which it accords to the state of nature and the social contract. Where Hooker had spoken of "times before there were civil societies" and of establishing government and law "by composition and agreement," Locke uses the term "the state of nature," in one case amending the text in order to attribute it to Hooker (see Locke's footnote to section 91 of the *Second Treatise,* where the words "i.e., such as attend men in the state of nature" are interpolated in the quotation from Hooker), and he makes the agreement to form government a contractual one dependent on the protection of natural rights. Moreover, in contrast to Hooker, Locke expressly provides for revolution, "the appeal to heaven," as a safeguard of those rights, although it should be noted that the decision to revolt against the government must be taken by the majority to whom the individual has irrevocably agreed to submit if he has given his express consent.[10]

9 Leo Strauss, *What is Political Philosophy?* (New York, 1959), ch. 9, also in *American Political Science Review,* Vol. LII, no. 2 (June, 1958), pp. 490–501.

10 See *Second Treatise,* sec. 95 and 121. See also the discussion in Willmoore Kendall, *John Locke and the Doctrine of Majority Rule* (Urbana, Illinois, 1941, paperback reprint, 1964) ch. 7.

Locke assumes, of course, that his majority will not itself be oppressive, since it will in fact be made up principally of solid middle-class property holders who will be careful to protect individual rights especially that of property.[11]

The state of nature is not the war of all against all of Hobbes. It is a state of "peace, good-will, mutual assistance, and preservation" (section 19) in which the mutual obligations of the law of nature are recognized. It is a state of equality, not in physical power as in Hobbes, but in political authority based on nature, made up of "creatures of the same species and rank, promiscuously born to all the same advantages of nature and the use of the same faculties . . . without subordination or subjection" (section 4). In support of his doctrine of equality, Locke quotes Hooker in the next section, but omits, apparently intentionally, his recognition of the possibility of a natural right of the rationally superior to rule. For Locke nature decrees original natural equality, and from natural equality he derives the necessity of consent to government.

Consent based on natural equality had appeared in the writings of political theorists before Locke, including Nicholas of Cusa, Richard Hooker, and Francisco Suarez. However, for them consent was a corporate act of the community at some point in the past, while for Locke it was an individual act. He allowed for tacit consent in his theory, but it was tacit consent *by the individual* to abide by the rules of the community. An explicit social contract replaced the implicit governmental contract of late medieval thought and moral equality was given an individualistic political application.

Locke's emphasis on natural liberty also represented a shift in natural law thinking. The individual possessed natural freedom in the state of nature. He surrendered some of that freedom (that of executing the law of nature) when he entered civil society and submitted to government. Yet the purpose of that government was to make his freedom more secure by guaranteeing his natural

11 For an analysis of the class bias of Locke's majority, see C. B. McPherson, *The Political Theory of Possessive Individualism* (Oxford, 1962), ch. 5; but note that McPherson is wrong in claiming that only property holders are citizens. See M. Seliger, *The Liberal Politics of John Locke* (London and New York, 1968), pp. 290 ff.

rights. The social contract did not permit him to submit himself to absolute government or to enslave himself, as Grotius and Pufendorf had argued that he could do. According to Locke, man's natural freedom was a moral *right,* not merely a fact of the state of nature as in Hobbes' theory. "Every man is born with . . . a right of freedom to his person which no other man has a power over . . ." (sec. 190).

In Locke's view society and government are established because of the "inconveniences" of the state of nature, especially that of personal bias in settling conflicts regarding respective moral rights. The role of government is to provide a common judge to enforce and protect the natural rights of the individual to life, liberty, and property, which are recognized before, during, and after the contract or agreement to form or enter into government. In recognizing that man has moral obligations to other men in the state of nature, Locke marks his fundamental divergence from Hobbes. Man is naturally social and moral, and "when his own preservation comes not in competition ought he, as much as he can, to preserve the rest of mankind, and not take away or injure the life, or what tends to the preservation of the life, the liberty, the health, limb or goods of another" (section 6).

The reference to man's duty to preserve himself has been cited by two writers already mentioned, Professors Strauss and Cox, to demonstrate that Locke's natural law is really the same as that of Hobbes.[12] However Locke holds that self-preservation may only be exercised "within the limits of the law of nature" (section 4). "The individual in the state of nature acts as executor of the law of nature by the right he hath to preserve mankind in general" (section 8). In Locke's state of nature self-preservation will not lead to conflicts with others except in cases where personal prejudice interferes with one's judgment of the application of the law of nature. To attempt to reduce his view of the state of nature to that of Hobbes, as do the writers mentioned above, is to distort the clear meaning of Locke's statements in the interest of an *a priori* theory of his hidden intentions. Locke criticized Hobbes in section 13 of the *Second Treatise,* where he attacked

---

[12] Leo Strauss, *Natural Right and History* (Chicago, 1953), p. 224; Richard Cox, *Locke on War and Peace,* (Oxford, 1960), p. 83.

the doctrine that the rule of "one man commanding the multitude" is preferable to the situation in the state of nature; as well
as in section 19, where he distinguished between the state of
nature and the state of war, "which some men have confounded."
Locke also distinguished between the just and unjust war (see ch.
xvi "Of Conquest"), which would be impossible under the Hobbesian theory, since nations are in a state of nature with respect
to one another, and there is no justice in the state of nature for
Hobbes, but only the right of self-preservation by whatever means
appear appropriate.

Locke's concern with the property right is another distinctive
element in his natural law theory. In contrast to most earlier
theorists who had been ambivalent about the natural law status of
property for Locke it arises out of the requisites of man's nature
and is a fundamental characteristic of human activity.[13]

In the *Second Treatise* Locke uses the term, property, in
several senses. Sometimes it is extended to include "life, liberty,
and estate" (para. 87 and 123). At other times he speaks of the
"property which man has in his own person" (para. 23 and 44).
But the doctrine with which he is most closely associated is that
which derives a right to exclusive material possession, i.e., property in the strict sense (which he sometimes calls "estate"), from
the mixture of man's labor ("property in his own person") with
land or material goods which have previously belonged to no one
(para. 25–51). But Locke's argument goes further than this, for
it is only through individual appropriation that the goods of the
earth can be effectively used for the preservation of mankind, as
God intended. When a man uses his labor to pick acorns or plow
a field, they become his by the intention of God and the law of
nature. There are natural limits on the accumulation of property,
however, for a man can acquire only as much as he can use before
it spoils. Yet, as a number of Locke's critics have pointed out, the
institution of money, which is not perishable and can be used in
indefinite amounts for investment purposes, removes the limit on

13 But note that Locke shared with earlier Christian theorists the view that
before the Fall man had "the free use of all things," but "private possessions and
labor" became necessary thereafter because of God's "curse on the earth." See
Bodleian Library, MS. c. 28 cited by Richard Ashcraft in chapter II, note 91 of his
forthcoming book, *Natural Rights, Toleration, and Liberation.*

accumulation (see ch. v, "Of Property," in the *Second Treatise*).

Even after the invention of money the property right is not absolute. Those that are starving are entitled to something from "he that hath and to spare" (section 183). The majority or their representatives may regulate property and levy taxes. For the property owner has consented to be bound by the laws that they adopt—although they are bound to impose only those taxes which are necessary for the common good (sections 131 and 139–40). As noted above, Locke is confident that the majority will not be oppressive, and he provides no remedy against it for those who have expressly consented to majority rule. No real conflict is envisioned between the requirements of the common good and individual property rights if a representative legislature regulates property by "established standing laws."

Locke's *Essay Concerning Human Understanding* (1690) has presented certain problems in relation to his natural law theory.[14] The best-known section of the *Essay*, Locke's attack on the doctrine of innate ideas, has been interpreted as implying the denial of natural law, but a closer analysis of his criticism reveals that this is not the case. Although Locke did not believe that moral ideas were innate, he held that they could be arrived at by the rational individual and he specifically reaffirmed his belief in natural law in the chapter in which he attacked the doctrine of innate moral ideas. "There is a great deal of difference between an innate law and a law of nature; between something imprinted on our minds in their very original and something that we, being ignorant of, may attain to the knowledge of, by the use and due application of our natural facilities."[15]

It is true that Locke was not confident that the average man could or would achieve a knowledge of that law but he had previously shown the same pessimism on this subject in his early *Essays on the Law of Nature*. In fact, the necessity for a surer guarantee of morality was one of his principal arguments for

---

[14] See W. von Leyden, ed., *John Locke, Essays on the Law of Nature* (Oxford, 1958), *Introduction*, sec. 7; Peter Laslett, ed., *John Locke, Two Treatises of Government*, 2nd edition (Cambridge, 1967), pp. 79–84.

[15] *Essay Concerning Human Understanding*, Book I, ch. 2, sec. 13 (p. 78 in A. C. Fraser edition, Oxford, 1894).

The Reasonableness of Christianity in 1695, but even while making this point he accepted the existence of natural law.[16]

A more difficult problem is presented by his description of moral good and evil as "nothing but pleasure and pain or that which occasions or procures pleasure or pain to us" (*Essay*, II, 28, 5; cf. also II, 20, 2, and II, 21, 42). This appears to assert a hedonistic ethic at variance with the belief in a moral law inherent in nature. Yet in the same chapter (section 8), Locke divides the divine law into that "promulgated by the light of nature or by the voice of revelation."

The notion of natural sanctions attached to the natural law may help to resolve the problem. Earlier theorists had always believed that observance of the law of nature would bring with it good results in the natural course of events and that its violation would bring the contrary, a belief to which Locke had referred in his early *Essays on the Law of Nature* (VI and VIII). Pleasure and pain, then, are the natural sanctions attached to the natural law. They are the *causes* which lead most men to follow the natural law even if they have not analyzed it carefully, but they are not the *reasons* for the moral good or evil of the acts themselves, which derive from their inherent character rather than their effects.[17] Locke's statements on pleasure and pain influenced later utilitarian theories, but they do not mean that Locke himself was a utilitarian or a hedonist. His views changed on many subjects during his life but he continued to believe in the existence and potential knowability of the natural law. Early and late he affirmed "the existence of a perfect parallel between the calculus of rationally apprehended truths and the divinely furnished system of hedonic sanctions."[18]

In the writings of the seventeenth century theorists, natural law was transformed from a basic order in the universe which

[16] "It is true that there is a law of nature but who is there that ever did or undertook to give it to us all entire as a law? . . . Where was it that they [the rules of morality] [were] received as precepts of a law—of the highest law, the law of Nature?" *The Reasonableness of Christianity*, sec. 242–243 (Gateway edition, Chicago, 1965), pp. 174–76.

[17] See R. Singh, "John Locke and the Theory of Natural Law," *Political Studies*, Vol. IX, No. 2 (June, 1961), pp. 105–18; and Hans Aarsleff, "The State of Nature and the Nature of Man," in John W. Yolton, ed., *John Locke: Problems and Perspectives* (Cambridge, 1969), pp. 99–136. Note especially the evidence presented by Aarsleff on the role of pleasure and pain in Locke's early writings.

[18] John Dunn, *The Political Thought of John Locke* (Cambridge, 1969), p. 193.

depended on God's sovereign will and the inherent rationality of the cosmos into a guarantee of individual rights and a ground for political equality. The rational individual, rather than the ordered universe, was now the starting point. The old hierarchies had disappeared. The earlier assumption that in all but the most obviously unjust societies the existing order represented God's will and reflected the order of the universe was now challenged by a new awareness of the possibilities of a restructuring of society by autonomous, rational, and equal individuals. The eighteenth century, the period in which these ideas gained nearly universal acceptance, was also the period in which the doctrine of natural law began to be attacked and belief in its validity began to decline.

BIBLIOGRAPHY

Abrams, Philip, ed. *John Locke, Two Tracts on Government*. Cambridge, 1967, Introduction.

Brown, K. C., ed. *Hobbes' Studies*. Oxford, 1965, ch. 2–4.

Cox, Richard. *Locke on War and Peace*. Oxford, 1960.

Cranston, Maurice. *John Locke: A Biography*. London, 1957.

Dunn, John. *The Political Thought of John Locke*. Cambridge, 1969.

Gauthier, David. *The Logic of Leviathan*. Oxford, 1969, esp. ch. 5.

Goldsmith, M. M. *Hobbes' Science of Politics*. New York, 1966.

Gough, John W. *John Locke's Political Philosophy*. Oxford, 1950.

Hood, F. C. *The Divine Politics of Thomas Hobbes.* Oxford, 1964.

Krieger, Leonard. *The Politics of Discretion, Pufendorf and the Acceptance of Natural Law.* Chicago, 1965, ch. 3–4.

Laslett, Peter, ed. *John Locke, Two Treatises of Government.* Second edition, Cambridge, 1967, Introduction.

McPherson, C. B. *The Political Theory of Possessive Individualism.* Oxford, 1962.

Munz, Peter. *The Place of Hooker in the History of Thought.* London, 1952.

Oakeshott, Michael. *Rationalism in Politics.* London, 1962, pp. 248–300.

Polin, Raymond. *La Politique morale de John Locke.* Paris, 1960, ch. 3.

Seliger, M. *The Liberal Politics of John Locke.* London and New York, 1968.

Strauss, Leo. *Natural Right and History.* Chicago, 1953, pp. 165–251.

von Leyden, W., ed. *John Locke, Essays on the Law of Nature.* Oxford, 1958, Introduction.

Warrender, Howard. *The Political Philosophy of Hobbes.* Oxford, 1957.

Watkins, J. W. N. *Hobbes' System of Ideas.* London, 1965, ch. 5.

Yolton, John W., ed. *John Locke, Problems and Perspectives.* Cambridge, 1969.

Essays on the Law of Nature (1660) *

JOHN LOCKE

I. Is there a rule of morals or law of nature given to us? Yes.

. . . This law, denoted by these appellations, ought to be distinguished from natural right: for right is grounded in the fact that we have the free use of a thing, whereas law is what enjoins or forbids the doing of a thing.[1]

Hence, this law of nature can be described as being the decree of the divine will discernible by the light of nature and indicating what is and what is not in conformity with rational nature, and for this very reason commanding or prohibiting.[2] It appears to me less correctly termed by some people the dictate of reason, since reason does not so much establish and pronounce this law of nature as search for it and discover it as a law enacted by a superior power and implanted in our hearts.[3] Neither is reason so much the maker of that law as its interpreter, unless, violating the dignity of the supreme legislator, we wish to make reason responsible for that received law which it merely investigates; nor indeed can reason give us laws, since it is only a faculty of our mind and part of us. Hence it is pretty clear that all the requisites of a law are found in natural law. For, in the first place, it is the decree of a superior will, wherein the formal cause of a law appears to consist; in what manner, however, this may become known to mankind is a question perhaps to be discussed later on. Secondly, it lays down what is and what is not to be done, which is the proper function of a law. Thirdly, it binds men, for it contains in itself all that is requisite to create an

---

* From W. von Leyden, ed., *John Locke, Essays on the Law of Nature* by permission. Copyright © 1958 by Clarendon Press, Oxford.

1 Cf. Hobbes, *Leviathan,* Part 1, ch. 14; also Pufendorf, *Elementa Jurisprudentiae Universalis,* 1660, lib. 1, def. xiii, par. 3.

2 For this sentence and the following definition of natural law as *dictatum rationis* see Grotius, *De Jure Belli ac Pacis,* lib. i, c. 1, sec. 10, par. 1.

3 Cf. Culverwel, *Discourse of the Light of Nature,* 1652, ch. ix, p. 99 (ed. Brown, 1857); also Hooker, *Laws of Ecclesiastical Polity,* Bk. 1, ch. 8, par. 3 (Keble's ed. of Hooker's *Works,* 1865, i, 228).

obligation. Though, no doubt, it is not made known in
the same way as positive laws, it is sufficiently known to men
(and this is all that is needed for the purpose) because it
can be perceived by the light of nature alone. . . .

I admit that all people are by nature endowed with reason,
and I say that natural law can be known by reason, but from
this it does not necessarily follow that it is known to any
and every one. For there are some who make no use of the light
of reason but prefer darkness and would not wish to show
themselves to themselves. But not even the sun shows a man
the way to go, unless he opens his eyes and is well prepared for
the journey. There are others, brought up in vice, who
scarcely distinguish between good and evil, because a bad
way of life, becoming strong by lapse of time, has established
barbarous habits, and evil customs have perverted even
matters of principle. In others, again, through natural defect
the acumen of the mind is too dull to be able to bring to
light those secret decrees of nature. . . .

II. Can the law of nature be known by the light of nature? Yes.

. . . The last way of knowledge that remains to be
discussed is sense-perception, which we declare to be the basis
of our knowledge of the law of nature. However, this must
not be understood in the sense that the law of nature appears
somewhere so conspicuously that we can either read it off
with our eyes, examine it with our hands, or hear it proclaiming
itself. But since we are searching now for the principle
and origin of the knowledge of this law and for the way in
which it becomes known to mankind, I declare that the
foundation of all knowledge of it is derived from those things
which we perceive through our senses. From these things,
then, reason and the power of arguing, which are both distinctive
marks of man, advance to the notion of the maker of these
things (there being no lack of arguments in this direction
such as are necessarily derived from the matter, motion, and
the visible structure and arrangement of this world) and at
last they conclude and establish for themselves as certain
that some Deity is the author of all these things. As soon as

this is laid down, the notion of a universal law of
nature binding on all men necessarily emerges; and this
will become clear later on. From what has been said, however,
it is quite certain that there is a law of nature that can be
known by the light of nature. For whatever among men
obtains the force of a law, necessarily looks to God, or nature,
or man as its maker; yet whatever man has commanded or
God has ordered by divine declaration, all this is positive law.
But since the law of nature cannot be known by tradition, all
that remains is that it becomes known to men by the light
of nature alone. . . .

VII. Is the binding force of the law of nature perpetual and universal? Yes.

. . . In fact, this law does not depend on an unstable
and unchangeable will, but on the eternal order of things.
. . . Since man has been made such as he is, equipped with
reason and his other faculties and destined for this mode
of life, there necessarily result from his inborn constitution
certain definite duties for him, which cannot be other than
they are. In fact, it seems to me to follow just as
necessarily from the nature of man that, if he is a man,
he is bound to love and worship God and also to fulfil other
things appropriate to the rational nature, i.e. to observe the
law of nature, as it follows from the nature of a triangle that,
if it is a triangle, its three angles are equal to two right angles,
although perhaps very many men are so lazy and so thoughtless
that for want of attention they are ignorant of both these
truths, which are so manifest and certain that nothing can
be plainer. Hence no one can doubt that this law is binding
on all human beings. . . .

VIII. Is every man's own interest the basis of the law of nature? No.

. . . Our answer to this objector is this: Utility is not
the basis of the law or the ground of obligation, but the
consequence of obedience to it. Surely, it is one thing for an

action of itself to yield some profit, another for it to be
useful because it is in accordance with the law, so that if the
law were abolished, it would have in it no utility whatever:
for example, to stand by one's promise, though it were to
one's own hindrance. In fact, we must distinguish between an
action as such and obedient action, for an action itself
can be inexpedient—for example, the restitution of a trust
that diminishes our possessions—whereas obedient action
is useful in so far as it averts the penalty due to a crime.
But this penalty would not be due and hence would not be
shunned, if the standard of rightness of an action were immediate
advantage. And thus the rightness of an action does not
depend on its utility; on the contrary, its utility is a result
of its rightness. . . .

The Second Treatise of Civil Government[*]

JOHN LOCKE

Chapter II: Of the State of Nature

4. To understand political power aright, and derive
it from its original, we must consider what state all men
are naturally in, and that is a state of perfect freedom to
order their actions and dispose of their possessions and persons
as they think fit, within the bounds of the law of nature,
without asking leave, or depending upon the will of any
other man.

A state also of equality, wherein all the power and
jurisdiction is reciprocal, no one having more than another;
there being nothing more evident than that creatures of the
same species and rank, promiscuously born to all the
same advantages of nature, and the use of the same faculties,
should all be equal one amongst another without subordination
or subjection, unless the Lord and Master of them all should
by any manifest declaration of his will set one above
another, and confer on him by an evident and clear
appointment an undoubted right to dominion and
sovereignty. . . .

Chapter III: Of the State of War

19. And here we have the plain difference between the
state of nature and the state of war, which however some
men have confounded, are as far distant as a state of peace,
good-will, mutual assistance, and preservation, and a state
of enmity, malice, violence, and mutual destruction, are one
from another. Men living together according to reason,
without a common superior on earth with authority to

judge between them, is properly the state of nature. But force, or a declared design of force, upon the person of another, where there is no common superior on earth to appeal to for relief, is the state of war, and it is the want of such an appeal that gives a man the right of war even against an aggressor, though he be in society and a fellow-subject. . . .

Chapter IV: Of Slavery

22. The natural liberty of man is to be free from any superior power on earth, and not to be under the will or legislative authority of man, but to have only the law of nature for his rule. . . .

23. This freedom from arbitrary power is so necessary to, and closely joined with, a man's preservation, that he cannot part with it but by what forfeits his preservation and life together. For a man not having the power of his own life cannot by compact, or his own consent, enslave himself to any one, nor put himself under the absolute arbitrary power of another to take away his life when he pleases. . . .

24. This is the perfect condition of slavery, which is nothing else but the state of war continued between a lawful conqueror and a captive.

Chapter V: Of Property

27. Though the earth and all inferior creatures be common to all men, yet every man has a property in his own person; this nobody has any right to but himself. The labor of his body and the work of his hands we may say are properly his. Whatsoever, then, he removes out of the state that nature hath provided and left it in, he hath mixed his labor with, and joined to it something that is his own, and thereby makes it his property. It being by him removed from the common state nature placed it in, it hath by this labor something annexed to it that excludes the common right of other men. For this labor being the unquestionable property of the laborer, no man but he can have a right

to what that is once joined to, at least where there is enough
and as good left in common for others.

SOURCES

Hobbes, Thomas, *Leviathan,* Pt. I, ch. 13–15, Pt. II, ch. 26,
   30–31.
Hooker, Richard, *Laws of Ecclesiastical Polity,* Bk. I, ch. 2–3,
   5–10.
Locke, John, *Essays on the Law of Nature.*
——, *Second Treatise of Civil Government,* ch. 2–5, 8, 11.
——, *Essay Concerning Human Understanding,* Bk. I, ch.
   2–3; Bk. II, ch. 20 and 28; Bk. III, ch. 6.
Pufendorf, Samuel, *On the Law of Nature and Nations,*
   Bk. II, ch. 2–3; III, ch. 2; VII, ch. 2.

6.
NATURAL LAW
IN AMERICA

It is well known that the Declaration of Independence was based on the natural rights philosophy of John Locke. Its opening paragraphs declaring that government is based on consent and established for the protection of natural rights which, if violated, justify revolution, are essentially a restatement of the argument in the *Second Treatise*.

Yet Locke was not the only writer on natural law who influenced American thinking, and his *Second Treatise* was not as widely known nor as influential as later commentators have believed.[1] When it became necessary to appeal to a standard beyond that of English law, the colonists also turned to international law, and they looked to such writers as Grotius and Pufendorf for justification of their actions. In the latter part of the eighteenth century, the most frequently cited work on interna-

---

[1] Cf. John Dunn, "The Politics of Locke in England and America," in John W. Yolton, ed., *John Locke, Problems and Perspectives* (Cambridge, 1969), pp. 45–81, and Clinton Rossiter, *Seedtime of the Republic* (New York, 1953), p. 358. Dunn shows that the *Treatise* was not well known in the colonies until the 1760s. Locke's *Essay Concerning Human Understanding*, however, was widely read.

tional law was a recently translated treatise by the Swiss Emmerich de Vattel, *The Law of Nations or the Principles of the Natural Law Applied to the Conduct and Affairs of Nations and Sovereigns.*[2] Published in 1758, it was translated into English in 1759, and Benjamin Franklin is known to have received a copy in 1775. Vattel's discussion of the right of revolution was generally similar to that of Locke, and in Vattel the colonists found another notion which harmonized with the colonial experience, that of a fundamental law which binds the legislature and can only be changed by the whole people, for "It is from the constitution that the legislators hold their power. How can they change it without destroying the foundation of their authority?"[3]

The relationship between this fundamental law and natural law became a close one, although conceptually the laws were distinct. In the one case, the source of legitimacy was the will of the people; in the other, it was "nature and nature's God." Yet the two could be equated, since the people would presumably have willed that the natural law act as limitation on the legislature in a more precise and explicit way than the exclusively moral limitations (enforced, it is true, by the possibility of resort to revolution) in the theory of Locke.

Another source of colonial political thought at the time of the American Revolution was Sir William Blackstone's *Commentaries on the Laws of England,* first printed in the colonies in 1771. Its introductory section contains a discussion of the natural law which is a restatement of the doctrines of the Swiss professor of ethics, Jean Jacques Burlamaqui, whose *Principes du droit naturel* had been published in 1747. Following Burlamaqui, who was influenced by Pufendorf, Blackstone relates the natural law directly to individual self-love. "The Creator . . . has so intimately connected, so inseparably interwoven the laws of eternal justice with the happiness of each individual that the latter cannot be attained but by observing the former. . . . In consequence of which mutual connection of justice and human felicity, he has not perplexed the law of nature with a multitude of abstracted

---

[2] See figures on American citations between 1789 and 1820, quoted in Arthur Nussbaum, *A Concise History of the Law of Nations* (New York, 1947), p. 161.

[3] deVattel, *The Law of Nations,* Book I, ch. 3, par. 34, quoted in Ernest Barker, *Traditions of Civility* (Cambridge, 1948), p. 315.

rules and precepts . . . but has graciously reduced the rule of obedience to this one paternal precept, 'that man should pursue his own true and substantial happiness.' This is the foundation of what we call ethics or natural law. . . . This law of nature, being coeval with mankind and dictated by God himself, is superior in obligation to all others. . . . No human laws are of any validity if contrary to this."[4]

Yet it is an indication of how far English practice had departed from Lockean theory that Blackstone combines this higher law theory with a view of sovereignty and of parliamentary supremacy which is fundamentally at variance with it. He defines law, as the will of a superior; consequently, every government must have "a supreme, irresistible, absolute, uncontrolled authority in which . . . the rights of sovereignty reside." In England, that authority is the Parliament, which has no limits on its power except that of natural impossibility. "I know it is generally laid down more largely that acts of Parliament contrary to reason are void. But if parliament will positively enact a thing to be done which is unreasonable I know of no power in the ordinary forms of the constitution that is vested with authority to control it. . . ." Parliament is internally balanced between the King and the Houses of Lords and Commons, but there is no higher body, including the judiciary, which can review its acts, for "that were to set the judicial power above that of the legislature which would be subversive of all government."[5]

Parliamentary sovereignty so stated would seem difficult to reconcile with a higher natural law, or with Blackstone's insistence on the "absolute" natural rights of Englishmen to liberty, security, and property (the last of which, he says, "is probably founded in nature" but subject to "modifications" by society [Blackstone, p. 137]). Yet there are ways of resolving the apparent contradiction. One might make a distinction between moral and legal validity, ascribing Blackstone's assertions about the superiority of the natural law to the moral sphere while maintaining his belief that, legally, Parliament must be supreme. A second and more likely

4 Sir William Blackstone, *A Commentary on the Laws of England*, London, 1765, pp. 40–41. (A slightly abridged paperback edition is available as *Ehrlich's Blackstone*, 2 vols., New York, 1959.)

5 *Ibid.*, p. 91.

solution of the problem is to assume that properly constituted parliaments, will observe the natural law, and if they do not, will correct themselves when their error is brought to their attention by the courts.[6] Blackstone clearly rejects any attempt to give judges the power to declare legislation void because of its opposition to a superior natural law and this has remained the prevailing doctrine in British law since the eighteenth century.

The colonists, however, were operating under different assumptions. The colonial lawyers knew the writings of the seventeenth-century judge, Sir Edward Coke, whose *Institutes* and *Reports* were the standard works on British law until the publication of Blackstone's *Commentaries*. Editions of Coke were very widely distributed in the colonies,[7] and through them the colonists knew his decisions in *Calvin's Case* (1608) and in *Bonham's Case* (1609), which defended the superiority of the natural and common law to acts of Parliament and seemed to claim for the judiciary the right to enforce those limits on Parliamentary legislation. Coke's doctrines have been interpreted as stating a principle of judicial construction by a lower court of the law enunciated by "the High Court of Parliament" rather than the assertion of a general right of judges to strike down parliamentary legislation.[8] However, the plain words of the cases are "the common law will control the acts of Parliament and sometimes adjudge them to be utterly void" (*Bonham's Case*) and "the law of nature cannot be changed or taken away" and "should direct this case" (*Calvin's Case*). Justice Hobart made a similar statement in another case a few years later: "An act of Parliament made against natural equity would be void" (*Day v. Savadge*, 1615).

The doctrine of the supremacy of natural law had been asserted by earlier English writers on law, and in *Calvin's Case*

---

6 Universal suffrage was *not* a prerequisite for a properly constituted Parliament since Blackstone believed that a property qualification was necessary "to exclude such persons as are in so mean a situation, that they are esteemed to have no will of their own" [Blackstone, p. 171].

7 A study of 47 colonial libraries found Coke's *Institutes* in 27 of them. Grotius appeared in 16 and Locke's *Second Treatise* in 13. See A. E. Dick Howard, *The Road from Runnymede* (Charlottesville, Va., 1968), p. 119.

8 See Bernard Bailyn's introduction to *Pamphlets of the American Revolution* (Cambridge, Mass., 1965), pp. 99–103, and Samuel E. Thorne, "Dr. Bonham's Case," *Law Quarterly Review*, Vol. LIV (1938), 545–551.

Coke could cite Bracton in the thirteenth century, Fortescue in the fifteenth, and St. Germain (*Doctor and Student*) in the sixteenth.[9] However, none of them had drawn from their belief in the supremacy of natural law the conclusion that judges could declare legislation void. Whatever may have been Coke's own theory on the subject, his decisions were cited by James Otis in *The Rights of the British Colonies Asserted and Proved* (1764) to demonstrate that the courts should declare the Sugar Act void on the grounds that it taxed the colonists without their consent. Using an argument that Grotius and the late medieval scholastics had utilized for a different purpose, Otis said, "The Parliament cannot make two and two, five; omnipotency cannot do it . . . Should an act of Parliament be against any of his [God's] natural laws, their declaration would be contrary to eternal truth, equity, and justice, and consequently void." Confusingly, he admitted that the British Parliament was the supreme legislative body and added that it would repeal the act when "informed by the executive in the King's courts of law" but he noted that in the past "judges have declared the act of a whole Parliament void." In an appendix to the work he quoted extensively from de Vattel on fundamental law and argued that English judges like Coke, Hobart, and Holt (in *City of London v. Wood,* 1701) recognized that it was "contrary to reason" to give Parliament the right to alter the constitution and violate "natural equity" by infringing on the Englishmen's rights enshrined therein.[10]

At the very time, then, that British lawyers were ascribing to the English Parliament an unlimited right to make law, American theory was using earlier doctrines of the superiority of natural and common law to assert general limits on the legislature and,

---

[9] Cf., for example, Sir John Fortescue, *De Natura Legis Naturae*, I, 10: "For this law is the mother of all human laws. If they depart from it, they are not worthy to be called laws" translated from the Latin quotation in R. W. and A. J. Carlyle, *A History of Medieval Political Theory*, Vol. V [London, 1950], p. 172).

[10] James Otis, "The Rights of the British Colonies Asserted and Proved," in Bernard Bailyn, ed., *Pamphlets of the American Revolution* (Cambridge, Mass., 1965), pp. 454–55, 476–77. Otis also claimed that taxation without representation was against "the fundamental principles of the British Constitution." The mixture of appeals to common and natural law was typical of the American colonists' argument. See Ernest Barker, "Natural Law and the American Revolution," in *Traditions of Civility* (Cambridge, 1948), pp. 263–355.

by the close association of higher law doctrines with those of the supremacy of fundamental or constitutional law, preparing the way for the characteristically American institution of judicial review.

Although they also referred to the historic rights of Englishmen, it was to natural law that the colonists principally appealed in the Declaration of Independence; specifically they appealed to the natural right of a "people" to revolt when its rights have been abused. The *Declaration,* as composed by Jefferson and adopted by the Second Continental Congress, was based on the principles enunciated in Locke's *Second Treatise*—although with one difference. The enumerated inalienable rights were said to be life, liberty, and "the pursuit of happiness," rather than the Lockean trilogy of life, liberty, and property. V. L. Parrington, one of the "progressive historians" of the first part of this century, described this alteration as "a revolutionary shift."[11] However, the notion of a right to the pursuit of happiness was a commonplace of eighteenth-century thought. Locke had mentioned it in his *Essay Concerning Human Understanding* (II, 21, 47) and the Virginia Declaration of Rights, written by George Mason a few weeks earlier, had spoken of rights to "the enjoyment of life and liberty, the means of acquiring property, and pursuing and obtaining happiness." It is significant that the Virginia Declaration spoke of property, but the Declaration did not. There is some evidence that Jefferson did not consider property a natural right, notably his suggestion to Lafayette that it be omitted from his draft of the *Declaration of the Rights of Man.* Yet in other writings he spoke of a natural right to the means of subsistence while recognizing that society could alter the definition and extent of that right, a view similar to that of his mentor, John Locke. It is more likely that there were stylistic reasons for his choice of the more felicitous triad finally adopted.[12] The Lockean formulation

[11] Vernon L. Parrington, *Main Currents in American Thought,* Vol. I (New York, 1927), p. 344.

[12] This is the opinion of Adrienne Koch, *Jefferson and Madison* (New York, 1950), pp. 78–80. For other views, see Howard Mumford Jones, *The Pursuit of Happiness* (Cambridge, Mass., 1953), pp. 12–17; Edward Dumbauld, *The Declaration of Independence and What It Means Today* (Norman, Okla., 1950), pp. 60–61; Gilbert Chinard, *Thomas Jefferson* (Ann Arbor, 1957), pp. 83–85; Julian P. Boyd, *The Declaration of Independence* (Princeton, 1945), pp. 3–4.

of life, liberty, and property reappeared subsequently in the "Due Process" clauses of the Fifth and Fourteenth Amendments to the American Constitution.

It is one of the ironies of American history that the first draft of the *Declaration,* as written by Jefferson, contained a condemnation of slavery among its list of complaints against George III. The passage was struck out by the Second Continental Congress, but it indicates that Jefferson, although a slaveowner, was aware that that institution was a violation of the natural right of human liberty.[13] Yet rather than weaken the appeal for national independence by alienating slaveholders, the Continental Congress decided to avoid any reference to slavery in *The Declaration.*

Natural law doctrines of limited government and inalienable rights prepared the way for the institution of judicial review, and it was by an appeal to the nature of a constitution as fundamental law that John Marshall in *Marbury v. Madison* (1803) claimed for the Supreme Court the right to decide on the constitutionality of legislative acts. Natural law thinking was evident in Supreme Court decisions well before the *Marbury* decision. In *Chisholm v. Georgia* in 1793, Chief Justice Jay appealed to "reason and the nature of things" to justify suits by a private citizen against a state. In *Calder v. Bull,* decided in 1798, Justice Chase spoke of "certain vital principles of our free government," "the great first principles of the social compact" (among them private property), and "the general principles of law and reason" which would forbid the enactment of *ex post facto* legislation even if there were no constitutional prohibition.[14]

---

[13] James Otis had been even more critical in his *Rights of the British Colonies,* where he called the slave trade "a shocking violation of the law of nature," and asserted that "The colonists are by the law of nature freeborn, as indeed all men are, white or black." See James Otis, "The Rights of the British Colonies," in Bailyn, ed., *Pamphlets of the American Revolution* (Cambridge, Mass., 1965), p. 439.

[14] But note that in a concurring opinion Justice Iredell implicitly criticized this view: "If the legislature of the Union or the legislature or any member of the Union shall pass a law within the general scope of their constitutional power, the court cannot pronounce it to be void merely because it is in their judgment contrary to the principles of natural justice. The ideas of natural justice are regulated by no fixed standard; the ablest and purest men have differed upon the subject; and all that the court could properly say, in such an event, would be that the legislature (possessed of an equal right of opinion) has passed an act which in the opinion of the judges was inconsistent with the basic principles of natural justice . . ."

Blackstone had recognized that there were limits on the absolute rights of property. It could be taken by eminent domain if compensation were paid, and it could be taxed provided the consent of the property-holder or his representative were given. Justice Cooley, who commented on Blackstone for American readers and wrote an influential book on the interpretation of the constitution, *Constitutional Limitations* (1868), while recognizing these limitations, made an effort to ensure for the judiciary a general right to review legislative interference with private property. In his discussion of what he called "vested rights" he interpreted the clauses of the Fifth and Fourteenth Amendments prohibiting the taking away of property without "due process of law" as giving the judge the right to decide not only whether improper procedures had been used, but also whether the legislature was justified in terms of the needs of the government in interfering with property rights.

This doctrine of "substantive due process" as applied to property rights was not immediately adopted by the Supreme Court, but it worked its way into judicial thinking in the latter part of the nineteenth century, partly under the influence of a single justice, Stephen Field. In 1871, in the *Legal Tender Cases,* Field wrote a dissent in which he attacked the Congressional law making greenbacks acceptable for the payment of debts on the grounds that it contravened the "unchangeable principles of right and morality without which society would be impossible . . ." and "fundamental principles of eternal justice upon the existence of which all constitutional government is founded." A few years later, in the *Slaughterhouse Cases* (1873), Field dissented again, finding a constitutional basis for his natural law thinking in the Fourteenth Amendment guarantee of "the privileges and immunities of United States citizens" which he said, guarantee all privileges and immunities "which of right belong to citizens of all free governments" against abridgement by the states. He added, however, that a slaughterhouse monopoly such as the one in question would be invalid even without that amendment, for it was "opposed to the whole theory of free government." Finally, in 1877, his dissent in the case of *Munn v. Illinois* interpreted the due process clause of the Fourteenth Amendment as a guarantee of private property against any interference which the judge deemed "unreasonable."[15]

All of these quasi-natural law appeals were made in dissenting opinions. However, the majority opinion in *Munn v. Illinois* had indicated that "in some circumstances" state regulation might be sufficiently arbitrary to be unconstitutional. In 1886, while upholding a railroad rate regulation statute, the Court indicated it would invalidate a statute which "amounts to a taking of private property for public use without just compensation or without due process of law," and in 1890 it struck down a Minnesota railroad statute because it deprived the railroad of a judicial appeal "by due process of law" on the reasonableness of the railroad commission's rates.[16] In 1897, in the case of *Allgeyer v. Louisiana,* a majority of the Court not only accepted the view that the due process clause protected property against "unreasonable" infringement, but extended the interpretation of the liberty which the clause guaranteed against abridgement to liberty of contract as well. The most notorious application of this doctrine took place in 1905, when in *Lochner v. New York* the Court struck down a maximum hours law of New York on the grounds that it was an unreasonable interference with liberty of contract and therefore in violation of the Fourteenth Amendment.

By this time, earlier appeals to vague natural law principles had been replaced by references to the equally vague guarantees of the due process clause. Yet the fact that the only liberty which had been defended by the Supreme Court had been liberty of contract laid it open to Justice Holmes' charge in his dissent in the *Lochner* case that it was using the Fourteenth Amendment to legislate its own social and economic prejudices into the constitution via a disguised version of natural law. For Holmes, the law should be what the majority wished it to be unless there was a clear and explicit constitutional prohibition to the contrary.

Beginning with the cases of *Meyer v. Nebraska* (1923) and *Gitlow v. New York* (1925), the Court began to apply the due

---

[15] On the background of the due process clause in English law and its origin in the Magna Carta, see Howard, *The Road from Runnymede,* cf. especially p. 301 for a discussion of its "natural rights" interpretation by the courts.

[16] *Stone v. Farmers' Loan and Trust Co.,* 116 U.S. 331 (1886): *Chicago, Minneapolis and St. Paul Railroad Co. v. Minnesota,* 134 U.S. 457 (1890).

process clause as a prohibition against interference with civil liberties as well as economic ones, and in *Near v. Minnesota* (1931) the Court struck down a state law as an abridgement of freedom of the press, which was understood as a substantive liberty guaranteed by the Fourteenth Amendment. In 1937 in the "switch in time that saved nine," the Court acceded to the Holmes view on limits on the property right, and began to uphold New Deal labor and welfare legislation. Yet at the same time it became increasingly concerned with the protection of civil and political liberties, and it was obliged to develop standards for the interpretation of the due process clause as a guarantee of liberty. While "natural law thinking" had now become a synonym for subjective prejudice and reactionary social views, the Court still had to use a rule of reason in determining when to strike down legislative actions which appeared to violate basic democratic freedoms. To do this it used formulas such as "the fundamental principles of liberty and justice in free government" (*Twining v. New Jersey,* 1908), or that which is "implicit in the concept of ordered liberty" (*Palko v. Connecticut,* 1937), or even the prohibition of "conduct which shocks the conscience" (*Rochin v. California,* 1952). These standards could be defended on a theory of legal positivism that a constitutional majority had opted in 1789 and 1868 (the date of the adoption of the Fourteenth Amendment) for a free society and that these guarantees were necessary conditions for freedom. Yet there seem to be natural law elements implied in the thinking behind them—based not on the nature of man but on the nature of a free society.

Justice Black in his dissent in the case of *Adamson v. California* (1947) accused the Supreme Court of engaging in natural law reasoning in its development of the due process clause. Black argued that the Fourteenth Amendment must be interpreted as applying to the states the specific guarantees of the first eight amendments of the Bill of Rights, or the Court would be guilty of substituting its own "natural law" concepts of decency for the specific language and intent of the Constitution.

Part of Black's bias against natural law arises from his interpretation of the Court's actions in the period between 1880 and 1937, when it read its own social and economic preferences into the Fourteenth Amendment, as a prohibition against state action.

Now as Black sees it, the Court is reading in its own political preferences as to the nature of a free society and using the same parts of the Constitution and the same essentially subjective standards to do so. However, one may ask whether the Court does not have a greater responsibility to protect human rights and access to the political processes than to preserve a given economic system. Justice Stone summarized this view in a footnote to the case of *United States v. Carolene Products Co.* (1938) in which he raised the question "whether legislation which restricts those political processes which can ordinarily be expected to bring about repeal of undesirable legislation is to be subjected to more exacting judicial scrutiny under the general prohibitions of the Fourteenth Amendment than are most other types of legislation." He used a similar justification for special consideration for racial and religious minorities, arguing that "prejudice against discrete and insular minorities may be a special consideration which tends seriously to curtail the operation of those political processes ordinarily to be relied upon to protect minorities and which may call for a correspondingly more searching judicial inquiry."[17]

Stone is not arguing for absolute or natural rights. He derives his rationale from the nature of a democratic system, which requires that access to the means of peaceful change be kept open. Some limitations on these rights have been accepted by the Court (e.g., Justice Holmes' denial in *Schenck v. United States* [1919] of a First Amendment right to shout "fire" falsely in a crowded theater). However, these political and personal rights are given a "preferred position" on the basis of a substantive interpretation of the due process clause of the Fourteenth Amendment.

The case in which a quasi-natural law interpretation of the Fourteenth Amendment was carried the furthest in recent years was *Griswold v. Connecticut* in 1965.[18] There the Court struck down a Connecticut statute forbidding any person from "aiding or abetting" the distribution of birth-control devices. The majority opinion by Justice Douglas argued that the right of marital privacy was guaranteed by "emanations" from the Bill of Rights as applied to the States by the Fourteenth Amendment. Two justices wrote separate opinions relating the right of privacy to the liberty guaranteed by the due process clause. Three concurring judges relied on the Ninth Amendment, which states that the enumeration in the Bill of Rights "shall not be construed to deny or disparage others retained by the people." In an appeal to the natural-rights doctrines of the Founding Fathers, Justice Goldberg, the author of their opinion referred to the "belief of the Constitution's authors that fundamental rights exist that are not expressly enumerated in the first ten amendments . . ." Predictably, Justice Black attacked the Court's use of the due process clause and Goldberg's vague interpretation of the Ninth Amendment as "natural law due process philosophy" which gave the Court power to "invalidate any legislative act which the judges find irrational, unreasonable, or offensive."

The Court has also substantially expanded its interpretation of the fair judicial procedure which is guaranteed by the same constitutional limitation against infringement by state or local government agents. The most controversial of these decisions, *United States v. Miranda* (1966) requires that accused persons be informed of their rights to silence and to counsel before answering any questions after arrest. Others include extension of the right to counsel to state legal procedures and the prohibition of evidence acquired through illegal searches and seizures.

As the examples cited indicate, the Court now has asserted for itself a very wide area of discretion in determining both the substance and procedure of a free and democratic society. This is based on constitutional provisions, principally the due process clauses of the Fifth and Fourteenth Amendments, which are so vague and general that the Court is open to the charge that it is simply legislating its own views on the nature of the good society. Yet the alternative is to leave the determination of the definition of democratic liberties to the often less-than-tender mercies of legislative majorities—which Americans have not been willing to do up to the present. The result is that despite a certain inevitable subjectivity in court decisions on these subjects we will continue to incorporate a type of quasi-natural law thinking as an important element in the American political system. As this chapter has indicated, this development follows a long tradition in American thought.

BIBLIOGRAPHY

Bailyn, Bernard. *The Ideological Origins of the American Revolution.* Cambridge, Mass., 1967, ch. 2 and 5.

Barker, Ernest. "Natural Law and the American Revolution," *Traditions of Civility.* Cambridge, 1948, pp. 263–355.

Berns, Walter. *Freedom, Virtue, and the First Amendment.* Baton Rouge, 1957, ch. 7.

Biddle, Francis. *Justice Holmes, Natural Law and the Supreme Court.* New York, 1961.

Cardozo, Benjamin. *The Nature of the Judicial Process.* New Haven, 1921.

Corwin, Edward S. *The "Higher Law" Background of the American Constitution.* Ithaca, N.Y., 1955.

Curtis, Charles P. *Law as Large as Life.* New York, 1959, ch. 8–11.

Haines, Charles G. *The Revival of Natural Law Concepts.* Cambridge, Mass., 1930, Pts. II–III.

Koch, Adrienne. *Jefferson and Madison.* New York, 1950, ch. 4.

Leboutillier, Cornelia Geer. *American Democracy and Natural Law.* New York, 1950.

McIlwain, Charles H. *The American Revolution.* New York, 1923, ch. 3.

Pound, Roscoe. *The Formative Era of American Law.* Boston, 1938.

Rossiter, Clinton. *Seedtime of the Republic.* New York, 1953, Part 3.

de Vattel, Emmerich. *The Law of Nations or the Principles of Natural Law.* London, 1797.

Wright, Benjamin F. *American Interpretations of Natural Law.* Cambridge, Mass., 1937.

The Rights of the British Colonies Asserted and Proved*

JAMES OTIS

. . . To say the Parliament is absolute and arbitrary is a
contradiction. The Parliament cannot make 2 and 2, 5:
omnipotency cannot do it. The supreme power in a state is
jus dicere only; *jus dare,* strictly speaking, belongs alone to God.
Parliaments are in all cases to *declare* what is for the good of
the whole; but it is not the *declaration* of Parliament that
makes it so. There must be in every instance a higher authority,
viz., God. Should an act of Parliament be against any of *his*
natural laws, which are *immutably* true, *their* declaration would
be contrary to eternal truth, equity, and justice, and
consequently void: and so it would be adjudged by the
Parliament itself when convinced of their mistake. . . .

By the laws of nature and of nations, the voice of universal
reason, and of God, when a nation takes possession of a desert,
uncultivated, and uninhabited country, or purchases of
savages, as was the case with far the greatest part of the British
settlements, the colonists, transplanting themselves and their
posterity, though separated from the principal establishment or
mother country, naturally become part of the state with its
ancient possessions, and entitled to all the essential rights of
the mother country. . . .

It is presumed that upon these principles the colonists
have been by their several charters declared natural subjects
and entrusted with the power of making *their own local laws,*
not repugnant to the laws of England, and with *the power of
taxing themselves.* . . .

. . . The common law is received and practiced upon
here and in the rest of the colonies, and all ancient and modern
acts of Parliament that can be considered as part of or in
amendment of the common law, together with all such acts of

Parliament as expressly name the plantations; so that the power of the British Parliament is held as sacred and as uncontrollable in the colonies as in England. The question is not upon the general power or right of the Parliament, but whether it is not circumscribed within some equitable and reasonable bounds. 'Tis hoped it will not be considered as a new doctrine that even the authority of the Parliament of *Great Britain* is circumscribed by certain bounds which if exceeded their acts become those of mere *power* without *right,* and consequently void. The judges of England have declared in favor of these sentiments when they expressly declare that *acts of Parliament against natural equity are void.* That *acts against the fundamental principles of the British constitution are void. . . .*[1]

1 "A very important question here presents itself. It essentially belongs to the society to make laws both in relation to the manner in which it desires to be governed, and to the conduct of the citizens: this is called the *legislative power.* The nation may entrust the exercise of it to the prince or an assembly, or to the assembly and the prince jointly, who have then a right of making new and abrogating old laws. It is here demanded whether if their power extends so far as to the fundamental laws they may change the constitution of the state. The principles we have laid down lead us to decide this point with certainty that the authority of these legislators does not extend so far, and that they ought to consider the fundamental laws as sacred if the nation has not in very express terms given them the power to change them. For the constitution of the state ought to be fixed; and since that was first established by the nation, which afterwards trusted certain persons with the legislative power, the fundamental laws are excepted from their commission. . . ." de Vattel.

"An act of Parliament made against natural equity, as to make a man judge in his own cause, would be void; for *jura naturae sunt immutabilia.*" Hob. 87. Trin-[ity Term], 12 Jac. [I], *Day v. Savadge,* S. C. and P. [same case and point] cited Arg[uendo] 10. Mod. 115 Hil[ary Term], 11 Anne C. B. [Common Bench] in the case of Thornby and Fleetwood, "but says, that this must be a clear case, and judges will strain hard rather than interpret an act void, *ab initio." This is granted, but still their authority is not boundless if subject to the control of the judges in any case. . . .*

Palko v. Connecticut (1937)*

Mr. Justice Cardozo delivered the opinion of the Court. . . .
. . . the due process clause of the Fourteenth Amendment
may make it unlawful for a state to abridge by its statutes the
freedom of speech which the First Amendment safeguards
against encroachment by the Congress . . . or the like
freedom of the press . . . or the right of peaceable assembly,
without which speech would be unduly trammeled. . . . [some]
immunities that are valid as against the federal government
by force of the specific pledges of particular amendments
have been found to be implicit in the concept of ordered liberty
and thus through the Fourteenth Amendment become valid
as against the states.

The line of division may seem to be wavering and
broken if there is a hasty catalogue of the cases on the one side
and the other. Reflection and analysis will induce a different
view. There emerges the perception of a rationalizing
principle which gives to discrete instances a proper order and
coherence. The right to trial by jury and the immunity
from prosecution except as the result of an indictment may
have value and importance. Even so, they are not of the very
essence of a scheme of ordered liberty. To abolish them is not to
violate a "principle of justice so rooted in the traditions and
conscience of our people as to be ranked as fundamental." . . .
Few would be so narrow or provincial as to maintain that a
fair and enlightened system of justice would be impossible
without them. What is true of jury trials and indictments
is true also, as the cases show, of the immunity from
compulsory self-incrimination. . . .

On which side of the line the case made out by the
appellant has appropriate location must be the next inquiry
and the final one. Is that kind of double jeopardy to which
the statute has subjected him a hardship so acute and shocking
that our polity will not endure it? Does it violate those
"fundamental principles of liberty and justice which lie at

* 302 U.S. 319; 58 S.Ct. 149; 82 L.Ed. 288.

the base of all our civil and political institutions?" . . .
The answer surely must be "no."
The judgment is
Affirmed.

Adamson v. California (1947)*

. . . Mr. Justice Black, dissenting. . . .

This decision reasserts a constitutional theory spelled out
in *Twining v. New Jersey, supra,* that this Court is endowed
by the Constitution with boundless power under "natural law"
periodically to expand and contract constitutional standards
to conform to the Court's conception of what at a particular
time constitutes "civilized decency" and "fundamental liberty
and justice." Invoking this *Twining* rule, the Court
concludes that although comment upon testimony in a federal
court would violate the Fifth Amendment, identical comment
in a state court does not violate today's fashion in civilized
decency and fundamentals and is therefore not prohibited by
the Federal Constitution as amended.

The *Twining* case was the first, as it is the only decision of
this Court which has squarely held that states were free,
notwithstanding the Fifth and Fourteenth Amendments, to
extort evidence from one accused of crime. I agree that if
Twining be reaffirmed, the result reached might appropriately
follow. But I would not reaffirm the *Twining* decision.
I think that decision and the "natural law" theory of the
Constitution upon which it relies degrade the constitutional
safeguards of the Bill of Rights and simultaneously appropriate
for this Court a broad power which we are not authorized
by the Constitution to exercise. . . .

My study of the historical events that culminated in the
Fourteenth Amendment, and the expressions of those who
sponsored and favored, as well as those who opposed its
submission and passage, persuades me that one of the chief
objects that the provisions of the Amendment's first section,
separately, and as a whole, were intended to accomplish was to
make the Bill of Rights applicable to the states.

And I further contend that the "natural law" formula
which the Court uses to reach its conclusion in this case should
be abandoned as an incongruous excrescence on our Constitution.
I believe that formula to be itself a violation of our

* 332 U.S. 46; 67 S.Ct. 1672; 91 L.Ed. 1903.

Constitution, in that it subtly conveys to courts, at the expense of legislatures, ultimate power over public policies in fields where no specific provision of the Constitution limits legislative power. And my belief seems to be in accord with the views expressed by this Court, at least for the first two decades after the Fourteenth Amendment was adopted. . . .

I fear to see the consequences of the Court's practice of substituting its own concepts of decency and fundamental justice for the language of the Bill of Rights as its point of departure in interpreting and enforcing that Bill of Rights. . . .

Conceding the possibility that this Court is now wise enough to improve on the Bill of Rights by substituting natural law concepts for the Bill of Rights, I think the possibility is entirely too speculative to agree to take that course. I would therefore hold in this case that the full protection of the Fifth Amendment's proscription against compelled testimony must be afforded by California. This I would do because of reliance upon the original purpose of the Fourteenth Amendment. . . .

SOURCES

Blackstone, Sir William. *Commentaries on the Laws of England,* Vol. I, London, 1765, pp. 38–61, 123–45, 153–62, 250–52.

Calvin's Case (1608) and *Bonham's Case* (1609), excerpted in Sidney Simpson and Julius Stone, *Law and Society,* Vol. I, St. Paul, 1949, pp. 372–76.

Otis, James, "The Rights of the British Colonies Asserted and Proved," in Bernard Bailyn, ed. *Pamphlets of the American Revolution,* Cambridge, Mass., 1965, pp. 419–82.

de Vattel, Emmerich, *The Law of Nations or the Principles of Natural Law,* London, 1797, prologue.

Cases of the United States Supreme Court:

Chisholm v. Georgia (1793).

Calder v. Bull (1798).

Marbury v. Madison (1803).

Gibbons v. Ogden (1823)—opinion by J. Johnson.

The Legal Tender Cases (1871).

The Slaughterhouse Cases (1873).

Munn v. Illinois (1877)—dissent by J. Field.

Stone v. Farmer's Loan and Trust Co. (1886).

Chicago, Minneapolis and St. Paul Railroad v. Minnesota (1890).

Lochner v. New York (1905).

Twining v. New Jersey (1908).

Powell v. Alabama (1932).

Palko v. Connecticut (1937).

Adamson v. California (1947).

Rochin v. California (1952).

Griswold v. Connecticut (1965).

7.

ROUSSEAU AND BURKE: CRITICS OR EXPONENTS OF NATURAL LAW?

A case can be made that Jean Jacques Rousseau (1712–1778) was opposed to the theory of natural law. In the first version of his *Social Contract* he devoted a chapter (Bk. I, ch. 2), originally entitled *On Natural Law and General Society (Du droit naturel et de la société générale)*, to an attack on Diderot's article on *Natural Law* in his *Encyclopedia*. There Rousseau challenged the prevalent conception that either in the state of nature or in his present state of civilization man could learn the principles of natural law by using his reason. "The sweet voice of nature [was] unperceived by the stupid men of primitive times [and] unavailable to the enlightened men of later times. . . . Notions of the natural law, which we would rather call the law of reason, only develop after the prior development of the passions have rendered all its precepts impotent." Even the well-intentioned man "will be mistaken on the rule or its application and follow his own inclination."[1]

In his *Emile* (1762), Rousseau put into the mouth of the Vicar of Savoy a hymn of praise for the "inner light" or "inner voice" of conscience, whose decrees "are not judgments but feelings." Apart from conscience, says the Vicar, man finds "nothing but the sad privilege of wandering from one error to another by the help of an unbridled understanding and a reason which knows no principle."[2] In the *Discourse on the Origin of Inequality* (1754) and the final version of *The Social Contract* (1762) Rousseau also attacked the natural law theories of the Roman lawyers, as well as those of Grotius, Hobbes, Pufendorf, and Burlamaqui.[3] In these passages Rousseau appears as a critic of natural law for its excessive intellectualism and a defender of an emotive or intuitionist theory of morals.

Yet to see Rousseau simply as a romantic sentimentalist is to underestimate the complexity of his thought. Despite his suspicion of reason, he believes that it can enable man to come to an understanding of a "natural" morality, but only if it is guided by conscience towards a concern for the good of others. In the *Emile,* Rousseau promises that he will show that "justice and kindness are . . . no mere moral conceptions framed by the understanding, but true affections of the heart enlightened by reason, the

---

[1] The first (Geneva Manuscript) version of the *Social Contract,* written between 1755 and 1759, is printed in French in C. E. Vaughan, ed., *The Political Writings of Jean Jacques Rousseau,* Vol. I (Cambridge, 1915), pp. 446–511. The same volume also includes Diderot's article "Droit naturel" (pp. 429–33), an English translation of which appears in Stephen J. Gendzier, ed. and trans., *Denis Diderot, The Encyclopedia, Selections* (New York, 1967), pp. 171–75.

[2] J. J. Rousseau, *Emile, or Education* (Barbara Foxley, trans.) (London, 1911), pp. 231, 259, 253, 254.

[3] Grotius is criticized in *The Social Contract,* Book I, chapters 4 and 5; and Book II, chapter 2. Rousseau mentions his differences with Hobbes in *Discourse on the Origin of Inequality,* Part I (pp. 165 and 181 in Jean Jacques Rousseau, *The Social Contract and Discourses* [G. D. H. Cole, trans.], London, 1913) and in *The Social Contract,* Book I, chapter 2. Pufendorf is referred to critically twice in the *Discourse on the Origin of Inequality* (pp. 165 and 211 of the Cole translation) and Jean Jacques Burlamaqui is mentioned in the preface to the same work, along with critical references to the natural law theories of the Roman lawyers. The only natural law writer mentioned favorably is John Locke, who is cited with approval for his comments on property and against patriarchal rule (Cole translation, pp. 298 and 209).

natural outcome of our primitive affections; that by reason alone, unaided by conscience, we cannot establish any natural law, that all natural right is a vain dream if it does not rest upon some instinctive need of the human heart." In a footnote Rousseau adds that the observance of the Golden Rule "has no true foundation but that of conscience and feeling." It cannot be justified on the basis of rational self-interest. "From this I conclude that it is false to say that the precepts of natural law are based on reason only. They have a firmer and more solid foundation. The love of others springing from self-love is the source of human justice."[4]

Reason alone is inadequate as a guide to morality, because our intellects are weak and subject to self-deception. Moreover, as he says in the Preface to the *Discourse on the Origin of Inequality*, the modern natural law theorists "have established it on such metaphysical principles that there are very few persons among us capable of comprehending them, much less of discovering them for themselves."[5] Our feelings of pity and altruism and the promptings of conscience are a better indication of "the law of nature, that holy and imprescriptible law which speaks to the *heart and reason* of man."[6]

Rousseau rejects natural law as a rationalistic and deductive system and also as the law which governed or can be imagined to have governed the original state of man. He does not reject the nature of man as a guide to basic principles of morality and politics, nor the belief that there is an overall purpose and harmony in nature. We can discern the purposes of nature as prefigured in man's earlier evolution and from the direction of his instinctive feelings of concern for his fellows. However, it is only at the end of man's development that we can see his *true* nature as a free man living according to self-imposed laws.

Rousseau used the analytical tools of the state of nature and the social contract developed by the modern natural law writers,

---

4 *Emile*, pp. 196–97.

5 *Discourse on the Origin of Inequality*, Preface (p. 156 in the Cole translation). The subject which was the occasion for the work was proposed by the Academy of Dijon as "What Is the Origin of Inequality among Men and Is It Authorized by Natural Law?"

6 *Considerations on the Government of Poland*, ch. VI (p. 185 in Frederick Watkins, ed., *Rousseau, Political Writings* [London, 1953]).

but his application of them was radically different. Unlike Pufendorf and Locke, Rousseau saw the state of nature as one in which man was not yet capable of moral relations with his fellows. Governed by emotion, living in a solitary state, he was not the naturally social and moral being of the earlier theorists. Yet neither was he the timid yet aggressive being of Hobbes' model. His principal emotions were self-love and pity, and the latter emotion made it possible for him to follow the "maxim of natural goodness," "Do good to yourself with as little evil as possible to others."

As Rousseau describes the subsequent development of morality in the *Discourse on the Origin of Inequality* man only began to develop moral relationships with the emergence of social relationships, as the human race increased, and man began to improve himself by cooperative endeavors. First patriarchal society replaced the original self-sufficiency of each man; permanent unions replaced the transient sexual encounters of the earlier period; men began to communicate with one another through speech; and some understanding of their moral obligation to others began to replace the rule of the emotions. The common use of the earth gave way to property distinctions and the idea of justice developed.

Rousseau describes this state as the "very best man could experience," and yet he sees in it the source of the evils which were to emerge in later stages. Healthy self-love (*amour de soi*) gave way to vanity (*amour-propre*); some acquired larger amounts of property; and men attempted by various maneuvers to increase their holdings at the expense of others. Property conflicts ensued, and it was finally recognized that the only way to secure peace in society was to establish a government, a supreme power to assure order, harmony, and mutual defense. Having done so, men found, however, that their rulers exploited them, that the government which they had established to make a more civilized life possible only increased the inequality among men and their mutual competition and warfare. Moreover, and here Rousseau states his disagreement with Hobbes, there was no obligation for men to obey governments which exploited them, since mere superior strength does not establish right, and one could not expect those who had established government in order to improve their situations to continue to support it when it had enslaved them. Yet at the end of the *Discourse on Inequality* Rousseau admitted that he and those who had now grown dependent on civilization could not go back to the earlier state, and therefore were condemned to abide by "a constitution . . . from which . . . there always arise more real calamities than even apparent advantages."

The Social Contract was Rousseau's attempt to resolve the problem posed in the *Discourse on Inequality,* how to retain the advantages of society and government while avoiding the attendant evils of inequality, exploitation, self-deception, and falseness in society. To put it into moral terms, Rousseau wished to have the moral life which is only possible in society and under government, while retaining on a higher level the original freedom which man had enjoyed before government emerged. This freedom was desirable not merely because it had existed at some point in the past, but because all men are *by nature* free and equal. And just as man's earlier freedom in the state of nature prefigured a higher moral freedom in a just society, so his emotional feelings of self-love and pity ("natural law properly speaking") prefigured a higher morality which combined both the insights of his reason and the prompting of his conscience ("reasoned natural law").[7] Rousseau's criticism of the classical natural-law conceptions, then, did not involve a rejection of all reference to nature as a guide to morality, but only a more sophisticated and realistic account of the evolution of morality, a recognition of man's capacity to rationalize his egoism, and an attempt to relate the promptings of conscience to the reason in the moral life.

"Men are by nature free and equal" is the basic principle of Rousseau's theory of natural law. On this basis he rejects Grotius' argument that man can be enslaved, and argues against Aristotle that what appear to be slaves by nature are only in this state because they have first been enslaved against nature. He follows this argument with an account of the moral basis of human liberty ("to renounce liberty is to renounce being a man") and an attack on slavery and absolutist government as contrary to the freedom that man has by nature.[8]

[7] *The Social Contract,* first (Geneva) version, Book II, ch. 4 (Vaughan, *The Political Writings,* I, 494).

[8] *The Social Contract,* Book I, chapters 2–4. Note that in chapter 4 he speaks of duelling and private war as "contrary to the principles of natural law." Cf. also Book I, chapter 5 of the first version, where, in discussing paternal authority, Rousseau adds, "I do not speak of slavery, since it is contrary to nature and nothing can authorize it" (Vaughan, *The Political Writings,* Vol. I, p. 465).

The next step in Rousseau's theory is to reconcile man's natural freedom and equality with society and government. To do this he describes (and prescribes) a social contract in accordance with which man will receive the protection and advantages of society and "each while uniting himself to all may still obey himself alone, and remain as free as before."[9] This is done by a unanimous surrender to the general will—the collective legislation on general subjects which is to be made by all and applied to all. These laws must be impartial; there can be no selfishness in arriving at them, and no interest groups participating in their formulation. Legislation must take place with the direct participation of all the members of the community and cannot be arrived at by representatives since they are likely to have selfish interests of their own which are opposed to those of the community. The general will must be willed by each man thinking not of his selfish interest but of the good of the community.[10] It will be supreme, and no fundamental rights or preexisting laws can limit it.

Normally this general will can be achieved by a meeting face-to-face of the whole community, but if the people are not yet able to act unselfishly, they must be educated by a legislator. Moreover, if an individual consistently disagrees with the general will, he must be "forced to be free," i.e., he must be compelled to obey what is his real will, even if he does not recognize it.

The process which Rousseau describes for the emergence of a general will or consensus among the citizens assembled together appears to be almost a mystical one, but it can also be related to the natural law tradition. One of the fundamental assumptions of that tradition had been the belief in a harmony or order in the universe—and between the individual and society. Rousseau shares this belief in his theory of the general will, and assumes that if the individuals unselfishly will the general good, a natural harmony of wills will produce a general law equally applicable to all.

Yet the general will should not be equated directly with

9 *The Social Contract,* Book I, ch. 6.

10 The sum of the selfish wills is called by Rousseau "the will of all," and distinguished from the general will in a manner similar to the distinction, made by the Roman and canon lawyers, between *omnes ut singuli* and *omnes ut universi.* For this and other usages of traditional legal terms, see Ernest Barker, ed., *The Social Contract* (New York, 1947), Introduction.

natural law. In Book II, chapter 6 of *The Social Contract*, Rousseau states that "when we have defined a law of nature we shall be no nearer the definition of a law of the state." As his explanation of the general will indicates, the process of group consultation determines only the good of a given political entity, not that of man in general. The general will does not embrace foreigners, and Rousseau gave advice to the Poles and the Corsicans on developing their particular national spirit and culture, warning against an excessive cosmopolitanism.[11] Patriotism and devotion to one's country are necessary for the creation and maintenance of the general will in each state, and the general wills of two states may come into conflict.

Yet even here the teleological cast of Rousseau's thinking emerges. *The Social Contract* was originally intended to be part of a general work on political institutions which would include discussions of federalism and international relations. In its relations to other states, the general will of any particular state is "a particular and individual will which has its rule of justice in the law of nature. . . . The great city of the world becomes the body politic whose general will is always the law of nature and of which the different states and peoples are individual members."[12] Thus the differences among the various nations are ultimately capable of being resolved, and we may finally attain the "true foundations" of the "reasoned natural law" which is "that each one prefer the greatest good of all."[13] Yet there is no certainty that this development will take place. It is more likely that the egoism, the competitiveness, and falsity which characterize all societies which are not based on the general will will also characterize international relations. In international as in national politics, it is possible but unlikely that a natural harmony of individual and group wills can be attained.[14]

A similar belief in the possibility but not the likelihood of

---

11 Cf. *Considerations on the Government of Poland,* ch. III (Watkins translation, pp. 167 ff.).

12 *A Discourse on Political Economy,* in G. D. H. Cole, trans., *Jean Jacques Rousseau, The Social Contract and Discourses* (London, 1913), p. 237.

13 *Social Contract,* first version, Book IV, chapter 2 (Vaughan, *The Political Writings,* I, 494–95).

14 Cf. Stanley Hoffmann, "Rousseau on War and Peace," *American Political Science Review,* Vol. LVII (June, 1963), 317–33.

harmony characterizes Rousseau's views on the relation of reason and feeling, the intellect and the will, rationality and conscience. This attempt to harmonize human faculties had underlain many earlier theories of natural law, but Rousseau's distinctive contribution was to focus renewed attention on the role of conscience and of society in the development of our moral conceptions and to criticize the elitism and excessive intellectuality of the eighteenth-century versions of natural law thinking.

Rousseau also placed human freedom at the center of his theory. The idea of natural freedom had been part of the natural law tradition since the time of the Roman lawyers, but it had been relegated to a subordinate position. For Rousseau, it was central, and governments and laws which operated in defiance of it were lacking in legitimacy.

A third contribution to natural law thinking was Rousseau's insight into the nature of legal and moral obligation. As Kant recognized later, under the influence of Rousseau (he called him "the Newton of the moral world"),[15] moral obligation is only understandable in terms of the free and uncoerced acceptance of general principles which apply to all men, and only man has the capacity to accept such obligations.

Rousseau's thinking, then, is not antithetical to a type of natural law.[16] His concepts of freedom, equality, and moral legislation are rooted in his view of the nature of man. He also shares the natural law belief in the possibilities of the integration of human faculties and a harmony of individual and group interest. He departs from the tradition as he knew it in his pessimism about the capacities of the individual philosophic reason to arrive at a detailed knowledge of a deductive code of natural law, and in

15 For Kant's comments on Rousseau, see Vaughan, *The Political Writings*, Vol. II, p. 20, 1.

16 Ernest Barker, ed., *The Social Contract*, p. xxix, and Robert Derathé, *Jean-Jacques Rousseau et la science politique de son temps* (Paris, 1960), p. 159, believe that Rousseau's social contract assumes a preexisting natural law obligation of promises to give it binding force. Vaughan, *The Political Writings of Jean Jacques Rousseau*, I, 441 also cites this as the reason for the omission of the chapter attacking natural law from the final version of *The Social Contract*. However, from Rousseau's description, it appears that the contract is entered into in order better to assure the self-preservation of the members in the manner of Hobbes. Subsequently with the emergence of the general will, it is recognized that a new and higher stage of moral freedom under law has developed, by which the citizens feel themselves obliged.

his evolutionary approach to the development of moral conscious-
ness from pity through conscience to the general will of particular
societies to the not-yet-attained general will of mankind, which he
equates with the law of nature.

It is easy to criticize the potential abuses present in Rousseau's theory—the possibilities of the tyranny of the majority or
the legislator, the naïveté of the assumption that individual and
group interests will automatically be reconciled, the impossibility
of democratic government in modern society without resort to a
representative principle—which he rejects; but Rousseau's importance and his impact on political thought can only be explained
by the fact that in his writings for the first time a belief in human
freedom became the central organizing principle of society and
government.

Edmund Burke (1729–97) is also often considered a critic of
natural law. His opposition to the doctrine of natural rights in his
Reflections on the Revolution in France and his emphasis on the
importance of history, tradition, and prescription are often considered as arguments against the attempt to derive values from
nature. In an early satirical work, *A Vindication of Natural Society* (1756), he attacked "the proponents of natural religion" by
attempting to demonstrate that the argument from nature which
had been used against organized religion could be turned against
all of organized society with the same destructive effect. Throughout his writings, politics is viewed as a practical rather than a
theoretical pursuit (reproducing the distinction made in Aristotle's *Nicomachean Ethics*); and prudence, rather than abstract
reasoning, is considered the characteristic virtue of the politician.
This emphasis on practical consequences has led one well-known
writer of political philosophy to describe Burke as a utilitarian
for whom expediency takes precedence over the demands of abstract right.[17]

Yet this view of Burke does not take into account the fact
that among the traditions which he was trying to preserve in a revolutionary age was a belief in certain fundamental moral principles inherent in the universe, in short, a belief in natural law.

---

[17] C. E. Vaughan, *Studies in the History of Political Philosophy,* Vol. II (Manchester, 1925), ch. 1.

Burke was a devout Christian, and as such believed in divine providence, and an ordered universe presided over by a rational God. He also had received a classical and legal education and was familiar with the works of Aristotle, Cicero, Sir Edward Coke, Grotius, and Pufendorf, in which the concept of natural law figured prominently. We know that at Trinity College, Dublin, he read and approved of a work by Bishop Sanderson on the subject of natural law which was strongly influenced by Thomism.[18] In 1767 and 1768 he also read and reviewed Blackstone's *Commentaries,* the opening section of which contains a discussion of natural law.[19]

The mere fact of exposure to these ideas would not prove Burke's adherence to natural law, but in certain of his works there is a direct appeal to its principles. The most notable of these is the *Tract on the Popery Laws* (1761), an attack on the legislation adopted by the English Parliament against Catholicism in Ireland. Irish himself, but not a Roman Catholic, Burke criticized these laws as violating the "will of Him who gave us our nature and in giving impressed an invariable law upon it."[20] In Burke's view, the legal limits on the exercise of religion, the interference with the property of Irish Catholics, their exclusion from education and from many professions were violations of the laws of God and nature. In arguing against them, he indicated where he parted company with the contemporary natural rights theorists. He rejected the state of nature as a standard for the determination of men's rights in society. It is not the consent of the individual which determines law, but "equity and utility." The latter is understood as the "general and public utility, connected in the same manner with and derived directly from, our rational nature." It is a mistake, therefore, to call Burke a utilitarian. Utility has a function in his thought—but it is a consequence or indication of morality rather than its determinant. There is an objective moral law which political laws, however various, should not violate. If they do so, such laws are void.

18 Francis P. Canavan, *The Political Reason of Edmund Burke* (Durham, N.C., 1960), pp. 209–10.

19 Cf. Burleigh T. Wilkins, *The Problem of Burke's Political Philosophy* (Oxford, 1967), p. 35.

20 "Tract on the Popery Laws," Ross Hoffman and Paul Levack, eds., *Burke's Politics* (New York, 1959), p. 152.

As late as 1788 in his speech on *The Impeachment of Warren Hastings,* Burke appealed to "the eternal laws of justice to which we are all subject" and "the primeval indefeasible unalterable law of nature and of nations" which Hastings had violated in his conduct in India.[21] In 1783, in a statement introducing the East India Bill, he observed that "the rights of man, that is to say the natural rights of mankind, are indeed sacred things, and if any public measure is proved mischievously to affect them, the objection ought to be fatal to that measure." Burke added that in English laws these rights have been "further affirmed and declared" by covenants such as the Magna Carta. The charter of the East India Company, in Burke's opinion, violated both "the chartered rights of man" recognized in the Magna Carta and "the natural rights of mankind at large."[22]

It was more on the basis of historic than of natural rights that Burke supported the American colonists in their struggle against the mother country. In his *Speech on American Taxation* (1774) he criticized the "metaphysical distinctions" to which the colonists appealed and advised "Leave the Americans as they anciently stood, and these distinctions, born of our unhappy contest, will die along with it. . . ." In his *Speech on Conciliation with the Colonies* (1775) he proposed that the colonists be allowed to tax themselves, since their love of liberty "according to English ideas and on English principles" had become "fixed and attached on this specific point of taxing."[23]

Burke did not oppose the American Revolution when it finally broke out. He approved of the Glorious Revolution which had overthrown James II in 1688 and of the revolutionary changes at the time of the Protestant Reformation, since "when tyranny is extreme, and abuses of government intolerable, men resort to the rights of nature to shake it off."[24] Burke strongly *disapproved* of the French Revolution, however, and in the course of his argument against it he made clearer his view on the relationship of natural law and politics. In his *Reflections on the Revolution in France* (1790) he criticized the abstract character of the revolutionists' arguments and rejected the belief that every man has a

---

21 *Works of Edmund Burke,* 5th edition (Boston, 1877), Vol. IX, 458–59.
22 *Works,* Vol. II, 437–38.
23 *Works,* Vol. II, 73 and 120–21.
24 *Works,* Vol. VI, 178; Vol. VII, 16.

right to participate in government. Politics is a practical affair, and political arrangements will vary, even though there are some real rights of man which government should protect. "The rights of man are in a sort of middle, incapable of definition but not impossible to be discerned." They include the right to justice, to property, to inheritance, to "a fair portion of all which society . . . can do in his favor," but not to a share in government, which is "a thing to be settled by convention." In direct opposition to Rousseau, Burke also denied that men have a natural right to liberty. Inevitably society and government will curtail individual liberty, but they bring many other advantages by way of compensation. The same thing also seems to be true of equality. "Men have equal rights but not to equal things." "A perfect democracy is the most shameless thing in the world." There is no pre-established or natural right to equal participation in government.

While his statements on the Glorious Revolution may seem to give the impression that he accepted a contractual theory of government similar to that of Locke, the *Reflections* indicate that his view of the contract is more like that of Hooker than that of Locke. Society is a collective undertaking, and the individual has obligations to past and future generations transcending the calculations of individual self-interest. The British constitution works "after the pattern of nature. . . . Our political system is placed in a just correspondence and symmetry with the order of the world. . . . By preserving the method of nature in the conduct of the state, in what we improve we are never wholly new, in what we retain, we are never wholly obsolete. . . . Each contract of each particular state is but a clause in the great primeval contract . . . which holds all physical and moral natures, each in their appointed place."[25]

Does Burke believe in natural law, then? He believes in it in the sense that he holds that there are fundamental principles of justice which are derived from man's nature by the intention of the Creator. He does not believe in the use of natural law to evaluate the various forms of government and the details of the law on the basis of an abstract and deductive scheme, for resort to theo-

[25] *Reflections on the Revolution in France,* in Hoffman and Levack, eds., *Burke's Politics,* pp. 295, 303, and 318.

ries of this sort is "one sure symptom of an ill-conducted state."[26]

For Burke, there is a large area of the morally neutral and of practical compromise which is the normal sphere of politics. Occasionally, as in Ireland or India, the government may clearly violate the fundamental principles of justice and in this case its decrees are void by reason of their contravention of a religiously based natural law, but in most circumstances laws are to be made in accordance with the varying traditions of the individual countries, and should only be changed when there is an urgent need for their modification.

There are important differences between Burke's view and those of theorists such as Hobbes and Locke. Yet as the *Tract on the Popery Laws* indicates, his thinking on politics is grounded in a classical natural law approach which resembles that of Cicero, both in its generality and in the way in which he applies it to current problems of legislation. In its subordination to and integration with a Christian view of the action of divine providence in a hierarchically ordered universe, it also resembles the natural law theory of Aquinas, by whom Burke was influenced at least through intermediaries.[27] Yet there is a distinctive emphasis on history and tradition ("the collected reason of ages") which is not present in the theories of either Cicero or of St. Thomas. His adherence to the doctrine of prescription, the belief that existing laws and institutions have a presumption in their favor, leads him to justify rotten boroughs, an ineffectual monarchy, a decadent aristocracy, and an established church in a way which would be difficult to relate either to utilitarianism or natural law, at least in its more rationalistic forms. Burke's writings, then, constitute something of a departure from the natural law-natural rights theories of his own day, but he continues to believe that there are some basic moral principles inherent in nature which can be perceived by man. This view, like his attitude toward history and politics and his suspicion of individualism and rationalism, can only be understood in the context of his deeply Christian outlook

[26] *Letter to the Sheriffs of Bristol,* 1777, in *Works,* Vol. II, 230.

[27] The argument for a connection between Burke and Thomism is stated (or rather overstated) in Peter Stanlis, *Edmund Burke and the Natural Law* (Ann Arbor, Michigan, 1958). See the author's critical review in *The Natural Law Forum,* Vol. IV, no. 1 (1961), 166–74.

and his reverence for the British constitution as it had evolved to his day. These are the central themes of Burke's political theory, and it is for these views that he is remembered. Nevertheless, natural law thinking is an important, if subordinate, element in his thought.

BIBLIOGRAPHY

Rousseau

Cassirer, Ernst. *The Question of Jean-Jacques Rousseau*. New York, 1954.

Derathé, Robert. *Jean-Jacques Rousseau et la science politique de son temps*. Paris, 1960.

———. *Le Rationalisme de Jean-Jacques Rousseau*. Paris, 1948.

Haymann, Franz. "La Loi naturelle dans la philosophie politique de J. J. Rousseau," *Annales*. Vol. XXX (1943–45), pp. 65–109.

Hendel, Charles W. *Jean-Jacques Rousseau, Moralist*. Vol. I, London, 1934.

Hoffmann, Stanley. "Rousseau on War and Peace," *American Political Science Review*. Vol. LVII (June, 1963), pp. 317–33.

Kelly, George Armstrong. *Idealism, Politics and History: The Sources of Hegelian Thought*. Cambridge, 1969, Pts. I–II.

Lovejoy, Arthur O. "The Supposed Primitivism of Rousseau's Discourse on the Origin of Inequality," *Essays in the History of Ideas*. New York, 1960, ch. 2.

Masters, Roger. *The Political Philosophy of Rousseau*. Princeton, 1968, chs. 2, 6, 7.

Ogden, Henry. "The Antithesis of Nature and Art and Rousseau's Rejection of the Theory of Natural Rights," *American Political Science Review*. Vol. XXII (August, 1938), no. 4, pp. 643–54.

Shklar, Judith N. *Men and Citizens: A Study of Rousseau's Social Theory*. Cambridge, 1969.

Burke

Canavan, Francis P. *The Political Reason of Edmund Burke*. Durham, N.C., 1960.

Parkin, Charles. *The Moral Basis of Burke's Political Thought*. Cambridge, 1956.

Sigmund, Paul. "Edmund Burke and the Natural Law," *Natural Law Forum*. Vol. IV, no. 1 (1961), pp. 166–74.

Stanlis, Peter. *Edmund Burke and the Natural Law*. Ann Arbor, Michigan, 1958.

Vaughan, C. E. *Studies in the History of Political Philosophy*. Manchester, 1925, Vol. II, ch. 1.

Wilkins, Burleigh T. *The Problem of Burke's Political Philosophy*. Oxford, 1967.

Discourse on the Origin of Inequality (1754)*

JEAN JACQUES ROUSSEAU

The right of property being only a convention of human
institution, every man may dispose of what he possesses as
he pleases: but this is not the case with the essential gifts
of nature, such as life and liberty, which every man is permitted
to enjoy, and of which it is at least doubtful whether one
has the right to divest oneself. By giving up the one, one
degrades his being; by giving up the other, one destroys himself
insofar as he can and, as no temporal good can indemnify
us for the one or the other, it would be an offense against
both reason and nature to renounce them at any price whatsoever.
But, even if one could alienate his liberty, as if it were his
property, there would be a great difference with regard
to the children, who enjoy the father's goods only by the
transmission of his right; whereas, liberty being a gift which
they have from nature as men, their parents have no right to deprive
them of it. So that just as to establish slavery, it was necessary to
do violence to nature, so, to perpetuate it, nature would have
to be changed. Jurists who have gravely pronounced that the child
of a slave comes into the world a slave, have decided, in other
words, that a man shall come into the world not a man. . . .

* Translated by Paul E. Sigmund from "Discours sur l'Inegalité" in C. E.
Vaughan, ed., *The Political Writings of Jean Jacques Rousseau*, Vol. I. Copyright ©
1915 by Cambridge University Press.

The Social Contract: First Version*

[*Geneva MS. f. 225*] (*1755–59*)

JEAN JACQUES ROUSSEAU

Book I, Chapter 2: On the General Society of the Human Race
(*Original title: On Natural Law and General Society*)

. . . Let us imagine the human race as a moral personality
with a sentiment of common existence which gives it
individuality and unity [and] a universal motivating principle
which makes each part act for a general purpose relative
to the whole. Let us imagine that that common sentiment is
one of humanitarianism and that the natural law is the
actuating principle of the whole machine. Let us then observe
what results from man's constitution in his relations to his
fellows. To the contrary of what we supposed, we will find that
the progress of society stifles humanitarianism in men's hearts
by awakening personal interest and that notions of the
natural law, which we would rather call the law of reason,
only develop after the prior development of the passions have
rendered all its precepts impotent. Hence we see that the supposed
social bond dictated by nature is a veritable chimera, since
its conditions are always unknown and impossible to practice
and it is necessary either to ignore them or to violate them. . . .
. . . In fact no one will disagree that the general will
is in each individual a pure act of understanding which reasons
in the silence of the passions concerning what man can ask
of his fellow-man and what his fellow-man has the right
to ask of him. But where is the man who can thus separate
himself from himself in this way? And if concern with his

* Translated by Paul E. Sigmund from "Du Contrat social ou essai sur la
forme de la republique," in C. E. Vaughan, ed., *The Political Writings of Jean
Jacques Rousseau*, Vol. I. Copyright © 1915 by Cambridge University Press.

self-preservation is the first law of nature, can one thus force
him to consider the species as a whole and impose on himself
duties which do not seem to him connected with his own
particular constitution? Do not the preceding objections still
continue, and does it not still remain to see how his personal
interest requires that he submit himself to the general will?

Moreover, since the art of generalizing ideas in this way
is one of the most difficult and delayed exercises of the
human understanding, will the ordinary man ever be able
to derive the rules of his conduct through this kind of
reasoning? And when it is necessary to consult the general will
on a particular action, how many times will it not happen
that the well-intentioned man will be mistaken on the rule
or its application and follow only his own inclination
while he thinks he is obeying the law? What will he do as
a guarantee against error? Will he listen to the inner voice?
But that voice, they say, is only formed by the habits of
judgment and feeling of society and its laws. It cannot
therefore serve to establish them. In addition, he must have
avoided arousing the passions in his heart which speak
louder than the conscience, cover its timid voice, and support
the philosophers who say that it does not exist. Is he to consult
the principles of written law, the actions in society of all
peoples, the tacit conventions of even the enemies of
the human race?[1] The first difficulty recurs—it is only
from the social order established among us that we draw
the ideas of the one we imagine. We conceive of a general
society according to particular societies; the establishment
of petty republics makes us think of the great Republic; and
we only begin properly to become men after we have become
citizens. Everywhere one sees what we are to think of
those pretended cosmopolites who justify their love for their
native country by their love for the human race and boast
of loving the whole world so as to have the right to love no one.

---

[1] A reference to Diderot's recommendations in his article on *Droit naturel* in
the *Encyclopedia* as to how to discover the general will. On the earlier use of the
term, "the general will," by Diderot and Montesquieu, see Vaughan, ed., *The Political Writings*, Vol. I, pp. 424–26; Judith N. Shklar, *Men and Citizens: A Study of
Rousseau's Social Theory* (Cambridge, 1969), p. 168, fn. 2.

What reasoning demonstrates to us on this point is
entirely confirmed by the facts, and however little one goes
back into antiquity, one easily sees that sound ideas of natural
law and common fraternity among men were disseminated
rather late and made such slow progress in the world that
it was only Christianity that gave them sufficiently general
currency. . . .

Book II, Chapter 4: On the Nature of the Laws

. . . The greatest advantage which results from this notion
[the general will] is to show us the true foundations of justice
and natural law. In fact, the first law, the only true
fundamental law which follows immediately from the social
compact is that each one prefer the greatest good of all in
every case. . . .

. . . Extend to general society the maxim of which the
state gives us the idea. Protected by the society of which we
are members or by that in which we live, our natural
repugnance to doing evil no longer restrained by the fear of
having it done to us, we are drawn at the same time by
nature, by habit, and by reason to treat other men a bit like
we treat our fellow citizens, and from that disposition translated
into action arise the rules of reasoned natural law, which is
different from natural law properly speaking, which is only
based on a feeling which is sound but very vague, and often
stifled by love of self.

. . . It is therefore in the fundamental and universal
law of the greatest good of all and not in particular relationships
of one man with another that we must look for the true
principles of justice and injustice; and there is no particular
rule of justice which cannot be easily deduced from that
first law. . . .

The Social Contract (1762)*

JEAN JACQUES ROUSSEAU

Book I, Chapter VIII: The Civil State

This passage from the state of nature to the civil state
produces a very remarkable change in man, by substituting
justice for instinct in his conduct, and giving his actions
the morality they had lacked before. It is only then when the
voice of duty takes the place of physical impulses and law
that of appetite, that man, who so far had considered
only himself, finds himself forced to act on different principles,
and to consult his reason before listening to his inclinations.
Although, in this state, he deprives himself of some
advantages which he had from nature, he gains in return
others so great, his faculties are so exerted and developed,
his ideas so extended, his feelings so ennobled, and his
whole soul so uplifted, that, if the abuses of this new condition
did not often degrade him below that which he left, he would
be bound to bless continually the happy moment which took
him from it for ever, and, instead of a stupid and unimaginative
animal, made him an intelligent being and a man. . . .

. . . We might also add, to what man acquires in the
civil state, moral freedom, which alone makes man truly
master of himself; for the mere impulse of appetite is slavery,
while obedience to a law which we prescribe to ourselves is
freedom. . . .

* Translated by Paul E. Sigmund from "Contrat social" in C. E. Vaughan, ed., *The Political Writings of Jean Jacques Rousseau*, Vol. II. Copyright © 1915 by Cambridge University Press.

SOURCES

Burke, Edmund, *A Vindication of Natural Society.*
——, *Tract on the Popery Laws.*
——, *Reflections on the Revolution in France.*
Rousseau, Jean Jacques, *Discourse on the Origin of Inequality.*
——, *Discourse on Political Economy.*
——, *Emile,* especially "The Confession of Faith of the Vicar of Savoy."
——, *The Social Contract, First Version,* Bk. I, ch. 2; Bk. II, ch. 4.
——, *The Social Contract* (final version), Bk. I; Bk. II, ch. 3, 4, 6, 11 and 12.

8.
THE UTILITARIAN CRITIQUE

Probably the most devastating criticism of the doctrine of natural law appears in two short chapters devoted to a completely different subject. In his *Treatise of Human Nature* (1739), David Hume (1711–76) discusses "The Influencing Motives of the Human Will" (Bk. II, Pt. III, sec. 3), and attacks the belief in reason as a moral faculty which lay at the base of much of the earlier natural law thinking. In defense of his assertion that "reason is and ought to be the slave of the passions," Hume argues that reason can carry on logical and mathematical operations and can perceive empirical reality, but is incapable of making judgments of value. Reason cannot tell me why I should not "prefer the destruction of the whole world to the scratching of my finger," or "my own acknowledged lesser good to my greater," "my total ruin to prevent the uneasiness of a . . . person wholly unknown to me." These are matters of preference, related in origin to anticipated pleasure or pain, and governed by the emotions. What has been taken for the rule of reason is in reality the predominance of "calm passions" such as benevolence or kindness over violent passions such as anger.

In a later section Hume develops this point further. A

chapter entitled "Moral Distinctions Not Derived from Reason" is devoted to refuting those who believe "that there are eternal fitnesses and unfitnesses of things which are the same to every rational being that considers them; that the immutable measure of right and wrong imposes an obligation not only on human creatures but also on the Deity himself. . . ." In reply, Hume observes that "in every system of morality which I have hitherto met . . . the author proceeds for some time in the ordinary way of reasoning . . . when of a sudden I find that instead of the usual copulation of propositions, *is,* and *is not,* I meet with no proposition that is not connected with an *ought* or *ought not.* . . . As this *ought* or *ought not* expresses some new relation or affirmation . . . a reason should be given . . . how this new relation can be a deduction from others which are entirely different from it" (Bk. III, Pt. I, ch. 1). In the terms which later commentators were to use, a statement of value, an "ought," cannot be derived from a statement of empirical fact or logical deduction, an "is." The assertion that there are values inherent in nature or man is a logical fallacy. "It is impossible to show those relations upon which such a distinction (of right and wrong) may be founded and . . . we cannot prove, a priori, that those relations, if they really existed and were perceived, would be universally forcible and obligatory." There are empirical observations and logical relationships perceived by the senses and reason, but they cannot tell us anything about what is good.

In the next section (Bk. III, Pt. I, ch. 2), Hume observes that "natural" is an equivocal term which can be used in three senses. It can mean the opposite of supernatural; it can mean frequent or common; or it can be opposed to that which is artificial. None of these meanings is helpful in determining that which is moral. "Virtue is distinguished by the pleasure and vice by the pain that any action, sentiment, or character gives us by the mere view or contemplation."

Hume thus seems to expound a moral theory of hedonism, and if his earlier statements about the basis of value in subjective preference are to be taken seriously it seems to be an anarchic, egoistic hedonism at that. His theory of morality involves more than destructive criticism and subjective hedonism however. According to his theory, after society develops rules of justice to limit human partiality and selfishness and to provide security and stability, we derive "pleasure from the view of such actions as tend to the peace of society." What we call morality is built upon the disinterested approval elicited by our emotion (or calm passion) of sympathy for the interests of society. Its content consists of conventional rules which are found to be socially useful and then acquire an independent force of their own which makes us feel morally obligated by them.

Hume's theory thus attempts to explain the phenomenon of moral choice and yet preserve his central belief in the emotional basis of valuation. The choice of the milder pleasure derived from disinterested approval of acts beneficial to society rather than the immediate (and more "natural") pleasure induced by satisfaction of other emotions is what is called virtue. Reason does not lie at the basis of this choice but rather, emotion. If someone chooses to prefer anti-social acts, reason or nature cannot prove that he should not do so. One can argue from logical or empirical consequences, but not to any inherent obligation in human nature or society which demands that the individual prefer the interests of society or even his own long-run interests. As an empiricist, Hume can only point to the empirical facts of emotional preference, and the probable empirical results of such choices.

With this view of the relation of morals and nature, Hume explains the concepts of justice and moral and political obligation which had previously been explained by an appeal to natural law. "Natural" virtues, he says, are those based directly on a passion or emotion which all men feel. (He thus adds a fourth meaning of nature to the three mentioned above.) All men do not feel the obligation of justice by nature. More natural is the emotional feeling which would lead one, for instance, to take from the rich and give to the poor, or to prefer an immediate personal advantage to the social good. The idea of justice, then, is artificial, being created or evolved by society because it realizes that man's benevolence is limited and his egoistic impulses are strong. It indoctrinates him with the habitual belief that certain principles which are in fact derived from the long-run interest of society have an independent moral validity. Thus property relations, their transfer by agreement, and the keeping of promises are considered to be laws of nature, and they may be so described "if by natural we understand what is common to the species, or . . . inseparable from the species" (Bk. III, Pt. II, ch. 1). Yet in fact they are artificial conventions made necessary by the fact that society can exist only if these conventions are respected. Later, by dint of repetition and habit, man begins to consider them as absolute or moral "natural" principles rather than conventional human inventions.

Hume applies the same analysis to the social contract theory and to the origin of government which it was supposed to explain. If the obligation to keep promises is based on the good of society and is conventional in origin, there is no particular point in reducing political obligation to promise-keeping, as the contract theorists did (Bk. III, Pt. II, ch. 2). Political obligation can be better explained as arising out of the interest of society in order and security. Obedience and consent, resistance and revolution—all are justified in terms of the interest of society, not because of the conditions of some original contract. In a sense, all governments are based on consent, since they could not survive if men did not agree that they were useful and in their interest.

Hume's view seems to bear some resemblances to that of Hobbes, but it also differs significantly from it. Like Hobbes, he speaks of laws of nature, but subverts the traditional notion of natural law by his explanation of their conventional origin. Even self-preservation which is viewed by Hobbes as a universal desire of man, is for Hume simply a matter of emotional preference. However, the problem which Hobbes never solves—how the selfish pleasure–loving animals in his state of nature ever get into society or stay there—is resolved by positing the existence of a sympathetic passion in men. There is such a thing as human nature, but it is made up of opposing impulses of egoism and altruism, and law is only indirectly derived from it as a reinforcement of the altruistic impulses, through the establishment of rules that make a stable and secure life possible. Moreover, in terms of Hume's original analysis, there is no *reason* why one should prefer one's altruistic to his egoistic impulses, or even his existence over non-existence. Nevertheless, men do in fact prefer them and erect governments and systems of justice to reinforce them.

Despite his destructive criticism of the theory of natural law, one can build a natural law theory on the basis of Hume's analysis He admits as much himself when he says that his three principles may be called laws of nature in that they are common to all human societies. In his explanation he goes further, asserting that the individual must accept some kinds of property arrangements and contractual or promissory obligations in order for society to survive. Thus Hume develops a certain minimal set of principles out of the need for societal survival, which one might call a "natural" human need—and by implication he has given us, in addition to a psychological explanation of the nature of morality, a philosophical justification for it, derived, however, more from the nature of civilized living together than from the nature of man. (If the need for survival in society is not accepted however, no amount of argument can persuade the Humean sceptic, since his fundamental assumption is that there are only facts of experience and emotional preferences.) If one should ask whether, taking Hume's example, a secret loan, i.e., a debt known only to the debtor and creditor, would be repaid by an adherent of his moral philosophy, Hume would presumably reply that respect for promises as a general system would demand repayment even in this limiting case, or the framework of society would be endangered by undermining the habit and moral code respecting the payment of debts.

In addition, Hume's explanation of virtue and vice as distinctions based on disinterested approval of acts which benefit society assumes a constancy in human nature which gives rise to moral standards which are applicable to all men and persuade them to prefer the general interest over particular ones. Hume provides an emotional basis for this preference and limits the role of reason to connecting certain actions or characteristics with good results for society, but he arrives at conclusions which are similar to those of traditional moralists including the natural law theorists.

Yet the attitude to morality which Hume's theory suggests makes it much easier to depart from moral principles, since they are seen as artificial and socially conditioned. As Hume himself recognizes, mere disinterested approval of the interests of society is "too remote" and "too sublime" a motive for the performance of virtuous acts. Habit, convention, and moral conditioning are necessary to reinforce the requirements of life in society. Moreover, this minimal moral theory does not explain or justify the demands of human beings for a higher level of morality—for the full self-development and freedom which Rousseau articulated so well a few years later. That Hume and Rousseau had a famous quarrel almost immediately after their meeting is explicable not only in terms of the differences in their personalities but also in a fundamental philosophical divergence between the rather smug Scottish sceptic who was convinced that, in general, governments were improving over time in their ability to meet human needs, and the radical paranoid from Geneva who saw the human personality as repressed and distorted by contemporary society and government.

There is a tension which is never fully resolved in Hume's thought between his conception of moral values as a matter of subjective preference and his belief that men will agree in their disinterested approval of the public interest and evolve a system of laws and justice including the three artificially derived "laws of nature" to assure it. Jeremy Bentham (1748–1832) attempted to resolve this tension by erecting an objective science of morals and legislation on a more explicitly hedonistic basis. In arguing for his system he was savagely critical of all alternative moral theories, and in particular that of natural law and natural rights.

For Bentham, the argument from natural law was an attempt to ascribe to nature what were essentially subjective prejudices. "A great multitude of people are continually talking of the Law of Nature; and then they go on giving you their sentiments about right and wrong [as] so many chapters and sections of the Law of Nature."[1] The precepts which are ascribed to nature either say too little or too much. Either they are empty truisms, such as "Render to every man his due," or they assert that whatever exists is by nature and thus inhibit reform, or they comprise a second set of legal and moral principles which are counterposed as absolutes in a subjective or "anarchical" fashion to the compromises and limited rights arrived at by society.[2] To the argument from

[1] Jeremy Bentham, *An Introduction to the Principles of Morals and Legislation*, ch. 2, par. 14, fn. 1.

[2] Cf. Jeremy Bentham, *A Commentary on the Commentaries on the Laws of England* (Oxford, 1928), pp. 38 ff.

the need to recognize human rights in order to promote human happiness, Bentham gives a terse reply: "Hunger is not bread."[3]

Bentham's ire was particularly aroused by the *Declaration of the Rights of Man and the Citizen,* put forward during the French Revolution. "Natural rights is simple nonsense," he said, "and natural and imprescriptible rights . . . nonsense on stilts." Every right is limited, granted by society, and subject to qualifications. The social contract theory based on the doctrine of natural rights is "a pure fiction, or in other words, a falsehood."[4]

In his opposition to the French Revolution Bentham agreed with conservatives such as Edmund Burke, who shared his antipathy to the theories of the revolutionists. When in the section attacking the contract theory, he describes political obligation as psychologically based on habit, one might expect him to deduce from it a practical belief in conservatism as Hume had done before him. Yet this is not the case, because Bentham's destructive criticism was all aimed at preparing the way for his own theory of utilitarianism, which was thoroughly reformist in its implications.

It is utility, defined as the greatest good or greatest happiness of the greatest number, which is the standard of value for Bentham. Happiness in turn can be reduced to pleasure and pain, which determine both how we should act and how we do act. The moralist and the legislator are concerned with ensuring that the attractiveness of man's long-run pleasure, the greatest good of the greatest number, will coincide with the attractiveness of the short-run pleasure of the individual. Legislation thus attaches artificial pains to an immediate pleasure which is opposed to the greatest good of the greatest number. The only unit is pleasure, and all types of pleasure are commensurate. "Quantity of pleasure being equal, push-pin is as good as poetry."[5]

All other theories of morality and politics can, in Bentham's view, be reduced to utility. We distinguish among the many moral precepts in Scripture on this basis, and the legitimate insights of the natural law theory are derived not from an understanding of the purposes of nature, but from generalizations based on utility.

When Bentham applied this theory to law and politics, it had

---

[3] Jeremy Bentham *Anarchical Fallacies,* "The Declaration of Rights," Art. 2.
[4] *Ibid.*
[5] Jeremy Bentham, *Dissertations,* II, p. 389, quoted in Leslie Stephen, *The English Utilitarians,* Vol. II (London, 1900), p. 304.

important reformist implications. He originally favored autocracy as the best method of creating the artificial harmony of individual and social goods, but he soon realized that the monarchs of eighteenth-century Europe were more likely to legislate their own short-run pleasure than the greatest good of the greatest number, and he therefore espoused representative democracy as the best way to assure it by legislation. If his theory is consistently applied, this form of government still would not assure the greatest good of the greatest number, since, as Rousseau recognized, the legislators might also pursue their own short-run pleasure rather than being concerned with society; but Bentham seems to believe, with some justification, that there is less likelihood of this occurring in a democracy than under an autocratic system. To keep legislators responsive to the interests of those they represented, he proposed institutions such as annual parliaments in which the members could not be elected for two consecutive terms.

Bentham's principal practical concern was with legislative reform, and he used his theory to argue against excessive legal penalties for trivial offenses. (A heavy penalty, in terms of pain, was not necessary to discourage the slight pleasure produced by minor offenses such as petty theft.) The political and legal reforms introduced by Bentham's followers had an important influence on English politics in the first part of the nineteenth century. The reformist strain in Benthamism helps to explain the opposition of the Benthamites to natural-law thinking, since it seemed either too conservative or too radical to be helpful in reforming English politics and law.

It is easy to find fault with Bentham's theory, although it is not as easy to reply to his criticisms of natural law. Certainly his attempt to work out a "calculus of pleasures" was naïve in the extreme. It is evident that, despite Bentham's efforts to classify and quantify pleasures, such a subjective and variable experience is impossible to measure. Moreover, as John Stuart Mill later pointed out, it is a common human conviction that some pleasures are qualitatively superior to others. Push-pin is not as good as poetry in qualitative terms, and some conception of the nature of distinctively human activities seems to lie at the root of our conviction that it is not.

The examination of what we mean by moral activity raises further questions about the utilitarian calculus. As Bentham describes it, it appears that if one is to be rational, the calculation of the greatest happiness (pleasure) of the greatest number is to be made in each case—a theory which was later to be called act-utilitarianism. Yet, as Kant pointed out, moral conduct seems to involve some notion of universalization rather than the mere calculation of immediate advantage. The so-called "rule-utilitarians" recognize this, although, as one commentator has argued, their theory cannot eliminate some notions of fairness, equal opportunity, and welfare which are not reducible to mere summary rules of utility.[6]

Behind Bentham's theory lie certain assumptions which resemble those made by natural law theorists. Thus, in computing the greatest good of the greatest number, he assumes that each individual is to count for one and none for more than one. Otherwise the greatest happiness of a minority might outweigh the lesser happiness of a majority. And in a way Bentham bases his whole argument on the nature of man as a pleasure-seeking animal. And because this is what he is, it is also what he ought to be. It is part of man's nature to seek pleasure, and Bentham is simply advising him on how to do so more rationally.

Even if we reject the simplistic hedonism of Bentham, he has called attention to the importance of a concern with the effects of moral action—and shifted the focus of moral argument from the discussion of inherent moral obligations to a consideration of the results of a given moral decision. Yet in judging those results, it is necessary to have some standard of utility, and if Bentham's undifferentiated pleasure is inadequate, what can replace it?

John Stuart Mill (1806–73), brought up in the Benthamite creed of his father, James Mill, rejected Bentham's hedonism, since it did not distinguish as to qualitative differences among pleasures. For Mill it was "better to be Socrates dissatisfied than a fool satisfied" (*Utilitarianism*, ch. 2). In *On Liberty* he defended the right of the individual to free expression even when a democratic majority wished to restrict it in the interest of what it assumed to be the greatest good of the greatest number. It is true that his argument rested partly on the social utility of free speech,

---

[6] David Lyons, *Forms and Limits of Utilitarianism* (Oxford, 1965). See also John Rawls, "Two Concepts of Rules," *Philosophical Review*, Vol. LXIV (1955), pp. 3–32, and literature cited therein.

but he also derived it from a conception of man as a rational and moral being, from "the Greek ideal of self-development" (ch. 3). Similarly, in chapter 3 of his essay on *Representative Government* he argued that democracy was morally preferable to the most benevolent despotism or rule by a philosopher-king, even if the ruler had a perfect insight into what would ensure the happiness (whether Platonic or Benthamite) of his subjects.

Mill never gives us anything more definite than "the permanent interests of man as a progressive being" (*On Liberty*, ch. 1) as a standard for his qualitative utilitarianism, but permeating his writings is the moral ideal of the self-controlled active reformer who freely chooses to develop his potentialities and to contribute to the advancement of human freedom and diversity. This idea sounds suspiciously like some kind of appeal to man's higher nature along idealist or natural law lines, but Mill still attempts to relate this ideal to pleasure of a higher kind, to which "those who are equally acquainted with, and equally capable of appreciating and enjoying both, do give a marked preference" (*Utilitarianism*, ch. 2).

Mill rejects a recourse to nature or human nature as a source of the distinction between higher and lower faculties. In his essay on *Nature*, he describes all man's moral progress as the result of a struggle against physical nature and against his natural passions and emotions. In Mill's view, nature in the sense of the physical universe, was either amoral, or if evaluated morally, could be considered as evil rather than good. As far as human nature was concerned, it included many impulses and inclinations, some evil and some good, and much of morality consisted in conquering the natural but anti-social impulses in human nature.

As the discussions of the natural law theorists in the previous chapters of this book indicate, Mill did not accurately state their arguments. They did not believe that everything in nature or man was to be followed—least of all his emotions or impulses—but only that there are certain essential rational goals or patterns or "natural inclinations" in man which can be recognized as good, and which form the basis of moral and political obligation. These immanent goals are not very different, at least in some formulations, from those derived from Mill's ideal of socially responsible self-development.

Later in the nineteenth century, David G. Ritchie, writing on *Natural Rights* (London, 1894, reprinted 1952), proposed to replace Bentham's pleasure and pain with the standard of "the self as rational and universal" which will give us "the principles of a coherent and orderly society which will not throw away the hardwon achievements of man in his struggle with nature and with barbarism, and which will at the same time be progressive, in the sense of being capable of correcting its own faults." (p. 106). Influenced by Immanuel Kant and Charles Darwin, as well as by Mill, he grounded his moral theory in an evolving "social utility" as the basis of the moral principles of what he calls Evolutionist Utilitarianism.

This proposal was put forward in the context of an extended attack on the doctrine of natural rights—the main burden of the book. The principal point of Ritchie's criticism is a variation of Bentham's argument from subjectivity. He reviews the various arguments for natural rights and finds that they are mutually self-contradictory and are used to support many diverse theories, both reactionary and revolutionary. He proposes his own standard as more objective and at the same time capable of recognizing the undoubted moral progress of mankind.

Perhaps one might illustrate the differences in the views of the theorists under discussion with the example of slavery. Most natural law and natural rights theorists had held that slavery was opposed to nature. They appealed to the absolute standard of man's rational nature and/or to an earlier historical or analytical state of nature to prove that all men are by nature free and equal. Hume, on the other hand, might describe slavery as a conventional arrangement which is opposed to the sympathy which men feel in viewing the suffering of their fellows, finally leading them to the moral generalization that slavery is wrong.[7] Bentham would balance the pain inflicted on slaves by the pleasure to be gained

---

[7] When he discussed slavery (in "Of the Populousness of Ancient Nations" *Essays, Moral, Political, and Literary,* originally published 1741–42, reprinted in Oxford University Press edition, London, 1963, Part II, essay XI), Hume spoke of the Romans as having "shaken off all sense of compassion towards that unhappy part of their species," but he also said that one of the evils of slavery was that slaveholders "trample upon human nature" because of their "unbounded dominion" over their slaves, contrary to "the inviolable laws of reason and equity."

by their masters, and add a consideration of the numbers involved, deciding that slavery should be eliminated. Mill would refer to the contradiction between slavery and human perfectibility and dignity. For Ritchie, however, slavery was justified at one point in the past by its social utility.[8] It enabled the Greek civilization to reach great heights and contributed to the progress of the race. However, at a later point, it was no longer "socially useful" and therefore had to be abolished. Just how this view can be squared with the concept of "the self as rational and universal" he does not tell us.

As the illustration indicates, the standards used by utilitarians are less absolute than those of natural law. Hume recognizes that other principles develop out of the feeling of sympathy, and an attenuated approbation of the public interest, but they remain merely tentative generalizations. For Bentham the only principle is individual pleasure and pain, whereas for Mill and Ritchie a progressive social utility is the vague standard which comes to be filled in rather specifically in their writings with principles which are generally useful but can in extreme cases be violated.[9] Natural law theory, on the other hand, claims to perceive universal moral principles inherent in man and nature. And its defenders assert that in criticizing a given moral or political situation (such as the evils of a totalitarian regime or of slavery) the clarity and certainty of its principles provide a clearer guide than that of the greatest good of the greatest number, or social utility.

On the other hand, the two theories also have certain resemblances. Both in the form proposed by Bentham and in that of John Stuart Mill, utilitarianism makes certain assumptions about man which can be adequately justified only in terms of a theory about the nature of man which both describes what it is and prescribes what it should be. And on the other side, natural law theorists also hold that there are natural sanctions for the violation of the natural law, and they cannot help but believe that there are rewards for virtue, that "honesty is the best policy" and "crime

---

8 David G. Ritchie, *Natural Rights* (London, 1894), p. 104.

9 See chapter 3 of J. S. Mill, *Utilitarianism,* entitled "On the Connection between Justice and Utility."

does not pay"—that in response to Bentham's accusation that they adhere to the doctrine *"fiat justitia, ruat coelum,"* if justice is done, the heavens will *not* fall. For natural law theorists, then, utility is a result of the observance of natural law principles, whereas for utilitarians the principles of justice are an indication or codification of long-run utility. Both take account of the same moral experience and both often come to the same conclusions, but one emphasizes the *a priori* and universal character of our moral conclusions about man in society, and the other emphasizes the basis for these conclusions in human desires and in the *a posteriori* effects which follow their adoption.

BIBLIOGRAPHY

Baumgardt, David. *Bentham and the Ethics of Today*. Princeton, 1952.

Halevy, E. *The Growth of Philosophic Radicalism*. London, 1949.

Letwin, Shirley. *The Pursuit of Certainty*. Cambridge, 1965.

Plamenatz, John. *The English Utilitarians*. Oxford, 1958.

Sidgwick, Henry. *The Methods of Ethics*. 7th ed., London, 1907 (reissued 1962), ch. VI.

Stewart, John B. *The Moral and Political Philosophy of Hume*. New York, 1963, ch. IV.

von Leyden, W. "John Locke and the Natural Law," *Philosophy*. Vol. XXXI (1956), 23–35 (Locke's "confusions" analyzed from a utilitarian viewpoint).

Anarchical Fallacies*

JEREMY BENTHAM

The Declaration of Rights

. . . Article II: *The end in view of every political association is the preservation of the natural and imprescriptible rights of man. These rights are liberty, property, security, and resistance to oppression.*

Sentence 1. The end in view of every political association, is the preservation of the natural and imprescriptible rights of man.

More confusion—more nonsense,—and the nonsense, as usual, dangerous nonsense. The words can scarcely be said to have a meaning: but if they have, or rather if they had a meaning, these would be the propositions either asserted or implied:

1. That there are such things as rights anterior to the establishment of governments: for natural, as applied rights, if it mean anything, is meant to stand in opposition to *legal,* —to such rights as are acknowledged to owe their existence to government, and are consequently posterior in their date to the establishment of government.

2. That these rights *can not* be abrogated by government: for *can not* is implied in the form of the word imprescriptible, and the sense it wears when so applied, is the cut-throat sense above explained.

3. That the governments that exist derive their origin from formal associations, or what are now called *conventions:* associations entered into by a partnership contract, with all the members for partners,—entered into at a day prefixed, for a predetermined purpose, the formation of a new government where there was none before (for as to formal meetings

* Jeremy Bentham, *Works*, ed., John Bowring, Vol. II. Copyright © 1843 by Simpkin Marshall, London.

held under the control of an existing government, they are evidently out of question here) in which it seems again to be implied in the way of inference, though a necessary and an unavoidable inference, that all governments (that is, self-called governments, knots of persons exercising the powers of government) that have had any other origin than an association of the above description, are illegal, that is, no governments at all; resistance to them, and subversion of them, lawful and commendable; and so on.

Such are the notions implied in this first part of the article. How stands the truth of things? That there are no such things as natural rights—no such things as rights anterior to the establishment of government—no such things as natural rights opposed to, in contradistinction to, legal: that the expression is merely figurative; that when used, in the moment you attempt to give it a literal meaning it leads to error, and to that sort of error that leads to mischief—to the extremity of mischief.

We know what it is for men to live without government —and living without government, to live without rights: we know what it is for men to live without government, for we see instances of such a way of life—we see it in many savage nations, or rather races of mankind; for instance, among the savages of New South Wales, whose way of living is so well known to us: no habit of obedience, and thence no government—no government, and thence no laws—no laws, and thence no such things as rights—no security—no property: liberty, as against regular control, the control of laws and government—perfect; but as against all irregular control, the mandates of stronger individuals, none. In this state, at a time earlier than the commencement of history—in this same state, judging from analogy, we, the inhabitants of the part of the globe we call Europe, were;—no government, consequently no rights: no rights, consequently no property —no legal security—no legal liberty: security not more than belongs to beasts—forecast and sense of insecurity keener —consequently in point of happiness below the level of the brutal race.

In proportion to the want of happiness resulting from

the want of rights, a reason exists for wishing that there were such things as rights. But reasons for wishing there were such things as rights, are not rights;—a reason for wishing that a certain right were established, is not that right—want is not supply—hunger is not bread.

That which has no existence cannot be destroyed—that which cannot be destroyed cannot require anything to preserve it from destruction. *Natural rights* is simple nonsense: natural and imprescriptible rights, rhetorical nonsense,— nonsense upon stilts. But this rhetorical nonsense ends in the old strain of mischievous nonsense: for immediately a list of these pretended natural rights is given, and those are so expressed as to present to view legal rights. And of these rights, whatever they are, there is not, it seems, any one of which any government *can,* upon any occasion whatever, abrogate the smallest particle.

So much for terrorist language. What is the language of reason and plain sense upon this same subject? That in proportion as it is *right* or *proper,* i.e. advantageous to the society in question, that this or that right—a right to this or that effect—should be established and maintained, in that same proportion it is *wrong* that it should be abrogated: but that as there is no *right,* which ought not to be maintained so long as it is upon the whole advantageous to the society that it should be maintained, so there is no right which, when the abolition of it is advantageous to society, should not be abolished. To know whether it would be more for the advantage of society that this or that right should be maintained or abolished, the time at which the question about maintaining or abolishing is proposed, must be given, and the circumstances under which it is proposed to maintain or abolish it; the right itself must be specifically described, not jumbled with an undistinguishable heap of others, under any such vague general terms as property, liberty, and the like. . . .

The origination of governments from a contract is a pure fiction, or in other words, a falsehood. It never has been known to be true in any instance; the allegation of it does mischief, by involving the subject in error and confusion, and is neither necessary nor useful to any good purpose. . . .

Whence is it, but from government, that contracts derive their binding force? Contracts came from government, not government from contracts. It is from the habit of enforcing contracts, and seeing them enforced, that governments are chiefly indebted for whatever disposition they have to observe them. . . .

Nature*

JOHN STUART MILL

. . . In sober truth, nearly all the things which men are
hanged or imprisoned for doing to one another, are
nature's every day performances. Killing, the most criminal
act recognized by human laws, Nature does once to every
being that lives; and in a large proportion of cases, after
protracted tortures such as only the greatest monsters whom
we read of ever purposely inflicted on their living
fellow-creatures. If, by an arbitrary reservation, we refuse
to account anything murder but what abridges a certain term
supposed to be allotted to human life, nature also does this
to all but a small percentage of lives, and does it in all the
modes, violent or insidious, in which the worst human
beings take the lives of one another. . . .

But even though unable to believe that Nature, as a
whole, is a realization of the designs of perfect wisdom and
benevolence, men do not willingly renounce the idea that some
part of Nature, at least, must be intended as an exemplar, or
type; that on some portion or other of the Creator's
works, the image of the moral qualities which they are accustomed
to ascribe to him, must be impressed; that if not all
which is, yet something which is, must not only be a faultless
model of what ought to be, but must be intended to be our
guide and standard in rectifying the rest. It does not suffice
them to believe, that what tends to good is to be imitated
and perfected, and what tends to evil is to be corrected: they
are anxious for some more definite indication of the Creator's
designs; and being persuaded that this must somewhere be
met with in his works, undertake the dangerous responsibility
of picking and choosing among them in quest of it. A
choice which except so far as directed by the general maxim
that he intends all the good and none of the evil, must
of necessity be perfectly arbitrary; and if it leads to any

* From *Nature, The Utility of Religion, Theism, Being Three Essays on Religion.* Copyright © 1874 by Longmans Green, London.

conclusions other than such as can be deduced from that maxim, must be, exactly in that proportion, pernicious.

It has never been settled by any accredited doctrine, what particular departments of the order of nature shall be reputed to be designed for our moral instruction and guidance; and accordingly each person's individual predilections, or momentary convenience, have decided to what parts of the divine government the practical conclusions that he was desirous of establishing, should be recommended to approval as being analogous. One such recommendation must be as fallacious as another, for it is impossible to decide that certain of the Creator's works are more truly expressions of his character than the rest; and the only selection which does not lead to immoral results, is the selection of those which most conduce to the general good, in other words, of those which point to an end which if the entire scheme is the expression of a single omnipotent and consistent will, is evidently not the end intended by it.

There is however one particular element in the construction of the world, which to minds on the look-out for special indication of the Creator's will, has appeared, not without plausibility, peculiarly fitted to afford them; viz. the active impulses of human and other animated beings. One can imagine such persons arguing that when the Author of Nature only made circumstances, he may not have meant to indicate the manner in which his rational creatures were to adjust themselves to those circumstances; but that when he implanted positive stimuli in the creatures themselves, stirring them up to a particular kind of action, it is impossible to doubt that he intended that sort of action to be practiced by them. This reasoning, followed out consistently, would lead to the conclusion that the Deity intended, and approves, whatever human beings do; since all that they do being the consequence of some of the impulses with which their Creator must have endowed them, all must equally be considered as done in obedience to his will. As this practical conclusion was shrunk from, it was necessary to draw a distinction, and to pronounce that not the whole, but only parts of the active nature of mankind point to a special intention of the Creator in respect to their conduct. These parts it seemed natural to suppose, must be those in which the Creator's hand is manifested rather than the man's own: and hence the frequent antithesis between man as God made him, and man as he has made himself. . . .

It is only in a highly artificialized condition of human nature that the notion grew up or, I believe, ever could have grown up, that goodness was natural: because only after a long course of artificial education did good sentiments become so habitual, and so predominant over bad, as to arise unprompted when occasion called for them. In the times when mankind were nearer to their natural state, cultivated observers regarded the natural man as a sort of wild animal, distinguished chiefly by being craftier than the other beasts of the field; and all worth of character was deemed the result of a sort of taming; a phrase often applied by the ancient philosophers to the appropriate discipline of human beings. The truth is that there is hardly a single point of excellence belonging to human character, which is not decidedly repugnant to the untutored feelings of human nature. . . .

SOURCES

Bentham, Jeremy, *An Introduction to the Principles of Morals and Legislation,* ch. 2.
——, *A Commentary on the Commentaries,* Pt. I.
——, *Anarchical Fallacies,* "The Declaration of Rights."
Hume, David. *A Treatise of Human Nature,* Bk. II, Pt. III; Bk. III, Pts. I–II.
Mill, John Stuart, *On Liberty,* ch. 1.
——, *Utilitarianism,* ch. 2–3.
——, *Nature* in *Three Essays on Religion.*
Ritchie, David G., *Natural Rights,* London, 1894.

9.

NATURAL LAW IN LAW AND HISTORY

Kant, Marx, and Modern Legal Theory

It might appear to be an error to include Immanuel Kant (1724–1804) in a history of natural law theory, when the basic tendency of Kantian dualism is to make a sharp disjunction between the world of nature and the moral world. In Kant's view, nature as we perceive it, is governed by the principle of causality, and devoid of any morality. Man, insofar as he is a part of nature is rigorously determined in all his actions. Yet, at the same time, man is conscious of his own moral life and of his own freedom. Kant's moral theory is devoted to explaining this moral experience, and in doing so he develops a theory of morals and law which is ultimately derived from his view of human nature and more specifically from the nature of moral choice. However different his theory is from those which preceded it, Kant's moral and legal writings fall into the tradition of natural law, and he may even be considered the last of the great system-builders in natural law theory.

In this area as in many others, Kant accepted the criticisms of Hume but attempted to reconstruct a moral theory which would take account of the weaknesses in the traditional theory that Hume had pointed out. Physical nature, therefore, is not a source or standard of value for Kant. Neither, however, is the utilitarian standard of happiness or utility such a source of value, since (1) like nature, utility is externally imposed and dependent on changing circumstances; (2) there is no *a priori* self-evident reason why one should seek it as an end; and (3) seeking utility is different from acting morally, for the imperatives which it produces are prudential rather than moral, instrumental and hypothetical rather than categorical. Morality must be something different, not dependent on the external world, not a means to something else, but rather the action of a rational being on the basis of universal principle. As Kant defines it, moral action is not a calculation of alternative consequences in terms of some external end (even human happiness) but action on an *a priori* basis of duty alone. Only acts which are performed out of duty are moral actions, and in this sense alone can moral actions be said to be based on reason.

From this description of morality as action motivated by duty Kant derives the various forms of his categorical imperative. The essential characteristic of his imperative is that one act or refrain from acting on the basis of principle rather than on the basis of calculation of results, and that this principle be capable of extension to all mankind. Thus the categorical imperative can be phrased "So act that the maxim of your action can become a law for all mankind." By analogy with the universal extension of the physical laws of nature, it can be rephrased "So act that the maxim of your action can become a universal law of nature." (This is not to say that the moral principles are derived from nature, but only that they are similar in their universal applicability.)

In this way, Kant took the characteristics which Rousseau laid down as necessary for a moral political order—universality, generality, impartiality, and free consent—and made them the basis of individual ethics. Just as Rousseau's view of political obligation made freedom a precondition for legitimate rule, so Kant's interpretation of morality considers free choice in accordance with principle as the essential characteristic of morality. In order to be moral, this principle must be imposed upon oneself, not required by someone else or a means to the attainment of some other end.

Action according to a self-imposed law is a precondition for morality. If men are to act morally, the categorical imperative should therefore be rephrased "So act as to treat all men not simply as a means but always as at the same time ends in themselves."

When Kant comes to apply his moral teachings, his claim to have developed an *a priori* moral standard is somewhat compromised by the examples which he gives. Inevitably one must take into account the consequences in the natural world of the universal application of a given action in determining whether it is moral or not. Implied in the decision that a given action, e.g., lying or stealing, cannot be universalized is the acceptance of a standard of the good of mankind or of society—which, since it produces a hypothetical imperative, would not for Kant be a legitimate standard for morality. Kant's theory can be salvaged, however, by an alternative interpretation of the categorical imperative as a description of moral motivation rather than as a guide to moral action, so that although a concern with consequences is unavoidable the intuition of the duty of acting unselfishly on principle is what makes such actions moral.[1]

Kant tries to draw out the implications of the categorical imperative for law and government as well as for individual morality. Law becomes an imposed external order which makes possible the coexistence of free-willing moral individuals. It is characterized by compulsion, and therefore obedience to external law is not a moral act; but the subjects should obey it because it makes it possible for them to live together and act morally, and the ruler who makes the law should himself be guided by the categorical imperative in legislating. The ideal form of government to fulfill these requirements is a republic with a representative legislature and the separation of powers to assure that the law will maximize freedom and be enacted, applied, and judged objectively.

Kant only rarely refers to natural law as such. In the introduction to his *Metaphysics of Morals,* he describes natural law principles as "those external laws, the obligatoriness of which can be recognized by reason *a priori* even without external legislation." In the same work, he also makes use of the concepts of the state of nature, original contract, and natural rights. However, their meaning is changed to harmonize with Kant's basic view of

---

[1] Cf. T. C. Williams, *The Concept of the Categorical Imperative* (Oxford, 1968).

morality and law. The state of nature is an expression for the absence of agreed legal and moral restraints; the term natural law is applied only to external coercive legislation which is universally and rationally necessary for a legal system; and the social contract is an analytic construct signifying the recognition by the people that they can find a higher moral freedom in a civil state regulated by law if they give up the "wild lawless freedom of the state of nature." As for natural rights, there is only one right which man has by nature, that of moral freedom; and all other rights are derived from it.

This brief outline of Kant's moral and legal theory indicates in what sense he may be called a natural law theorist. Kant's belief that human desires and happiness have nothing to do with morality seems most *un*natural to those who do not share his views. If natural law theory is the attempt to derive moral and political principles from nature defined as the external world, Kant is not a natural law theorist. If, on the other hand, it signifies the derivation of principles from human nature, and the nature of law, he quite clearly belongs in that category. The categorical imperative, in its various forms, a natural right of freedom, the ultimate derivation of government from the people and its operation under legal principles, are all derived from human nature, not as in earlier theorists by an analysis of immanent purposes and goals in man, but through an examination of the preconditions for human moral action and the legal order required to make it possible.

In Part I of the *Metaphysics of Morals* which is concerned with legal theory, Kant derives further conclusions from the principle of the autonomy of the will and the nature of morals and law. He discusses contracts, property, marriage, the rights of parents, masters and servants, and international law—and relates these topics to moral freedom in a treatise that seems as thoroughly scholastic as any of the earlier natural law theorists. Kant analyzes marriage, for example, exclusively as a contract between two persons of different sex for the reciprocal possession of sex faculties, and he opposes revolution in any circumstances, because it is contrary to the concept of a legal state, since a law legalizing revolution would undermine the legal system and thus involve a contradiction. (See excerpt.)

Yet Kant welcomed the French Revolution because to him it stood for the advance of republicanism. In his *Idea for a Uni-*

versal History he posited a "secret plan of nature" for the emergence of the perfect constitutional state as the only condition in which the moral capacities of mankind could be fully realized. In his *Essay on Perpetual Peace* this goal was seen as one to be achieved in a federal union of republics. Yet in both cases Kant was conscious of the fact that he was imputing a teleology to nature and history which was not there. History was to be treated *as if* it were working towards these goals as long as the opposite could not be proved. Perhaps one might find in these passages another type of moral and political obligation which is related to nature and in a sense derived from it—the natural law that political forms are and should be working towards the establishment of republicanism. Although in Kant's view this theory received some support from the evidence of history, its real moral character was ultimately traceable to Kant's fundamental conception of man as a free-willing moral agent. This conception could not be demonstrated scientifically, but was based on the direct intuition of each man of his capacity to act in accordance with a self-imposed moral law—and his recognition that a republican constitution (i.e., representative government, the separation of the executive and legislature, and the rule of law) would maximize the possibilities for moral action by its citizens.

Whereas Kant did not derive a moral theory directly from history but rather imputed a moral purpose to it, other theorists have attempted to base their moral and political views on patterns which they perceived in history. Some might argue that the laws of history which Hegel and Marx derived could be called natural laws, and that they therefore could be classified as natural law theorists.[2] A distinction, however, must be made between the attempt to discern a pattern or law in history and the type of natural law thinking with which this book is concerned. History rather than nature is the source of norms, and moral and political imperatives are characterized by relativism and change rather than by the absolutism and universalism which characterizes natural law thinking. The natural law theories that Marx knew were considered by him as part of the ideological superstructure of capitalism. As he said in the *Communist Manifesto*, "The selfish misconcep-

---

[2] The subtitle of Hegels' *Philosophy of Right* is *Natural Law and Political Science Outlined,* but in it Hegel distinguishes clearly between nature and law.

tion that induces you [the bourgeoisie] to transform into eternal laws of nature and reason the social forms springing from your present mode of production . . . you share with every ruling class that has preceded you."

Yet there may be a sense in which we can relate the theory of Marx, at least, to the natural law which we have been examining. In order to do so, it is necessary to look at the final end product of the historical process. For Hegel, this is the triumph of the Idea in the world, so that what is real is rational, and what is rational is real. But in Marx, the last stage of the dialectic of history is the classless society, in which the alienation of man from nature, his fellow man, and his human nature, is overcome. All history is a story of the domination by the ruling class and its exploitation of human labor. However, when this domination is ended in the final stage of communism, and exploitation ceases, man's true nature is no longer repressed and oppressed by the division of labor, and he is at one with himself. "Man's natural behavior has become human for him . . . and . . . his human nature has become nature for him. . . . Communism . . . is the final resolution of the antagonism between man and nature and between man and man."[3] "A Communist society . . . makes it possible for me to do one thing today and another tomorrow, to hunt in the morning, fish in the afternoon, rear cattle in the evening, criticize after dinner, just as I have mind, without ever becoming hunter, fisher, shepherd, or critic."[4]

In these passages it seems clear that Marx has a conception of the nature of man which is universal, *a priori,* and a source of moral and political values. The last stage of history is superior not because it follows the others, but because it conforms to the innate needs of man, to his nature which requires spontaneity and freedom and a sense of union with other men and with nature—natural human values which have been distorted and suppressed

---

[3] Karl Marx, *Economic and Philosophical Manuscripts,* translated in Erich Fromm, *Marx's Concept of Man* (New York, 1961), pp. 126–27.

[4] Karl Marx, *The German Ideology,* in Fromm, *Marx's Concept of Man,* p. 206. Cf. also Marx's attack in *Capital* on Bentham's utilitarianism: "To know what is useful for a dog, one must study dog-nature. This nature itself is not to be deduced from the principle of utility. Applying this to man, he that would criticize all human acts, movements, relations, etc. by the principle of utility must first deal with human nature in general, and then with human nature as modified in each historical epoch" (*Capital,* Vol. I, Chicago, 1909, p. 668, no. 2).

in all other stages. It is no secret that for all his pretense at being a scientist, Marx was fundamentally a moralist, but it may be a bit startling to relate his theory to the argument from human nature, an argument which can even be formulated in terms of general moral principles which prescribe spontaneity, freedom, social life, and the aesthetic enjoyment of nature as moral requirements. With the new insights into the thinking of Marx which the translation of his *Economic and Philosophical Manuscripts* has provided, it seems undeniable that this was a major factor influencing his thought from an early point in his life.

Returning to the area of legal theory, it is possible to trace Kant's influence directly in a number of legal writers down to the present day. Two twentieth-century writers on jurisprudence acknowledge Kant's influence but come to rather different conclusions. The first, Rudolf Stammler, places himself squarely in the natural law tradition, but admits that his theory is based on the nature of law, not on the nature of man. "There can be no law of nature in the former sense of the word, but there may be methodical principles implied in the nature of law." The world of empirical reality, including human experience, is too varied and changing to say that one can derive natural moral laws or natural rights from human nature. "It is impossible to prove that man has definite native qualities for social life and certain *a priori* impulses guiding his conduct. . . . On the assumption of such impulses we can never arrive at an absolute and fundamental idea of just social volition." However, we can derive a conception of what the law should be from an understanding of its function in regulating "a community of free-willing individuals." We know that it must be rational and noncontradictory in its content, universal in its extent within the community, and that it must make social life possible among free men. From this we can derive a number of conclusions about the proper form for contract, property, and marriage law, although we cannot prescribe its content. Stammler thus espouses what he calls a "natural law with a changing content" on the basis of the Kantian analysis of law.[5]

On the other hand, Hans Kelsen, the author of *The General Theory of Law and the State,* and an avowed positivist and ardent

---

[5] Rudolf Stammler, *The Theory of Justice* (New York, 1925), ch. 3.

opponent of the idea of natural law, bases his opposition to natural law on Kantian thought. In his view, the Kantian theory of law is derived from "transcendental logical principles of cognition" which are the conditions of moral and legal experience and not in any sense an assertion about nature. Legal systems must be analyzed in terms of their logical consistency, conformity with the idea of law (which includes the ideals of order and equal treatment), and derivation from a basic norm which is the source of all legal obligation in the system. Kelsen admits that "despite its renunciation of any element of material justice" the basic norm may be justified in terms of some appeal to natural law, but he asserts that this "minimum of natural law" is necessary in order to have any law at all. In all other respects law is to be sharply distinguished from nature and from morality. As in Kant's own writings, law is defined as an order imposed on external action which makes social life possible and coercion legitimate. But unlike Kant, its relation to morality is dismissed as irrelevant, since moral conclusions are essentially subjective. Kant's *Fundamental Principles of the Metaphysics of Morals,* in which he develops the idea of the categorical imperative, is therefore dismissed by Kelsen as "the most perfect expression of the classical doctrine of natural law" and irrelevant to his philosophy of transcendental logic, which was "preeminently destined to provide the groundwork for a positivistic legal and political doctrine."[6] The central position of moral freedom in Kant's (and Stammler's) theories becomes a subjective moral preference rather than the basis of law and morality. Any basic norm will do, provided an internally consistent legal system can be derived from it.[7]

Stammler's attempt to derive moral and legal norms from the nature of law has also been pursued by other legal theorists who do not specifically acknowledge the influence of Kant. Lon Fuller, Professor of Jurisprudence at the Harvard Law School, has long maintained that the ideal of law implies certain moral standards,

---

6 Hans Kelsen, *General Theory of Law and the State* (Cambridge, Mass., 1949), pp. 437 ff.

7 "Even the purely capricious and personal rule of a despot is an order of law as long as the basic norm of his state sanctions this type of arbitrary regime." Edgar Bodenheimer, "The Natural-Law Doctrine: A Reply to Hans Kelsen," *Western Political Quarterly,* Vol. III, no. 3 (Sept., 1950), p. 362.

which are at least procedural or formal and may often possess substantive content as well. Thus the German state under Hitler, while it maintained some forms of law, was inevitably driven by its evil purposes to violate formal justice, to make special rulings, and to depart from the legal norms of predictability, universality, and rationality. Law, therefore, argues Fuller, has a certain purposive inner morality "a procedural or institutional kind of natural law" which provides us with standards to judge it. Moreover, in order for there to be any law at all, there has to be social communication; and Fuller has suggested that a more detailed set of principles along the lines of traditional natural law theory may be derived from the goal of meaningful social communication.[8]

H. L. A. Hart of Oxford University, who debated Fuller on the subject of law and morality in a well-known exchange in the *Harvard Law Review,* denies that law and morality are as closely connected as Fuller believes. We can have a law which is morally bad and still law, he says, and there is no use confusing the two kinds of activity. Law is external social regulation with a coercive sanction, while morality is internal action on the basis of principles of good and evil. A law can be so immoral that it should be disobeyed, but it is still a law, and the natural law theorists are in error in asserting that it is not.[9]

Yet in a book written since his encounter with Fuller, Hart has recognized that there is a "core of good sense" to the natural law doctrine. For Hart, there are certain basic requirements for human social existence which make law necessary. Men are vulnerable. They are in need of cooperation and yet are not sufficiently altruistic to live together in harmony at all times. Hence some legal regulations are necessary to enable them to survive. If it were not for man's altruism, it would not be possible for him to live in society at all, but since this altruism is limited, it is necessary to have a system of coercive sanctions to protect men from one another.[10]

It will be evident from this summary that Hart's view closely approaches that of David Hume, and has some resemblances to

---

[8] Lon Fuller, *The Morality of Law* (New Haven, 1964), p. 186.

[9] The Hart-Fuller debate appears in the *Harvard Law Review,* vol. 71, February, 1958, pp. 593–673, and is reprinted in Frederick A. Olafson, ed., *Society, Law, and Morality* (Englewood Cliffs, N.J., 1961), pp. 439–505.

[10] H. L. A. Hart, *The Concept of Law* (Oxford, 1961), ch. 9.

that of Thomas Hobbes. As with Hobbes and Hume, many different legal and political systems may conform with the requirements of his natural law. It is only necessary to recognize that if man is to survive he must live in society under certain coercive rules. Hart's theory resembles that of Hobbes in that survival is considered to be the inherently desirable good—an assumption with which not everyone would concur.[11]

In his attempt to answer an attack by Hans Kelsen upon the natural law doctrine, Edgar Bodenheimer points to certain minimal needs natural to man that limit the arbitrary will of the legislator. Among these needs are food, water, society, sex, and so on; without them man could not exist and, again assuming that existence is in itself desirable, interference with these goods is immoral and unnatural. Thus a law requiring only four hours sleep a day could be described as against nature and therefore illegitimate. Bodenheimer also alludes to the concept of "the interstices of the law" developed by Justice Benjamin Cardozo, in his *Nature of the Judicial Process*. In Cardozo's view natural law, in the sense of "what fair and reasonable men, mindful of the habits of life in the community and of the standards of justice and fairdealing prevalent among them ought in such circumstances to do" supplies "the main rule of judgment to the judge when precedent and custom fail. . . ."[12]

The need for an extralegal standard was most deeply felt by those who were concerned with the conduct of Germans under the Nazi regime. German writers who justified the resistance to Hitler, in particular the July, 1944 assassination plot, frequently found it necessary to appeal to natural law conceptions. The postwar German government has attempted to incorporate the notion of a higher moral responsibility in the oath for members of its armed forces and in legal and constitutional documents. This may be contradictory to the idea of a closed legal system and open the door to subjective moral interpretations, as some critics have

11 "As for the proposition that the overwhelming majority of men wish to survive even at the cost of hideous misery, this seems to me of doubtful truth" (Lon Fuller, *The Morality of Law*, p. 185). In his essay "Of Suicide," Hume argued that "the law of nature" does not forbid suicide. See David Hume, *Essays, Moral, Political, and Literary* (Oxford, 1963), pp. 585–96.

12 Benjamin Cardozo, *The Nature of the Judicial Process* (New Haven, 1921), p. 142; quoted in Bodenheimer, "The Natural Law Doctrine," p. 342.

argued,[13] but it has had an important political effect in under-
scoring the limited nature of political obligation. The specter of
anarchy which the positivists elicit has not yet materialized in
postwar German legal practice.

The Nuremberg War Crimes Trials were also the occasion
for discussion of the relationship of national, international, and
natural law. The International Military Tribunal appealed to
international law as the basis for the punishments which it imposed. However, it was difficult to find any justification in the positive law of nations for the punishment of the Nazi leaders for
"crimes against humanity," and there was only a very tenuous
basis in international law for a judgment by the victors of the
vanquished, especially for crimes involving third parties. In these
cases, some writers have argued that, try as they might, the defenders of the action of the victorious allies could not avoid an
appeal to a form of natural law.[14]

A natural law type of argument was involved (although not
stated as such) in the court's reply to the defense of the accused
that they were acting under superior orders. It was assumed that
men should know that mass murder, genocide, and similar acts
were criminal acts in themselves worthy of punishment, even if this
fact was not spelled out in the perverted legislation of the Nazi
state. The court referred to "the general principles of justice" or
"the conscience of mankind" in making this answer, but the
method of argument closely resembled that of the natural law
theorists.[15]

[13] Guenter Lewy, "Resistance to Tyranny: Treason, Right, or Duty," *Western
Political Quarterly*, Vol. XII, no. 3 (Sept., 1960), pp. 581–596.

[14] It should be noted that some natural law theorists hold that the War Crimes
trial of Adolf Eichmann in Jerusalem fifteen years later was that "genocide" was a
international) law that an individual can only be punished for a crime if its criminal
nature has been clearly pointed out by law before it was committed: the prohibition
of *ex post facto* legislation. The reply to this given at Nuremberg and also at the
trial of Adolf Eichmann in Jerusalem fifteen years later was that "genocide" was a
new crime and therefore could not have been anticipated in antecedent legislation.
Cf. Hannah Arendt, *Eichmann in Jerusalem* (New York, 1963); and W. Benton and
Georg Grimm, *Nürnberg, German Views of the War Trials* (Dallas, 1955), especially
pp. 87–97.

[15] "The question arises . . . whether we are rather confronted with one of
those rare cases in which natural law renders it permissible to make positive law
yield to the inexorable command of ethics. . . . It seems indeed that the idea of
natural law presents the only possible way of dealing with problems of such a kind
and magnitude" (August von Knierem, *The Nuremberg Trials* [Chicago, 1959], pp.
264–65).

When it is unable to cite any formal legal provisions international law attempts to give moral or natural law principles legal status by asserting that the international community has agreed to them by custom, but this assertion leads to a certain conceptual confusion in the argument. Thus, in the debate over the Vietnam war it is very difficult to distinguish between traditional just war arguments based on natural law, and those which appeal to accepted standards of international law.[16] Americans who consider the war immoral cite and sometimes confuse both the principles of morality and those of international law as enunciated at Nuremberg.

In the civil rights struggle in the South of the United States, the violation of the law was also justified in the name both of the positive law of the Constitution and of a higher law. Thus in his letter from the Birmingham City Jail, Martin Luther King asserted that "one has a moral responsibility to disobey unjust laws. I would agree with St. Augustine that 'An unjust law is no law at all.' . . . An unjust law is a code that is out of harmony with the moral law. To put it in the terms of St. Thomas Aquinas, an unjust law is a human law that is not rooted in eternal and natural law. . . ."[17]

It seems that those committed to the rule of law can neither live with nor live without natural law. On the one hand, it seems either too vague and subjective to provide any guidance to the hard-headed lawyer, or else so specific that it becomes a threat to the existing law which he is bound to apply and interpret. On the other hand, there is a recognized need for standards of interpretation, for guidance in the inevitable development of the law in which judges engage, and for higher standards of justice or a minimal level of internal consistency and order which will indicate whether a given law is legitimate substantively and procedurally. These standards may simply be called morality or ideal justice,

16 Compare, for instance, the arguments in Cornelius F. Murphy, Jr., "The Vietnam Conflict: A Moral Evaluation," *Natural Law Forum*, Vol. 12 (1967), pp. 196–209; and Mulford Q. Sibley, "The Morality of War: The Case of Vietnam," *Natural Law Forum*, Vol. 12 (1967), pp. 209–24, with those in Richard A. Falk, ed., *Vietnam and International Law* (Princeton, 1968).

17 Martin Luther King, Jr., "Letter from the Birmingham City Jail," *Why We Can't Wait* (New York, 1964), pp. 85–86.

but very often in the past and still today in certain parts of the world and in certain areas of inquiry they are known as the principles of the natural law.

BIBLIOGRAPHY

Arendt, Hannah. *Eichmann in Jerusalem*. New York, 1963.

Benton, W. E. and Georg Grimm. *Nürnberg, German Views of the War Trials*. Dallas, 1955.

Cardozo, Benjamin. *The Nature of the Judicial Process*. New Haven, 1921.

Fichte, J. G. *The Science of Right*. New York, 1869 (English translation of *Grundlage des Naturrechts*. Jena, 1796).

Fuller, Lon. *The Law in Quest of Itself*. Evanston, Ill., 1940.

———. *The Morality of Law*. New Haven, 1964.

———. "Positivism and Fidelity to Law," *Harvard Law Review*. Vol. 71, no. 4 (February, 1958), 630–73.

Hart, H. L. A. *The Concept of Law*. Oxford, 1961.

———. *Law, Liberty, and Morality*. Oxford, 1963.

———. "Are There Any Natural Rights?" in Anthony Quinton, ed. *Political Philosophy*, Oxford, 1967, pp. 53–66.

———. "Positivism and the Separation of Law and Morals," *Harvard Law Review*. Vol. 71, no. 4 (February, 1958), 593–629.

Hutchins, Robert. "Natural Law and Jurisprudence," in John Cogley, ed. *Natural Law and Modern Society*. Cleveland, 1963, pp. 29–47.

Kelsen, Hans. *The General Theory of Law and the State*. Cambridge, Mass., 1949.

——. *Le Droit naturel*. Paris, 1959.

——. *What is Justice?*. Berkeley, 1957; esp. pp. 137–97.

Krieger, Leonard. "Kant and Natural Law," *Journal of the History of Ideas*. April, 1965, pp. 191–210.

Ladd, John. Introduction to Immanuel Kant, *The Metaphysical Elements of Justice* (Part I of *The Metaphysics of Morals*). Indianapolis, 1965.

Lewy, Guenter. "Resistance to Tyranny: Treason, Right, or Duty," *Western Political Quarterly*. Vol. XII, no. 3 (Sept., 1960), pp. 581–596.

Paton, H. J. *The Categorical Imperative*. Chicago, 1945.

Reiss, Hans. Introduction to *Kant's Political Writings*. Cambridge, 1970.

Shklar, Judith. *Legalism*. Cambridge, Mass., 1964, pp. 64–110.

Tucker, Robert. *Philosophy and Myth in Karl Marx*. Cambridge, 1961, ch. 10.

Williams, T. C. *The Concept of the Categorical Imperative*. Oxford, 1968.

Woetzel, Robert K. *The Nuremberg Trials in International Law*. New York, 1960.

Wright, Lord. "War Crimes under International Law," *Law Quarterly Review*. Vol. 62 (January, 1946), pp. 40–52.

The Metaphysics of Morals*

IMMANUEL KANT

Introduction:

. . . *Moral Laws a priori and necessary.*—Moral laws, in
contradistinction to natural laws, are only valid *as* laws, insofar
as they can be rationally established *a priori* and comprehended as
necessary. In fact, conceptions and judgments regarding
ourselves and our conduct have no *moral* significance, if they
contain only what may be learned from experience; and
when any one is, so to speak, misled into making a moral
principle out of anything derived from this latter source, he is
already in danger of falling into the grossest and most
fatal errors.

If the philosophy of morals were nothing more than a
theory of happiness (*eudaemonism*), it would be absurd to search
after principles *a priori* as a foundation for it. For however
plausible it may sound to say that reason, even prior to
experience, can comprehend by what means we may attain to a
lasting enjoyment of the real pleasures of life, yet all that is
taught on this subject *a priori* is either tautological, or is
assumed wholly without foundation. It is only experience that
can show what will bring us enjoyment. The natural impulses
directed towards nourishment, the sexual instinct, or the
tendency to rest and motion, as well as the higher desires of
honor, the acquisition of knowledge, and such like, as developed
with our natural capacities, are alone capable of showing in
what those enjoyments are to be *found.* And, further, the
knowledge thus acquired, is available for each individual
merely in his own way; and it is only thus he can learn the
means by which he has to *seek* those enjoyments. All specious

* Translated by W. Hastie in Immanuel Kant, *The Philosophy of Law* (compared with original and corrected by Paul Sigmund). Copyright © 1887 by T. and
T. Clark, Edinburgh.

rationalizing *a priori,* in this connection, is nothing at bottom
but carrying facts of experience up to generalizations by
induction (*secundum principia generalia non universalia*); and
the generality thus attained is still so limited that numberless
exceptions must be allowed to every individual in order
that he may adapt the choice of his mode of life to his own
particular inclinations and his capacity for pleasure. And, after
all, the individual has really to acquire wisdom at the
cost of his own suffering or that of his neighbors.

But it is quite otherwise with the principles of morality.
They lay down commands for everyone without regard to his
particular inclinations, and merely because and so far as he is
free, and has a practical reason. Instruction in the laws of morality
is not drawn from observation of oneself or of our animal
nature, nor from perception of the course of the world in regard
to what happens, or how men act. But reason commands how
we ought to act, even though no example of such action
were to be found; nor does reason give any regard to the
advantage which may accrue to us by so acting, and which
experience could alone actually show. For, although reason
allows us to seek what is for our advantage in every possible
way, and although, founding upon the evidence of experience,
it may further promise that greater advantages will probably
follow on the average from the observance of her commands than
from their transgression, especially if prudence guides the
conduct, yet the authority of her precepts as *commands* does
not rest on such considerations. They are used by reason only as
counsels, and by way of a counterpoise against seductions to
an opposite course, to offset beforehand the equilibrium of a
balance which is partial to oneself in the sphere of practical
judgment, in order thereby to secure the decision of this
judgment, according to the *a priori* principles of a pure
practical reason. . . .

Natural and Positive Laws.—Obligatory laws for which an
external legislation is possible, are called generally *external
laws.* Those external laws, the obligatoriness of which can
be recognized by reason *a priori* even without an external
legislation, are called *Natural Laws.* Those laws, again, which
are not obligatory without actual external legislation, are

called *Positive Laws.* An external legislation, containing
pure positive laws, is therefore conceivable; but in that case
a previous natural law must be presupposed to establish the
authority of the lawgiver to subject others to obligation
through his own act of will. . . .

*Part I: The Metaphysical Foundations of the Science of Law
General Definitions and Divisions*

A. What the science of law is

The science of law has for its object the principles of all the
laws which it is possible to promulgate by external legislation.
. . . The theoretical knowledge of right and law in principle,
as distinguished from positive laws and empirical cases,
belongs to the pure science of law (*Jurisscientia*). The science
of law thus designates the philosophical and systematic
knowledge of the principles of natural law. And it is from this
science that the immutable principles of all positive legislation
must be derived by practical jurists and lawgivers. . . .

C. The universal principle of right law[1]

"Every action is *right* which in itself, or in the maxim on
which it proceeds, is such that it can coexist along with the
freedom of the will of each and all, according to a
universal law."
If, then, my action or my condition generally can coexist
with the freedom of every other, according to a universal
law, any one does me a wrong who hinders me in the performance
of this action, or in the maintenance of this condition. For such
a hindrance or obstruction cannot coexist with freedom
according to universal laws. . . .

Divisions of the science of law . . .
B. General division of law.

1 Kant's *"Recht"* has usually been translated as "right law" or as "law" rather
than Hastie's "right."—Ed.

I. Natural Law and Positive Law

Law, viewed as a scientific system of doctrines, is divided into Natural Law and Positive Law. Natural law rests upon pure rational principles *a priori;* positive or statutory law is what proceeds from the will of a legislator.

II. Innate Right and Acquired Right

The system of rights may again be regarded in reference to the implied power of dealing morally with others as bound by obligations, that is, as furnishing a legal title of action in relation to them. Thus viewed, the system is divided into innate rights and acquired rights. An innate right is that right which belongs to every one by nature, independent of all juridical acts. An acquired right is that right which is founded upon such juridical acts.

Innate right may also be called the "internal mine and thine" (*meum vel tuum internum*), for external rights must always be acquired.

There is only one Innate Right, the Birthright of Freedom

Freedom is independence of the compulsory will of another; and in so far as it can coexist with the freedom of all according to a universal law, it is the one sole original, inborn right belonging to every man by virtue of his humanity. There is, indeed, an innate equality belonging to every man which consists in his right to be independent of being bound by others to do anything more than that to which he may also reciprocally bind them. It is, consequently, the inborn quality of every man by virtue of which he ought to be *his own master by right (sui juris)* . . .

D. The principles of public law

Dignitaries in the State and the Original Contract.
. . . The act by which a people is represented as constituting itself into a state, is termed the original contract. This is

properly only an external way of representing the idea by
which the rightfulness of the process of organizing the
constitution, may be made conceivable. According to this
original contract, all the individuals give up their external
freedom in order to receive it back immediately as members of
a commonwealth. The commonwealth is the people viewed as
united altogether into a state. And thus it is not to be said
that the individual in the state has sacrificed *a part* of his
inborn external freedom for a particular purpose; but he has
abandoned his wild lawless freedom completely, in order to find
all his proper freedom again entire. . . .

Resistance on the part of the people to the supreme
legislative power of the state, is in no case legitimate, for it is
only by submission to the universal legislative will, that a
condition of law and order is possible. Hence there is no
right of sedition, and still less of rebellion, belonging to the
people. And least of all, when the supreme power is embodied
in an individual monarch, is there any justification, under
the pretext of his abuse of power, for seizing his person or taking
away his life (*monarchomachismus sub specie tyrannicidii*).
The slightest attempt of this kind is *high treason (proditio
eminens)*, and a traitor of this sort who aims at the *overthrow*
of his country may be punished, as a political parricide, even
with death. It is the duty of the people to bear any abuse
of the supreme power, even though it should be considered to
be unbearable. And the reason is that any resistance to the
highest legislative authority can never be anything other than
contrary to the law, and must even be regarded as tending to
destroy the whole legal constitution. In order to be entitled
to offer such resistance, a public law would be required
to permit it. But the supreme legislation would by such a law
cease to be supreme, and the people as subjects would be made
sovereign over that to which they are subject—which is a
contradiction. And the contradiction becomes more apparent
when the question is put: Who is to be the judge in a controversy
between the people and the sovereign? For the people and the
sovereign are to be constitutionally or juridically regarded
as two different moral persons, but the question shows that the
people would then have to be the judge in their own cause. . . .

Republicanism

The spirit of the original contract (*anima pacti originarii*)
contains and imposes the obligation on the constituting
power to make the mode of the *government* conformable to
the original idea; and, if this cannot be effected at once, to
change it gradually and continuously till it harmonize *in its
working* with the only rightful constitution, which is that
of a *pure republic*. Thus the old empirical and statutory
forms, which serve only to effect the political *subjection* of the
people, will be resolved into the original and rational forms
which alone take freedom as their principle, and even as
the condition of all compulsion and constraint. Compulsion
is in fact requisite for the realization of a juridical constitution,
according to the proper idea of the state, and it will lead at
last to realization of that idea, in actuality. This is the only
enduring political constitution, as in it the law is itself sovereign,
and is no longer dependent on a particular person. This is the
ultimate end of all public law, and the state in which every
citizen can be given his due directly . . .

SOURCES

Fuller, Lon, *The Morality of Law,* New Haven, 1964, ch. 4.
Hart, H. L. A., *The Concept of Law,* Oxford, 1961, ch. 9.
Kant, Immanuel, *Fundamental Principles of the Metaphysics
     of Morals.*
———, *Idea for a Universal History.*
———, *The Metaphysics of Morals,* Introduction, Pt. I.
Marx, Karl, *The Economic and Philosophical Manuscripts of
     1844.*
Stammler, Rudolf, *The Theory of Justice,* New York, 1925.

10.
NATURAL LAW AND RELIGIOUS THOUGHT

There is no question of the close historical links between the theory of natural law and Christian thought. In Roman Catholicism, the acceptance of the theology of St. Thomas Aquinas as the basis for teaching in seminaries and for much of the Catholic writing on philosophical and theological questions has meant that natural law in its Thomistic formulation is very much a part of the Catholic vocabulary. In Protestant thought, natural law is much less prominent. Luther and Calvin occasionally referred to the theory with approval (see the references cited in Chapter 5), and Protestant revolutionaries in the seventeenth and eighteenth centuries appealed to it.[1] Yet one of the key doctrines of the Reformation, the radical insufficiency of man's reason and weakness of his will as a result of sin, would tend to produce a certain pessimism about the possibility of finding values in nature by the use of reason, as natural law theories claim to do. If the Protestant emphasis is on Scripture as the sole rule of faith, religious and moral truth can be found there with a certainty that man's reason

---

[1] Cf. the frequent use of natural law arguments by the Levellers in the Putney Debates (1647) in A.S.P. Woodhouse, ed., *Puritanism and Liberty* (London, 1938).

cannot provide. In fact, in the writings of the contemporary Protestant theologian Karl Barth, the Scriptures are a more certain source of religious knowledge than the "illusions and confusions . . . of the so-called natural law. . . . The norm by which [the Christian community] should be guided is anything but natural; it is the only norm which it can believe in and accept as a spiritual norm and is derived from the clear law of its own faith, not from the obscure workings of a system outside itself."[2]

Yet it is difficult to extend this interpretation to all Protestant thought. In addition to the historical examples of appeals to natural law by Protestant writers, there is also the specific Scriptural reference to natural law by St. Paul in his Epistle to the Romans (2:14–15), where he speaks of the Gentiles as having "the work of the law written in their hearts." More generally, a belief in some kind of rational order in the universe would seem to follow from the Christian (and Jewish) doctrines of creation and divine providence. Unless one believes in a God who delights in irrationality and contradiction, or in the total corruption of human reason by sin, it is difficult for one who accepts Judeo-Christian premises not to arrive at a belief in a purposive universe which is a source of ethical imperatives for man.[3] If God is righteous and the source of morality, his creation is ordered morally, and this order can be perceived by mankind, if only in a dim and inadequate way.

The Protestant ambivalence towards natural law can be illustrated from the writings of Reinhold Niebuhr. Niebuhr has often criticized Catholic theories of natural law as rigid and inflexible, and excessively rationalistic. Throughout his writings he emphasizes sinful man's capacity to deceive himself individually and collectively through egotism; with this attitude he finds the conclusions of natural law thinking suspect—more rationalizing than rational. Yet when Niebuhr develops his own ethical theory, the law of love, it seems to be based on human nature as much as on

[2] Karl Barth, *Community, State, and Church* (Garden City, New York), 1960, p. 165. For an argument that Barth espouses a form of "revealed natural law" see Louis C. Midgley, "Karl Barth and Moral Natural Law," *Natural Law Forum*, XIII (1968), pp. 108–26, and *Beyond Human Nature* (Provo, Utah, 1969), Pt. IV, sec. 23.

[3] Cf. the arguments in Emil Brunner, *Justice and the Social Order* (New York, 1945), chapter 12, and Paul Tillich, *Morality and Beyond* (New York, 1963), chapter 2.

divine revelation. It is love, not only divine but also human, which is the basis of equality and justice. It is love which calls us to the higher expressions of morality—to self-transcendence. It is love too which combines both the universalizing and ordering tendencies of the reason and the emotional and community-oriented impulses of man's feelings. And this love arises out of the deepest needs of man. It is based on human nature—on an in-built purpose or "natural inclination" in Thomistic terms. In order for man to be fulfilled, it must be satisfied.

At times Niebuhr's argument appears to be a naturalistic one which differs very little from Erich Fromm's claim in *The Art of Loving* (New York, 1956) that if a man is to be happy he must fulfill the human need to love and be loved. Yet for Niebuhr this need for love has a theological basis in Christ's command, and the natural "law" of love is confirmed by supernatural revelation. It is also a single law from which other laws are derived and thus differs from the Thomistic pluralistic law related to a hierarchy of ends in man. As one commentator has analyzed it, the law of love is both the base and the apex of Niebuhr's theory of morality.[4] It underlies and transcends the requirements of human justice. It calls men not only to the ordinary requirements of justice, but to the fulfillment of the demands of an "impossible ethic" of self-sacrifice and even martyrdom, following the example of Christ.

A further difference of Niebuhr's theory from the traditional view is his acceptance of dilemma and contradiction in the structure of morality. His book, *Moral Man and Immoral Society* (New York, 1941), sums up in its title his view that social groups cannot and do not live by the requirements of individual morality. The most notable example of this conflict is in the recurrence of war between states. Niebuhr is not a pacifist. He accepts the necessity and even moral obligation of defense of one's country. Yet war is an evil, the lesser of two evils, but nevertheless an evil. This view contrasts with the theory of the just war which has been developed by natural law theorists to defend participation in certain wars, especially defensive wars, as a good—the lesser of two goods, but still a good. Both Niebuhr's view of an inevitable conflict between individual and social morality, and his belief in the necessity and

---

4 Paul Ramsey, *Nine Modern Moralists* (Englewood Cliffs, N.J., 1962), chapter 5.

inevitability of doing evil in some cases, contrast with the natural law belief in an ultimate moral order in the universe in which all contradictions are capable of being resolved and an ultimate harmony can prevail. Derived from a religious belief in the reality and pervasiveness of sin, Niebuhr's view insists that man has difficulty in knowing how he should act and that when he does know and does act he finds it impossible to avoid sin. Niebuhr, then, can only be called a natural law thinker in a very qualified sense, in that he finds a confirmation for Christian insights in a law of love built into man's nature.

By contrast, Catholic thought, with some significant exceptions (especially since the Second Vatican Council, 1962–65), has tended to place natural law in a central position in ethical, social, and political theory. While sharing with Protestantism a belief that man's intellect and will were weakened by the effects of original sin, Catholic thinkers, at least since the time of St. Thomas Aquinas, have subscribed to the belief that man's reason is potentially capable of perceiving the natural moral order which a rational and purposive God has created. This order does not exhaust the field of morality, since by direct revelation God has supplemented, enriched, and confirmed the findings of reason, but, in the words of St. Thomas, "grace does not contradict nature but perfects it."[5] Revelation as interpreted by the Church also acts as an external standard or guide for reason, but it can never contradict reason's findings. God reveals himself in two ways, directly through the revelation in the Old and New Testaments and the person of Christ; and indirectly, through a rational order in nature which can be known by man's reason.

There is much less emphasis, then, on the ambiguities of moral problems in Catholic thought than in Protestant thinking. The Catholic confessor must give answers to the moral problems of his penitents, and the Church has attempted to develop a systematic ethics to help him to do so. (The most extreme form of this approach appears in the manuals of casuistry, the attempt to apply general moral principles to individual cases [*casūs*].) This

---

[5] For a discussion by a contemporary Thomist of the relationship of natural law and revelation, see Josef Fuchs, *Natural Law: A Theological Investigation* (New York, 1965), p. 187.

ethical system is based partly on revelation, but much of it is based on reason, applying the Thomistic teleology to the solution of moral problems. And underlying the entire process is a belief in a rational order and an ultimate resolution of moral dilemmas, if only in the mind of God. In contrast to Niebuhr's discussion of "the relevance of an impossible ethical ideal,"[6] Catholic ethical theory holds that a law which is impossible to perform does not oblige. In contrast to the Protestant view of war as a necessary evil, Catholic thought sees it as the lesser of two goods, since man is never obliged to do evil, and he may be obliged to fight in a morally just war for his country. (It should be noted that some Catholic moralists are now questioning whether any nuclear war can be a just war, since it does not meet the natural law standard of proportionality—i.e., the good to be produced by the war does not outweigh the evil that is produced by the means employed. Similarly, Catholic moralists condemned the use of saturation bombing in World War II on the grounds that the numbers of innocent people totally unrelated to the war effort who were killed or wounded made this a morally illicit means of waging war.)[7]

The popes themselves have often appealed to natural law in their encyclicals on moral and social questions. Probably the best known of these appeals is the condemnation of artificial birth control in the encyclical *Casti Connubii (On Christian Marriage)* by Pius XI in 1930. Taking what appears to be an Aristotelian-Thomistic argument from the natural purpose of the sex act, the pope argued that it is intrinsically evil deliberately and directly to interfere with its natural and divinely intended purpose—the procreation of children. The pope recognized that the sex act also has the

---

[6] Reinhold Niebuhr, *An Interpretation of Christian Ethics* (New York, 1935), ch. 4.

[7] For a discussion, based on natural law principles of the just war theory, as applied to contemporary strategic problems, see Joseph McKenna, "Ethics and War: A Catholic View," *American Political Science Review*, LIV, 3 (September, 1960), 647–59. See also William J. Nagle, ed., *Morality and Modern Warfare* (Baltimore, 1960); and Walter Stein, ed., *Nuclear Weapons: A Catholic Response* (London, 1961). For Protestant views which also use a natural law approach, see Roland H. Bainton, *Christian Attitudes Toward War and Peace* (New York, 1960), esp. pp. 253–56; and Paul Ramsey, *The Just War: Force and Political Responsibility* (New York, 1968), and *War and the Christian Conscience* (Durham, N.C., 1961). Cf. also John C. Bennett, ed., *Nuclear Weapons and the Conflict of Conscience* (New York, 1962).

"secondary" purpose of fostering the mutual love of the marriage partners, but would not allow the procreative purpose to be frustrated in order to further the secondary purpose (although he implicitly approved birth control by means of periodic abstinence when he allowed marital relations under the conditions that "on account of natural reasons either of time or of certain defects, new life cannot be brought forth"). A majority of the members of a Papal Commission appointed at the time of the Second Vatican Council recommended a change in the traditional doctrine, but Pius XI's view was reaffirmed by Pope Paul VI in 1968. Much of the current controversy within the church over the ban on artificial birth control is carried on in terms of Thomistic natural law theory concerning the natural goals or purposes of sex and marriage. Those who favor a modification of the present teachings appeal to other natural purposes of sex in marriage, such as the fostering of mutual love, and argue that the periodic abstinence required by the papal position is more opposed to nature than other methods of avoiding conception.[8] Probably the most common objection criticizes the separation of the individual biological fact of sexual intercourse from the whole marital relationship, and argues that while it would be wrong for a married couple to avoid children altogether, temporary postponement of offspring for good and sufficient reasons is not against the natural purpose of the marital relationship as a whole. Nature and function, as used in the traditional view, are not moral terms at all—since it is as responsible persons with human purposes that men act morally. The teleological-biological method of moral analysis, it is argued, should be given up in favor of a concern with persons and their rights and duties as human beings in certain types of relationships.

The discussion has had another effect worthy of note for the history of natural law theory. It has called into question the papal claim to be the authoritative interpreter of natural law. Since the

---

8 The two sides of the current controversy are presented by two professors of philosophy at Georgetown University: Louis K. Dupré, *Contraception and Catholicism: A New Appraisal* (Baltimore, 1964); and German Grisez, *Contraception and Natural Law* (Milwaukee, 1964). For an articulate and theologically sophisticated criticism of the present position, see G. Egner, *Contraception vs. Tradition: A Catholic Critique* (New York and London, 1967), especially ch. 3. A historical survey of the development of the doctrine is contained in John Noonan, *Contraception* (Cambridge, Mass., 1965, paperback edition, New York, 1967).

pope did not rely on Scripture or revelation to support his stand, and since Paul VI's encyclical on the subject did not claim to be an infallible pronouncement within the meaning of the term as described by the First Vatican Council in 1871, the basis of his argument has been widely called into question on rational grounds alone. More fundamentally, his particular competence to define moral questions in the area of "natural law" (as distinct from revealed religion) has been challenged. This in turn may discourage future pontiffs from relying as heavily upon natural-law-type arguments in their doctrinal writings.[9]

Natural law principles have played an important role in the development of the Catholic theory of property. The Fathers of the Church had held that property was a departure from the original state of community of possession, made necessary by sin. Aquinas, however, influenced by Aristotle, argued that property was an "addition" to natural law for the convenience of men, and adapted Aristotle's formula of "private property, common use" to insist that property had both an individual and a social aspect, so that the property holder must observe the social responsibilities which come from its possession.[10]

Pope Leo XIII in his encyclical, *Rerum Novarum,* written in 1891, applied this teaching to contemporary social problems. He took St. Thomas one step further by stating that "every man has by nature the right to possess property as his own," and he condemned socialism (which he defined as a belief in the abolition of private ownership) as "contrary to the natural rights of man." However, the pope also insisted that the property holder must recognize his social obligations, and he criticized free-enterprise capitalism for ignoring the moral aspect of commercial activity, especially the right of the worker to a living wage. Citing the "natural right" of the workers to organize and associate to secure their

---

[9] The tendency to use a different vocabulary from that of natural law in dealing with questions of social and political morality was already evident in Paul VI's encyclical *On The Development of Peoples (Populorum Progressio)*, published in 1967. For the argument that Catholic moral teachings were not for the first ten centuries, and probably will not be in the future, linked to natural law theory, see Charles E. Curran, "Absolute Norms in Moral Theology," in Gene Outka and Paul Ramsey, ed., *Norm and Context in Christian Ethics* (New York, 1968), ch. 5.

[10] *Summa Theologica*, Pt. I–II, qu. 94, art. 5 (see discussion in ch. 4 *supra*).

rightful share of the product of their labor. Leo defended the incipient trade union movement.

Forty years later, Pope Pius XI in *Quadragesimo Anno* (1931) endorsed a pluralistic organization of society into natural "orders," especially industrial groups which included both workers and management and supported the association of workers with management in profit-sharing and similar schemes. Lower associations, including the family, which acted as buffers between the individual and the state and provided an outlet for his creative development, were to be encouraged as an expression of the social aspect of the human person. The question of when the state was to intervene in these associations was to be determined by a natural law principle of "subsidiarity"—when lower associations could do the job, they should be left to do so.

Pius spoke of a twofold character of ownership, both individual and social, and granted that "public authority, under the guiding light always of the natural and divine law, can determine . . . what is permitted and what is not permitted to owners in the use of their property," but he reaffirmed Leo's condemnation of socialism "if it truly remains socialism," while repeating his strictures against the excesses of capitalism.[11]

In the years after *Quadragesimo Anno* the principles of the welfare state became more widely accepted in Western Europe and the United States. Immediately after World War II, the governments of France and Italy, in which new Catholic-inspired Christian Democratic parties had an important role, nationalized a number of basic industries, and the Labour government in England, which also received the votes of most Catholics in that country, did the same. By the time of Pope John XXIII's encyclical *Mater et Magistra* in 1961, an increasing role of the state in the areas of social welfare and economic control had been accepted by the Vatican. Pope John's encyclical recognized the desirability in some cases of public ownership and state control of parts of the economy, although the pope reasserted the principle of subsidiarity and defended the right of private property if exercised with an awareness of its social function.

11 Abridged texts of the papal encyclicals are available in Anne Fremantle, ed., *The Social Teachings of the Church* (paperback ed., New York, 1963).

The change from *Rerum Novarum* in 1891 with its strong condemnation of socialism to the acceptance of public ownership in *Mater et Magistra* in 1961 could be explained as a difference of emphasis in changed circumstances. Less easy to conceal was the striking reversal of papal attitude on the question of the relations of church and state. Leo XIII's encyclical on *Human Liberty* (1888) spoke of liberty as flowing from the nature of man, but denied that man had a right to freedom of worship. Catholic states, said Leo, must publicly profess the one true religion and limit the public exercise of other faiths. Yet *Pacem in Terris*, Pope John XXIII's last encyclical, published in 1963, specifically mentioned "the right to worship God privately and publicly" in the list of human rights with which it began. The implications of the right of freedom of worship were drawn out in specific terms by the decree on religious liberty, adopted two years later by the Second Vatican Council, which gave its authoritative approval to the reversal of the traditional teaching which had previously favored the legal establishment of Catholicism where it was the prevailing religion of the citizenry.[12]

Natural law arguments in favor of religious liberty and of limits on private property were used by the Catholic-influenced Christian Democratic parties of Western Europe to justify limits on the free enterprise system, the extension of welfare measures, and the acceptance of religious pluralism and the secular state. Christian Democratic thinkers also defended democracy itself in natural law terms, arguing that it was the form of government which best conformed to man's rational and moral nature as a human being with a capacity for responsible free choice. This argument also marked a modification of nineteenth-century papal theory which had seen continental liberal democracy as the embodiment of the false "liberal" doctrine that the individual will was the sole source of morality and religion (cf. Pius IX, *Quanta Cura* and his *Syllabus of Errors* [1864], especially proposition 60).

In developing their programs, after World War II, the Christian Democrats attempted to apply Catholic natural law thinking

---

12 See the Council's "Declaration on Religious Freedom" in Walter M. Abbott S.J., ed., *The Documents of Vatican II* (New York, 1966), pp. 675–96. The Council based the right to religious freedom on "the very dignity of the human person, as this dignity is known through the revealed Word of God and by reason itself" (p. 679).

to the problems of postwar Europe. In keeping with Pius XI's support for intermediate groups and the principle of subsidiarity, the *Mouvement Republicain Populaire,* (MRP) the Christian Democratic party of France, proposed functional representation in the upper house of the new Fourth Republic after World War II. It did not achieve this goal, but an Economic and Social Council was created with advisory powers, and in 1969 President de Gaulle, before his defeat in a referendum on the subject, attempted to combine the Council with the Senate of the Fifth Republic so as to strengthen the role of functional groups in French politics. DeGaulle was also influenced by Catholic social thought in his proposals for worker participation in management and profits which he called *l'association capital-travail.* A similar idea was implemented by the Christian Democrats of Germany in 1951 with the adoption of a law recognizing the workers' right to "co-participation" *(Mitbestimmungsrecht)* on the directing boards of larger enterprises. All of these programs have common roots in a conception of society as composed of self-detemining "natural" social and economic groups between the individual and the state, a concept which was developed in Catholic natural law thinking. (A more authoritarian corporatist version of the same conception of society was also found in the political structures of Austria in the 1930's and in Portugal from the late 1920's to the present time.)

Despite papal criticism of capitalism, the Christian Democratic experiments in postwar Western Europe did not alter the basically capitalist orientation of their economies. However, some of the proponents of Christian Democracy in Latin America are now using similar natural law theories to develop a more distinctive middle way between individualism and collectivism. The Chilean Christian Democrats, who came to power in 1964, announced that their goal was a "communitarian" society. They adopted a strong agrarian reform law in which cooperatives were encouraged, bought a 25–51 percent interest in the American-controlled copper industry, establishing mixed private-public corporations to run the copper mines, and encouraged the organization of peasant unions and slum-dwellers in a program of "popular promotion" designed to give "marginal" groups access to the political process.

The left or "rebel" wing of Chilean Christian Democracy,

which seceded from the party in May 1969, wishes to go further. It calls for immediate steps to give the workers participation or even control in industry and sees as its goal a society based on "communitarian socialism."[13] Both the radicals and the moderates accept the notion of the "social function" of property, and natural law arguments figured prominently in the debates in the Chilean Congress in 1966 over the adoption of a constitutional amendment allowing compensation in bonds for agrarian lands taken under the agrarian reform law.

The single writer who has done most to apply Catholic natural law thinking to contemporary problems is the French philosopher Jacques Maritain. Particularly in the justification of democracy and the defense of the religiously neutral state, he has made a significant contribution to Christian Democratic political thought. His general theory appears to be organized along the lines of that of St. Thomas Aquinas, and he quotes him often. However, when his writings on natural law are examined more closely it becomes clear that he has introduced important modifications in the Thomistic theory. For one thing, he gives more emphasis to the notion of a progressive development in the understanding of the natural law. It is true that Aquinas had spoken of additions to, and subtractions from, the natural law, and he was aware of changes in moral standards since Old Testament times on the issue of polygamy. Yet it is doubtful that Aquinas would share Maritain's belief that the human race over time has, and will come to, a deeper understanding of the implications of the natural law.

Maritain also seems to place much more emphasis on an intuitive perception of the natural law, which he calls "knowledge by inclination" or "knowledge by connaturality." It is true that Aquinas speaks of a special faculty, *synderesis,* which enables man

---

[13] For an example of the anti-capitalist orientation of many Chilean Christian Democrats, see "The Chonchol Plan" in A. von Lazar and R. Kaufman, eds., *Reform and Revolution* (Boston, 1969), pp. 59–70. Julio Silva Solar and Jacques Chonchol in *Desarrollo sin Capitalismo* (Caracas, 1964) defend communitarian socialism on the basis of the Christian natural law principles of the Fathers of the Church but attack the doctrine of St. Thomas on property (pp. 31–60). An excerpt is translated in Paul E. Sigmund, ed., *Models of Political Change in Latin America* (New York, 1970), pp. 310–312. For the majority position in the Chilean party see Jaime Castillo, *Natural Law and Communitarianism,* translated at the end of this chapter.

to perceive basic moral principles, but this is described as a faculty of the reason, and natural law is the participation in the eternal law by *rational* creatures. The difference between the two theories can be illustrated through a shift in the way in which Maritain defines the *jus gentium* or law of nations in his writings. In his earlier *The Rights of Man and the Natural Law* (1943), Maritain defined the *jus gentium* as the principles which follow from the natural law "supposing certain conditions of fact, as for instance, the state of civil society or the relationships between peoples" (p. 70). In his later work, *Man and the State* (1951), this formulation was replaced by a definition of *jus gentium* as the basic principles of morality known "not through inclination but through the conceptual exercise of reason or through rational knowledge" (p. 98). Maritain tries to argue that this is similar to Aquinas' description of *jus gentium* as the "conclusions from the principles of natural law" (*Summa Theologica*, I–II, qu. 95, art. 4, concl.). Yet he is obviously uncomfortable with this explanation, since Aquinas clearly thought that the natural law could be expressed through rational propositions, whereas for Maritain it appears that once rational expression has been given to the direct intuitions of the natural law or further reasoning has taken place about them, it is no longer natural law, but *jus gentium*.

One can explain the difference in the two theories in terms of Maritain's own experience. He was originally a pupil of Henri Bergson, and perhaps some of Bergson's belief in the nonrational sources of morality (cf. *The Two Sources of Morals and Religion*, English translation, New York, 1935) was carried over into Maritain's natural law theory. Another possible source of this conception was his recognition that often men can agree on basic principles of morality because of a direct perception of their validity, but once they begin to rationalize and compare them, then disagreements in basic metaphysics and comparative values begin to appear—the realm of *jus gentium*.

Another evident difference between the theories of Aquinas and Maritain is the latter's emphasis on *rights* compared to the former's discussion of *law*. Maritain derives a doctrine of natural rights from the writings of Aquinas—arguing that the duties which the natural law imposes on man (to live, to mate, to reproduce, to learn, to worship), create rights, i.e., an obligation of non-interference by others.[14] However, Aquinas never used the term "natural rights," and only in modern times has it been recognized that natural law duties can be made the basis of a system of rights. It is also only in modern times that human freedom and capacity for choice has been understood by Thomist theorists such as Maritain as providing an argument for the moral superiority and desirability of democracy.

Human freedom and the purpose or end of the state as the promotion of the temporal common good are the bases of Maritain's argument for a religiously pluralistic state, united by a common faith in freedom. However, he allows for state action to "foster in its own way general morality by the exercise of justice and the enforcement of law, and by supervising the development of sound conditions and means in the body politic for good human life, both material and rational" (*Man and the State,* p. 174). Maritain does not explain his statement further, but it appears that the state, while excluded from legally enforcing religiously-based beliefs about morality, may regulate moral conduct if it can produce secular reasons for doing so. Whether natural law arguments about the relation of conduct to human nature would be sufficient to legitimize such action is not clear, although in the past Roman Catholic apologists have appealed to natural law to defend the retention on the statute books of laws prohibiting the dissemination of birth control information, and similar arguments are used in current debates on the liberalization of abortion laws. At this point, however, the term "natural law" has become so specifically identified with a religious (usually Catholic) position that contemporary discussions of the relation of law and morals do not usually give it much attention.[15]

Lest the impression be given that all Catholic thinking on morality and politics is expressed in natural law terms, reference must be made to the increase since the Second Vatican Council in

14 "The same natural law which lays down our fundamental duties and by virtue of which every law is binding, is the very law which assigns to us our fundamental rights" Jacques Maritain, *Man and the State* (Chicago, 1951), p. 95.

15 Basil Mitchell, *Law, Morality, and Religion in a Secular Society* (London, 1967), p. 105. For an attempt to relate the Catholic and Protestant positions to current efforts to redefine the relation of law and morals in a pluralist society, see Norman St. John-Stevas, *Life, Death, and the Law* (Bloomington, Indiana, 1961), especially chapter 1.

Catholic criticism of natural law as a method of approaching religious and ethical questions. While this criticism is especially common among opponents of the church position on birth control, it is also heard on more general grounds. Thus Gregory Baum O.S.A., an Augustinian theologian who was one of the *periti* or experts associated with the Council, has argued that the Catholic conception of morality is neither as legalistic nor as systematic as the natural law method implies, and has criticized the natural-supernatural dualism of some Catholic natural law writing on the grounds that it does not express the Catholic belief in a single human personality both endowed with reason and the object of divine grace.[16]

Other writers have expressed a similar unwillingness to separate the natural and the supernatural. The Jesuit anthropologist Pierre Teilhard de Chardin in *The Divine Milieu* (written in 1926–27) described the two as a continuum and saw the goal of evolution as an increasing spiritualization of man and nature. Michael Novak, a lay Catholic theologian, is now engaged in reinterpreting Aquinas in order to minimize the legalism and dualism of his moral theory. Both Teilhard de Chardin and Novak, from different perspectives, are aware of the need to be open to change and development. Novak, for example, calls for a new view of natural law "free of the associations of necessity, immutability, and logical rationality that once clung to it."[17]

This emphasis on change and development in the natural law reflects a basic problem in Christian thinking, and perhaps more generally in all thinking on morality. On the one hand, there is a belief in basic moral principles revealed by God and reflected in his creation, while, on the other hand, God is considered as the "wholly Other," the Infinite and Transcendent Being whose ways cannot be understood nor comprehended by finite man. On the one hand, there is the Catholic belief in a body of doctrine revealed by Christ and developed in the Church, and

[16] Gregory Baum, "The Christian Adventure: Risk and Renewal," *The Critic*, April–May, 1965, Vol. XXIII, No. 5, pp. 49–50 (see extract *infra*).

[17] Michael Novak, *A Time to Build* (New York, 1967), p. 326. Cf. also Robert Johann S.J.'s description of human nature as "a task to be accomplished . . . reason itself open to the Infinite," in "Love and Justice," Richard T. de George, ed., *Ethics and Society* (Garden City, N.Y., 1966), p. 34.

on the other, there is the attitude, associated in the past principally with Protestantism but now increasingly adopted by Catholics, which stresses human fallibility and the need for criticism of accepted truth and an appreciation of the validity of a variety of individual insights into religion.

In a parallel fashion, natural law responds on the moral level to this desire and need for the Absolute, but it must take into account man's fallibility in understanding and applying it. In Nietzchean terms, natural law is an instance of the Apollonian universalizing and rational elements in man, while the competing theories which recognize the importance of mysticism, individual intuition, and existentialist freedom in moral action correspond to the Dionysiac emotional and spontaneous element. Or to put it in terms of pre-Socratic philosophy, natural law is the attempt in morals and politics to find the one unchanging Being of which Parmenides wrote, but it cannot exclude the elements of change and Becoming which Heraclitus made the basis of his philosophy. Whether any of the writers discussed in this book have wholly succeeded in achieving this combination is for the reader to judge.

BIBLIOGRAPHY

Barth, Karl. *Community, State, and Church.* Garden City, N.Y., 1960.

Brunner, Emil. *Justice and the Social Order.* New York, 1945, ch. 12.

Fogarty, Michael. *Christian Democracy in Western Europe: 1820–1953.* Notre Dame, Indiana, 1957.

Ford, John C., S.J. and Gerald Kelly, S.J. *Contemporary Moral Theology.* Vol. I, Westminster, Md., 1958.

Fremantle, Anne, ed. *The Social Teachings of the Church.* New York, 1963.

Fuchs, Josef. *Natural Law, A Theological Investigation.* New York, 1965.

Midgley, Louis. *Beyond Human Nature.* Provo, Utah, 1969, Pts. III–IV.

Mitchell, Basil. *Law, Morality, and Religion in a Secular Society.* London, 1967.

Murray, John Courtney. *We Hold These Truths.* New York, 1960, Part III.

Outka, Gene H. and Paul Ramsey, eds. *Norm and Context in Christian Ethics.* New York, 1968.

Ramsey, Paul. *The Just War: Force and Political Responsibility.* New York, 1968.

———. *Nine Modern Moralists.* Englewood Cliffs, N.J., 1962, chs. 5, 7–9.

Rommen, Heinrich. *The Natural Law.* St. Louis, 1947.

Sigmund, Paul E., ed. *The Ideologies of the Developing Nations.* rev. ed. New York, 1967, pp. 383–404.

Simon, Yves. *The Tradition of Natural Law, A Philosopher's Reflections.* New York, 1965.

St. John-Stevas, Norman. *Life, Death, and the Law.* Bloomington, Indiana, 1961, ch. 1.

Tillich, Paul. *Morality and Beyond.* New York, 1963, ch. 2.

Natural Law*

JACQUES MARITAIN

. . . When I said a moment ago that the natural law of all
beings existing in nature is the proper way in which, by reason
of their specific nature and specific ends, they *should*
achieve fullness of being in their behavior, this very word
should had only a metaphysical meaning (as we say that a
good or a normal eye "should" be able to read letters on
a blackboard from a given distance). The same word *should*
starts to have a *moral* meaning, that is, to imply moral
obligation, when we pass the threshold of the world of free
agents. Natural law for man is *moral* law, because man
obeys or disobeys it freely, not necessarily, and because human
behavior pertains to a particular, privileged order which
is irreducible to the general of the cosmic order and
tends to a final end superior to the immanent common good
of the cosmos.

What I am emphasizing is the first basic element to be
recognized in natural law, namely the *ontological* element;
I mean the *normality of functioning* which is grounded on
the essence of that being: man. Natural law in general,
as we have just seen, is the ideal formula of development
of a given being; it might be compared with an algebraical
equation according to which a curve develops in space, yet
with man the curve has freely to conform to the
equation. Let us say, then, that in its ontological aspect,
natural law is an *ideal order* relating to human actions, a
divide between the suitable and the unsuitable, the proper
and the improper, which depends on human nature,
or essence and the unchangeable necessities rooted in it . . .

Thus we arrive at the *second* basic element to be recognized
in natural law, namely natural law *as known,* and thus
as measuring in actual fact human practical reason, which
is the measure of human acts.

* From *Man and the State* by permission. Copyright © 1951 by the University
of Chicago Press.

Natural law is not a written law. Men know it with
greater or less difficulty, and in different degrees, running
the risk of error here as elsewhere. The only practical
knowledge all men have naturally and infallibly in common
as a self-evident principle, intellectually perceived by virtue
of the concepts involved, is that we must do good and
avoid evil. This is the preamble and the principle of natural
law; it is not the law itself. Natural law is the ensemble
of things to do and not to do which follow therefrom in
necessary fashion. . . .

At this point let us stress that human reason does
not discover the regulations of natural law in an abstract and
theoretical manner, as a series of geometrical theorems.
Nay more, it does not discover them through the conceptual
exercise of the intellect, or by way of rational knowledge. I
think that Thomas Aquinas' teaching here should be
understood in a much deeper and more precise fashion
than is usual. When he says that human reason discovers
the regulations of natural law through the guidance of
the *inclinations* of human nature, he means that the very
mode or manner in which human reason knows natural law
is not rational knowledge, but knowledge *through inclination*.
That kind of knowledge is not clear knowledge through
concepts and conceptual judgments; it is obscure, unsystematic,
vital knowledge by connaturality or congeniality, in which
the intellect, in order to bear judgment, consults and listens
to the inner melody that the vibrating strings of abiding
tendencies make present in the subject.

When one has clearly seen this basic fact, and when,
moreover, one has realized that St. Thomas' views on the
matter call for an historical approach and a philosophical
enforcement of the idea of development that the
Middle Ages were not equipped to carry into effect, then at
last one is enabled to get a completely comprehensive concept
of Natural Law. . . .

Natural Law and Communitarianism*

JAIME CASTILLO

Property and Natural Law

. . . In response to those who claim that private property
is a matter of natural law, we hold that that system is not
required by natural law but only conforms to it when at a
given time it is the best method to regulate and permit
the most efficient use of all the goods of the earth. . . .

What is a matter of natural law is what we call the right
of common use, that the enjoyment of goods is a demand of
human nature because man should satisfy his needs with
the goods which have been placed at his disposal.

Nevertheless, there are those who, without denying that
the right of common use is essential and permanent and
that systems of appropriation are mutable, would deny the
existence of natural law itself. In my opinion to deny the theory
of natural law is as absurd as claiming to deny the theory of being.
It is an impossible claim. And if we deny the existence
of the natural law we will of necessity develop the same
solution under a different name. Ultimately it seems to me
that discussion on this matter is a dispute over terms rather
than over concepts.

What is meant by natural law has to be conceived, it
seems to me, as that minimum of rational terminology which
is necessary to explain an obvious fact—that there exists
in human nature a certain need to use and dispose of things in
a way which accords with the ethical and social character
of every human act. The formula, natural law, therefore
expresses something very minimal and perhaps excessively

* Translated by the editor from *Propriedad y Sociedad Comunitaria* (Instituto
de Estudios Politicos, Santiago, Chile 1966), in Paul E. Sigmund, ed., *The Ideologies
of the Developing Nations,* revised edition, by permission. Copyright © 1967 by
Frederick A. Praeger.

vague—that man proceeds in accordance with the integrity of his being. To concretize a theoretical system to reflect this exigency is inevitable from the point of view of logic, but it runs the risk of seeming to set down in precise terms what is a complex of visions. These then become for some a substitute for reality, abstractions in the bad sense of the word. The polemics of those who in their turn develop another set of abstractions or ideological fetishes exaggerate the problem and prevent simple and authentic reflection. . . .

The Communitarian Society

First, in a communitarian society there will be the full realization of community in the sense which we explained above. There will be a plenitude of human life in common. It will be a fraternal society [in which] the highest human values will prevail. This is the same as saying that the full human life of each man will be realized in its plenitude.

Second, the communitarian society will give preference to social values over those of the individual. On this point I must also refer to something which we have debated elsewhere—the opposition of communitarianism and socialism. I have said it already—I think that both terms point to the same thing. At least their relation is very intimate. Nevertheless, I personally think that the term *communitarianism* is an expression which is more vivid, more vigorous, and more expressive of our thinking. In addition, the term *socialism* implies certain doctrinal principles which are questionable as far as we are concerned and which are also linked to the experiences of totalitarian collectivism. Therefore, I prefer to use the term *communitarianism*. In any case the idea is the same, but to use the term *communitarian socialism* is to involve oneself in an unnecessary redundancy and at the same time to create certain doubts on our part.[1]

---

[1] This is a reference to the increasing use of the term "communitarian socialism" by the left wing and the youth organization of the Chilean Christian Democratic Party in order to indicate their opposition to the continued existence of "capitalist" property relationships in Chile.—Ed.

The communitarian society will possess a structure which is in accordance with what has been said above. Its decisive characteristic will be a communitarian type of property holding (by communities of workers, cooperatives, and other social forms), but it will allow for personal property when it has a social function as well as for the retention of some property by the national community. The dichotomy between capital and labor will be superseded by communitarian relationships, i.e., by uniting labor and capital in the hands of the workers themselves . . . .

Remarks on Natural Law*

GREGORY BAUM, O.S.A.

. . . There is no doubt whatever in my mind that morality
is intrinsic to human life itself. The good life is not the
pursuit or observance of a law imposed from without upon
human life. It is by growing according to an inner
principle that man achieves his destiny and enters into holiness.
But by calling this principle of the moral life "natural law"
we use a highly ambiguous expression, an expression
which lends itself to several misunderstandings.

In the first place, the expression "natural *law*" has
suggested to many that the principle of morality is present
in us as some kind of formulated law or set of laws. It has
sometimes created the impression that a good philosopher
should be able to write down a list of the universal
norms which make up this "natural law" in us. In reality,
however, the natural law is the deep inclination of man
to be faithful to himself, the orientation of man to grow
and mature, to seek the truth and to do good. This basic
orientation is in us, not in a conceptualized form, not as a
set of laws, but as a direction which our reason, reflecting
on experience, is able to discover. It is true that in analyzing
and systematizing the natural law as we discover it in our
life, or in the life of mankind, we may indeed express its
content in a series of laws, but we are deeply conscious
that these laws are not the reality but are derived from the
reality; that the formulated laws do not express the total
reality but, rather, present a useful abstraction of it. Any
formulation of the natural law, therefore, is capable of further
refinement and evolution. There will never be any ultimate
formulation of the natural law.

I am convinced, then, that the reality called natural
law is actually within us, that it is discoverable by the person
who lives deeply and is willing to reflect rationally on his

* From "The Christian Adventure: Risk and Renewal," in *The Critic,* April–
May, 1965, Vol. XXIII, no. 5, pp. 49–50, by permission. Copyright © 1965 by the
Thomas More Association, Chicago.

experience of life. This person, reaching out for maturity and responsibility, will discover the moral dimension of his own existence and the moral demands which others (society) make on him. Asserting natural law, therefore, implies that the conscience which is constantly attuned to reality will discover the objective norm of the good life.

The second difficulty I have with the term "natural law" is the ambiguity of the word "natural." Does this word signify that the common moral convictions of men obtained by rational reflection on their lives in society are derived from reason and not due to divine grace (the supernatural)? If this law is called "natural" in order to distinguish it from the supernatural law found in the Scriptures, I feel strangely uncomfortable. Since the Incarnation promises us the redemptive concern of God for *all* men and the death and resurrection of Jesus announced to us that *the whole world* has been redeemed by the God of mercy, I am convinced that the divine initiative to draw men away from self-love into generosity and charity is universal. Grace, as call, is active everywhere! We have, therefore, no way of knowing whether a moral conviction which matures in the consciences of men is simply natural, or whether it is not partially the work of redemptive grace in them, grace of which Jesus is the sole mediator. Is, for instance, the common conviction of the dignity of the human person simply based on a rational reflection on human life or is it brought about in men who, under the influence of divine grace, reflect on human existence? Since the dignity of man is so powerfully revealed in the Scriptures and lies at the heart of the Christian message, we may even ask the question whether modern society, even while largely abandoning the Christian creed, has not retained, assimilated and developed an inherited Gospel theme. This, at least, is a possibility. It is, therefore, quite impossible to say that a moral conviction which is alive in the consciences of all men is simply "natural." Since divine grace has entered history once and for all through the Incarnation, we may never be able to separate in the concrete order that which is of nature and that which is of grace, healing and elevating nature.

While, therefore, I affirm the reality called "natural law," it seems to me that this is neither natural nor is it law. . . .

SOURCES

Maritain, Jacques, *The Rights of Man and the Natural Law,* New York, 1943, ch. 2.

——, *Man and the State,* Chicago, 1951, ch. 4–6.

Niebuhr, Reinhold, *An Interpretation of Christian Ethics,* New York, 1935, ch. 4–7.

——, "Christian Faith and Natural Law," *Theology,* Vol. XL, February 1940, pp. 88 ff.

Papal Encyclicals:

Leo XIII (English texts in J. Husslein [ed.], *Social Wellsprings,* Vol. I, Milwaukee, 1940).

Libertas Humana (1888)

Rerum Novarum (1891)

Pius XI (English texts in Husslein, *Social Wellsprings,* Vol. II, Milwaukee, 1942).

Casti Connubii (1930)

Quadragesimo Anno (1891)

John XXIII (selections in Anne Fremantle, ed. *The Social Teachings of the Church,* New York, 1963).

Mater et Magistra (1961)

Pacem in Terris (1963)

CONCLUSION

As we have seen, natural law is one of the central themes in Western political theory. The preceding chapters have traced the development of this theme from fifth-century Greece to the present day. Nature first appeared as an ethical and political standard in Greek thought and it was appealed to both by Plato and Aristotle and by their opponents, the Sophists. The natural law theories subsequently developed by the Stoics related universal law to a rational order in the universe and in God, and their theories were carried on by Roman writers, chiefly Cicero and the Roman lawyers. Despite a certain ambivalence towards classical thought, Christian writers incorporated natural law into their writings—a process which was facilitated by specific references to Stoic theories in the writings and sermons of St. Paul. In the Middles Ages, natural law received differing treatments from the canon lawyers and from the scholastic theologians. The canon lawyers related it so closely to the divine law that it appeared to be identified with it, while St. Thomas Aquinas distinguished natural law from divine law in a complex theory which combined elements from Aristotle, the Stoics, and the Church Fathers. The late medieval controversies over the priority of will or reason in God and the differences between the nominalist and realist epistemology also affected natural law theory, although not as greatly as often believed.

The continuities between the medieval theories and those of

Hooker, Suarez, and Grotius are such that the real break in the history of natural law comes only with Hobbes. Although he used the traditional terminology, Hobbes redefined its content in such a way that his theory can only be associated with natural law if its egoistic and hedonistic elements are ignored or de-emphasized. There is more continuity with the past in Locke's theory despite his use of some of Hobbes' concepts in his thought. As reformulated by Locke in the theory of natural rights, and as transmitted through other writers such as Pufendorf, de Vattel, Coke, and Blackstone, natural law was one of the basic concepts in the political thought of the American Revolution. We have noted how American constitutional law was profoundly influenced by natural law, and it still makes use of such concepts as due process, which can be interpreted as a type of natural law.

Although they are not usually classified as natural law theorists, it has been necessary for us to consider the political theories of Rousseau, Burke, Hume, Mill and Kant in order both to evaluate their criticisms of natural law and, paradoxically, to demonstrate its continued relevance to their thought. In the case of Rousseau, we discovered a rather complex system of harmonies between feeling, conscience, the general will, and a natural law for all mankind in his writings. It was also argued that Edmund Burke was a defender of classical and Christian natural law ideas in morality, however opposed he may have been to contemporary theories of absolute natural rights. The criticisms by Hume and Mill of the attempt to derive moral and political principles from nature were evaluated, but an analysis of their thought revealed that they could not avoid relating their moral theories to certain assumptions about human nature. Immanuel Kant was considered from two opposing perspectives—as the last of the great natural law theorists, and as a thoroughgoing critic of the traditional theory. Even Karl Marx, at least in his early writings, was not found to be free from natural law thought. Contemporary applications of natural law to jurisprudence, international law, and religious thought were also examined in order to demonstrate the continuing importance of the natural law theory even after two centuries of attack.

This study has demonstrated that in the course of its history many different principles have been ascribed to natural law. It has been used to defend slavery and freedom; hierarchy and equality; revolution and reaction. In times of social change and criticism of existing political and legal institutions, the appeal to "nature" provided a standard for the evaluation of governmental and social arrangements in a reactionary, conservative, liberal, or revolutionary direction. In the disputed areas of international relations, property, slavery, resistance and revolution, and the development of new political institutions, it has been the source of a wide variety of norms and criticisms in Western political thought. Yet there are certain recurring themes in the natural law tradition besides the appeal to nature and human nature as the sources of objective standards for ethics, politics, and law. On the whole, and with important exceptions, natural law writers look for *purposes* in the world whether God's, man's or nature's. Natural law thinking emphasizes *reason,* as man's distinguishing characteristic, the source of his uniqueness and value, and the basis for the reconciliation of conflict in his social relations. While modern dynamic theories of natural law (e.g., Stammler, Maritain, Niebuhr) attempt to take into account the diversity of the moral insights of men, most natural law theories have aimed at achieving or working for a set of moral principles on which rational men can agree.[1] In an apparently disordered world, natural law theory assumes that harmonious *order* can be arrived at by the use of *reason* rather than by arbitrary will.

Most natural law theories have also attempted to defend some notion of human *equality* and have criticized artificial or ascriptive differences among men. In the modern period, natural law has given increased attention to man's capacity for *free choice* as the basis for moral and legal practices and institutions, and in recent years his need for *participation in the community* has been recognized as a moral demand of human nature.

While the natural law theory still exerts an influence on

---

[1] On natural law as an "ideology of agreement" see Judith N. Shklar, *Legalism* (Cambridge, Mass., 1964), Part I. Rudolf Stammler, *Theory of Justice* (New York, 1925), contains his theory of "natural law with a changing content." Jacques Maritain's theory is best expressed in *Man and the State* (Chicago, 1951), while Reinhold Niebuhr's revised version of natural law (based on the "law of love") appears in "Christian Faith and Natural Law," in George W. Forell, ed., *Christian Social Teaching* (Garden City, N.Y., 1966), pp. 393–402.

moral theologians (especially, although not exclusively, those in the Roman Catholic Church) and on writers on international law and relations, the appeal to nature is not now frequently made in the English-speaking world—at least not in explicit terms. The classical critics of natural law, such as the Sophists and Sceptics who argued against natural law by citing the diversity of human moral and legal codes; the Christian fideists who doubted the capacities of man's reason to attain moral truth; and the early modern theorists of sovereignty who demanded a single and incontrovertible source of law and justice in the nation-state, were not able to undermine men's faith in the ultimate rationality, objectivity, and intelligibility of the moral basis of civilized life. Today, however, we have come to look elsewhere for our philosophic models because of the pluralism of modern society; the important changes in our moral standards over time and space; and the obvious ethnocentrism and inadequacy of the eighteenth-century attempts to develop a systematic moral code based on nature. Natural law is considered either too rigid to apply to the modern world or too vague to provide a useful or intelligible standard. As the Danish philosopher, Alf Ross, puts the latter criticism, "Like a harlot, natural law is at the disposal of everyone. The ideology does not exist that cannot be defended by an appeal to the law of nature."[2]

From the point of view of modern philosophy, the most telling objection to natural law is still that made by Hume in Book III, Part I of *The Treatise of Human Nature,* where he demonstrates that it is logically and epistemologically impossible to derive a statement of value from a statement of fact about the natural world. To base one's values on nature appears to do just this—to derive an ethical judgment from some natural fact about man or the universe. But as this study has indicated, the protagonists of natural law do not really appeal to empirical data as *proof* that a given principle is contained in the natural law. Such evidence is cited as an *indication* of a more fundamental (or even "self-evident") purposive order, or goal in man, which is part of his essential being. The objection, then, to natural law thinking must go further than to deny that one can argue from fact to value—it must deny the possibility of perceiving purposive order or essential regulative principles in human existence.

And this is precisely what contemporary critics do deny. They separate nature and ethics as sharply as did Kant. They deny that there are purposes or essences in nature available to man. Natural law is rejected by most modern philosophers because they reject the "essentialism" (i.e., belief in fixed essences with definite properties) of the view of an ordered nature on which it is based. Values are viewed as ultimately reducible to personal preferences, although it is admitted that these preferences may be widely shared at a given time or place.[3] Human nature, in the sense of statistical regularities in human conduct and certain basic drives or instincts, may set limits on the possibilities for the implementation of moral ideals but it is not a source of those ideals. Occasionally the term "unnatural" is used to stigmatize certain types of unorthodox sexual conduct, but even this usage is becoming rare in this age of tolerance of sexual variety.

Furthermore, when a case is made for the use of natural law today, it usually turns out to be so ambiguous, misleading, and controversial, as to be nearly useless as a meaningful way of discussing ethics and politics. Too much time is spent on indicating what is *not* meant by natural law, and in tracing its history, or denouncing its opponents, rather than on showing how it can be applied today.[4] Natural law currently seems to have become more of a barrier than an aid to communication on moral and political problems.

But what is there that can replace the appeal to natural law as a source of norms to evaluate and criticize existing institutions and practices? Is there a modern equivalent to the natural law tradition which can be relevant to contemporary ethical and political theory?

Recognizing that an appeal to justice and morality beyond a given law and practice is inevitable and necessary, an analysis in

---

[3] Cf. Arnold Brecht, *Political Theory* (Princeton, 1959), chapter 10; Robert Dahl, *Modern Political Analysis* (Englewood Cliffs, N.J., 1963), p. 101.

[4] For examples of the three tendencies see John Courtney Murray, *We Hold These Truths* (New York, 1960), Part III; Scott Buchanan, *Rediscovering Natural Law* (Santa Barbara, Calif., 1962); and Leo Strauss, *Natural Right and History* (Chicago, 1953).

terms of "human needs and potentialities" could be used to develop standards and principles which are related to human nature without making the ontological claims that most natural law theorists make. An attempt to specify these needs and potentialities somewhat more concretely may produce a result which is remarkably similar to what the natural law theorists have been saying all along.

Starting from a universally-felt need for survival, it can be argued that, in order to survive, man must live in a society under common rules, which are necessary to protect human life and to defend the community.[5] Even the most primitive society must regulate the allocation and use of food, shelter, and material goods—i.e., property—although a wide variety of alternative arrangements are possible. Also, the area of sex and procreation is one which requires certain rules if only to provide a stable psychological and material environment for the offspring of the sexual union. Included among man's "natural" needs, then, are society, security, property arrangements, and sexual regulations.

It is more difficult to make a brief enumeration of those human potentialities which should be recognized. Surely, equality seems to be demanded if every man's potentialities are to be developed.[6] Man's capacity for knowledge and free choice will be recognized by any society that is concerned with developing the full potential of all of its citizens. The conditions for the responsible exercise of freedom in education, economic opportunity, and social welfare will be fostered in its institutions. The human need and potential for responsible participation in the community is also increasingly evident in the contemporary world, when industrialization and urbanization have focused attention on the problems of anomie and alienation. Christian theorists and some secular writers (e.g., Erich Fromm) would add a response to the human need and potential for love as one of the moral requirements of a developed and perfected society.

Security, social cooperation, equality, freedom, and, more

[5] Cf. H. L. A. Hart, "minimum content of natural law," *The Concept of Law* (Oxford, 1961), ch. 9.

[6] John Rawls, "Distributive Justice," Peter Laslett and W. G. Runciman, eds., *Philosophy, Politics and Society*, 3rd series (Oxford, 1967), pp. 58–82, has added the requirement that where inequalities exist they must be justified by their contribution to the good of all the individuals in the society.

difficult of accomplishment, community and love—these are some of the human needs and potentialities by which social, political, and economic institutions may be evaluated. The use of these goals as standards preserves something of the attempt of natural law theory to develop universal and objective norms related to human nature. It avoids, however, the "essentialism" implied by the older formulation. Like natural law theory this approach operates on the assumption that there are certain purposive goals in man that demand fulfillment. It gives a more prominent place to the recognition of human freedom than did the natural law theorists (except for Kant). But it assumes that this freedom will be used rationally—thus preserving the older emphasis on rationality. Like natural law thinking, it seeks to achieve agreement among rational men on the requirements of civilized societal life, and holds that some kind of consensus on basic principles is possible.

It must be admitted that this formula—human needs and potentialities—is subject to some of the same criticisms as the natural law theory. For example, the accusation that it is either too vague or too rigid can also be applied to it. It is better able to adjust to the recognition of new needs, capacities, and moral insights than the more static formulation of the natural law writers, but, by basing some of its moral claims on aspects of man's conduct that may be perceived as universal human potentialities, it lays itself open to considerable controversy, since views may differ on what constitutes the potential fulfillment of man. This is particularly true if any attempt is made to put these requirements and aspirations into laws. We are then involved in conflicts between moral principles, and we must develop a hierarchy of values among them. Yet if it is claimed that these needs and potentialities are universal among men and reciprocally binding, they must be expressed as general principles—although (unlike earlier natural law theories) such generalizations will be tentative in character and subject to revision in the light of new evidence on how best to achieve human fulfillment.

A number of modern writers on philosophy and law have developed theories which resemble the one just outlined. T. H. Green, the English liberal idealist philosopher, specifically alluded to a modern equivalent of natural law when he proposed his standard for the evaluation of political institutions. "The value, then, of institutions of civil life lies in their operation as giving reality to (human) capacities of will and reason. . . . They enable (man) to realize his reason, i.e., his idea of self-perfection, by action as a member of a social organization in which each contributes to the well-being of all the rest. So far as they do in fact thus operate they are morally justified and may be said to correspond to the law of nature, the *jus naturae,* according to the only sense in which that phrase can be intelligibly used." The contemporary philosopher, Frederick Olafson, also speaks of a "new and restricted version of natural law theory" which "expresses the only set of reciprocally applicable priorities that most people are really prepared to live by. . . . Its authority is simply that of the unwillingness or practical inability of the human beings who use a certain concept of human nature to accept . . . the implications for conduct of the abandonment of that concept."[7]

The idea of the reciprocal application of common goals through shared laws is given greater content in Carl Friedrich's attempt to derive an argument for democracy from the permanent characteristics of human nature. In *Man and His Government,* Friedrich begins with "the basic given of all political experience: the community." He then enumerates four characteristics of man in community—"pliability and adaptability, having and sharing of purposes, experiencing oneself as self, and communicating with each other through language." While noting that "all these traits are in a sense comprised in the old idea of reason" Friedrich is critical of what he considers the elitist rationalism of earlier natural law theories. For him involvement of all on the basic value choices of the community is a conclusion that follows from the human experience and moral potential of man in community.[8]

The closest analogue to our theory in contemporary writing on jurisprudence is Thomas E. Davitt's attempt in his monograph, *The Basic Values of Law,* to ground obligation on "certain basic

---

[7] "Essence and Concept in Natural Law Theory," Sidney Hook, ed., *Law and Philosophy* (New York, 1964, p. 239). Green's statement appears in his *Lectures on the Principles of Political Obligation* (London, 1882, reprinted 1959), pp. 32–33.

[8] Carl Joachim Friedrich, *Man and His Government* (New York, 1963), p. 38 ff.

drives which dynamically express what is fundamentally necessary for man's self-development." Using data from psychology, anthropology, and ethnology, Davitt attempts to outline the basic human values which all or most societies and legal systems take into account because they correspond to "elementary needs and tendencies" which demand fulfillment. Among these Davitt includes life, sex, knowledge and decision, "mine and thine," and protection and security.[9]

Similar arguments are made by Marxist writers concerned with human alienation. For what is man alienated from but his true self, the potential and need for which is suppressed by the real or supposed requirements of the capitalist system? Sidney Hook, elsewhere a critic of natural law, has attacked the theory of alienation as "foreign to Marx's concept of man" and "obscurantist legerdemain" but he recognizes that if Marx indeed did espouse such a theory "this would entail the acceptance of a natural law morality," the "standard of the unalienated self."[10]

Contemporary movements of protest against various aspects of modern industrial civilization also proceed from certain assumptions about the requirements of human nature. Young people, blacks, adherents of women's liberation, socialist critics of capitalism share the same basic perception that there are certain demands on society that arise from the way man is constituted and that society can and should satisfy them. Implicitly they reject the pessimism of Freud's view expressed in *Civilization and Its Discontents* that alienation and conflict are part of the human condition, arising out of a fundamental opposition between man's natural instincts and the requirements of civilized life. Nor do they partake of the despair of existentialist writers like Jean Paul Sartre who argue that the absurdity of man's existence makes it necessary for him to affirm a moral commitment while knowing that it is meaningless. Like the natural law theorists of the past, the contemporary moral critics believe that a harmonious order in human society can be found, that man's needs and potentialities are not destined to be forever frustrated. Perhaps this

---

[9] Thomas E. Davitt, *The Basic Values in Law*, Vol. 58, Part 5 (1968) of *The Transactions of the American Philosophical Society* (Philadelphia, 1968).

[10] Sidney Hook, *From Hegel to Marx,* paperback edition (Ann Arbor, Mich., 1962), pp. 6–7.

is a utopian ideal but it is one that has attracted man throughout the ages—and one of the reasons for the continuing attraction of natural law thinking. As increased economic progress makes it appear that the more elemental needs of mankind can be satisfied, is it too much to hope that the higher potentialities of his nature can achieve fulfillment? Today, when demands are increasing domestically and internationally for something more than mere lip service to the ideas which the natural law theorists did so much to develop we can perhaps look forward to the day when the "natural" human need and potentiality for the responsible exercise of freedom in community may be a reality as well as an ideal for the mass of mankind—when, in the words of Teilhard de Chardin, "the inevitable 'totalization' of humanity will take place in such a way as not to destroy but to enhance in each one of us, I will not say, independence, but—what is quite a different thing —the incommunicable uniqueness of the being within us."[11]

[11] Pierre Teilhard de Chardin, "Some Reflections on the Rights of Man," UNESCO ed., *Human Rights* (New York, 1949), p. 106.

BIBLIOGRAPHY

Benn S. I. and R. S. Peters, *The Principles of Political Thought.* New York, 1959, Pt. I.

Brecht, Arnold. *Political Theory.* Princeton, N.J., 1959. chs. 4, 5, and 8.

Buchanan, Scott. *Rediscovering Natural Law.* Santa Barbara, Calif., 1962.

Cogley, John, ed. *Natural Law and Modern Society.* Cleveland and New York, 1963.

Cohen, Morris R. *Reason and Nature.* Glencoe, Ill., 1931, ch. 4.

Davitt, Thomas E. *The Basic Values in Law*. Philadelphia, 1968.

Friedrich, Carl J. *The Philosophy of Law in Historical Perspective*. Chicago, 1958, esp. chs. 4, 6, and 19.

Hook, Sidney, ed. *Law and Philosophy*. New York, 1964, Pt. II.

Murphy, Joseph S. *Political Theory, A Conceptual Analysis*. Homewood, Ill., 1968, ch. 2.

Oppenheim, Felix. *Moral Principles in Political Philosophy*. New York, 1968, pp. 35–52.

Raphael, D. D., ed. *Political Theory and the Rights of Man*. Bloomington, Ind., 1967.

The Natural Law Forum. Notre Dame, Ind., volumes I–XIV (1956–69).

Watkins, Frederick. "Natural Law and the Problem of Value-Judgment," in Oliver Garceau, ed. *Political Research and Political Theory*. Cambridge, Mass., pp. 58–74.

The hippies' search for community and love, the New Left criticism of the quality of contemporary life, the demands of the women's liberation movement that the needs and potentialities of women be recognized — all mark a return to an ancient concept — the appeal to human nature as a moral standard. The dominant form of that appeal in Western political thought since the time of the Greeks has been the theory of natural law.

In this volume, Paul Sigmund shows how natural law has been used as a standard by which to judge legal and political actions. He pays special attention to the relationship of natural law to three important historical developments — Rome's extended influence over Western Europe, the fusion of Christianity and classical culture in the Middle Ages, and the emergence of liberal individualism from the 16th to the 18th centuries.

Most importantly, he analyzes more contemporary aspects of the theory and evaluates the relevance of an updated version of the theory of natural law to today's society.

(continued on back flap)